AMERICA'S CONDUCT

AMERICA'S CONDUCT

Inner City Escort

LARRY DAVIS

© 2015 by Larry Davis

This work is subject to copyright. All rights reserved.

No part of this publication may be reproduced, stored in a retrieval system, or transmitted in any form or by any means, electronic, mechanical, photocopying, or otherwise, without written permission of Larry Davis.

Published by No Fears, No Tears Publications

Letter from Birmingham Jail reprinted by arrangement with The Heirs to the Estate of Martin Luther King Jr., c/o Writers House as agent for the proprietor New York, NY.

ISBN-13: 978-1508730675

Dedication

To

LIL LARRY HAKEEM DAVIS
my son

Contents

SPECIAL THANKS i

FOREWORD iii

BENIGHTED 1

DISORDERLY CONDUCT 9

DISCOMBOBULATED 19

DETERIORATION 24

DESTROYED 33

CLONED 46

RETARDATION 62

SUBMERGED 80

ZOMBIES 91

RETRIBUTION 97

AVALANCHE 104

DEVASTATION 112

VOYAGE 120

ZONKED 133

INSANITY 143

LOST SOULS 164

ABYSS 178

GLADIATOR SCHOOL 187

REUNITED 198

MASQUERADE 202

CALLOUS 217

UNSOCIABLE 229

EPILOGUE: CATASTROPHE 241

Special Thanks

I'd like to thank these people for shaping my life and making a contribution, in one form or another, to the evolution of my life and this book.

First and foremost, I want to thank my parents, Mr. Willie James Davis and Jannie Mae Laffitte Davis for loving each other enough to bring me into the world. Thank you to my siblings for our experiences together. I am forever grateful.

To Raymond Washington, who started a movement of good that went astray, for reasons I've shared with you all in this book. We will never forget your legacy.

To Big John, John Louis McDaniel, you have always been the inspiration that leads me to being strong, even when you weren't always at your strongest. Because of you, I knew that I could endure this life's challenges.

To Big Quake, you are by far the biggest reason I will always love the Crips the way that I do. I have yet to see another man demonstrate the type of bravery, courage and determination you displayed for us during a critical time in our young lives. I will always respect you, and cherish our memories.

To Jackie R. Johnson, my ex-wife and my son's mother, you have given me the most precious gift on Earth, little Larry Hakeem Davis. Although times for us haven't always been glorious, we did spend some great times together. Our life was the essence of ups and downs. I think we done fair for squares. Thank you for sharing part of your life with me. I will always love you.

To my son, Lil Larry Hakeem Davis, I have attempted to share with you our history as best I could, in the hopes of you and other young men recognizing the importance of each of us recording our own history so it will never be lost. I attempted to give you a better understanding of who your father is, and who I was growing up here in America. I know that I have failed you, as black people have failed each other. I hope this book can, in some way, make a difference in your life. I love you to death. Your Father.

To Brother Abdur Raheem Hizbullah (Isaiah Thompson), I told you I wouldn't forget that you took time out of your busy schedule to help me realize this dream to help people like myself better understand the mistakes we continue to make. Thank you Brother Raheem. I am forever grateful.

To Lisa Carroll, the engineer who kept the fire under my feet to bring my experiences to the forefront so the world would know the truth about our daily lives throughout all of America's inner cities. Lisa, you are a shining star and I will always love you.

To Young Rob, Young Sadd, Big Sadd, Lil Sadd, Big Bubble, Baby Bubble, Loco, Ken Dog, Big Limes, Key Boss, Young Lala, Lil Fluxx, Big Spike and so many others. In life are lessons that enable us to grow and reach far beyond our imaginations. With each one of you I have learned so much and I will continue to appreciate the opportunities the universe blessed each of us with to move forward. However, Young Rob, Loco and Big Moe RIP, above all, have had the opportunity to know me best. It has been the utmost pleasure to call you all my comrades. You are the realest of the real. I love you all unconditionally, do or die. We all shall forever remain dipped in the flavor of the East Side. I will continue to shine in the midst of hate.

To Kristine, my editor, I am at a loss for words that describe the appreciation I hold in my heart for you. I am so grateful that you opened up your heart to assist me in telling my story to the world. People like you give people like me the belief that every person is capable of manifesting richness from within. You are so precious and will always be my chief editor. This is a promise from my heart. With all of the love in the universe, I thank you.

Foreword

For so many years, African Americans have been tricked, manipulated, deceived and threatened. We have been told to behave a certain way, even when that way goes against who we are as a people. We are unwilling to conform, so we act out, even against our better judgment, just to defy the people we hold responsible for slavery. It doesn't matter to us that these individuals are not actually the participants; the color white is good enough for us. Those of us who refuse to surrender, submit or succumb to these demands are punished, imprisoned, beaten, or even killed by the state. So we continue to disagree with America's conduct towards us. But today, African Americans do more harm to themselves than the Ku Klux Klan has ever done.

For far too long we have been traveling down the wrong path. How is it possible that you can look at someone who looks exactly like you do and hold hatred, disrespect or murderous thoughts for them? How did this happen to African Americans? What has caused us to abandon our history, something that holds all the answers this universe needs to breathe life into every existence? It is our responsibility to change these patterns. We must learn that in order to reap the benefits from our history we no longer have the right to blame others for our senseless abuse of one another's property, integrity, companionship and love for family. It is our own responsibility to correct this misbehavior. Our people must find the courage within ourselves to stand up and build our foundation stronger, fortifying it, by all means necessary.

I have written *America's Conduct: The Inner-City Escort* in hopes of shedding light on the problems that I believe contribute to the destructive behavior African Americans engage in here in America. I personally acknowledge my role in this destruction, while at no time do I want to give the impression that I am glorifying my past conduct. My goal is to provide the readers with an escort through the inner city of my youth, to provide insight into how I thought and what I believed in during those experiences. I simply want to illustrate what a sick, abused, mistreated mind looked and acted like here on America's soil from the time Africans were forced to reside here.

Today we have an opportunity to change history and make it suitable for all human beings here in America. We all must look deep within ourselves to discover the gifts of strength, power, intelligence, bravery, insight, knowledge, fortitude and so much more that we inherited from our forebears. It is my hope that the younger generation of all races will work together towards reversing this destructive conduct that has been poured all over the souls here and abroad in one form or another. It is essential that African Americans become conscious of their ancestors' past experiences in order that we learn the importance of unity, strength, determination, faith and love to better prepare us for the journey ahead of us. Once this transformation has occurred and an awakening has manifested, we no longer have the right to complain, protest, cry or point fingers at anyone other than ourselves. Now is the time that we must act in accordance with balance, so that we can blossom like the kings and queens of our ancestors. And so it is.

Benighted

> **AMENDMENT 13**
>
> *SECTION 1: Neither slavery nor involuntary servitude, except as a punishment for crime whereof the party shall be duly convicted, shall exist within the United States, nor any place subject to their jurisdiction.*
>
> *SECTION 2:* Congress shall have power to enforce this article by appropriate legislation.
>
> *Proposed January 31, 1865; ratified December 6, 1865; certified December 18, 1865.*

1911 was the year my maternal grandfather, Mr. Arthur Laffitte Jr., was born. He was an intense man, 6 feet 4 inches tall, bald, dark skinned, long and slender. His eyes made him appear as though he was saddened, yet truly determined to overcome the hand life had dealt him. His face had the structure of an African king, full of strength and wisdom, yet deceptively ambiguous. If one looked directly into his eyes he appeared to have been unwillingly subdued and seemed perplexed. He had been engaged in a battle only God had the power to win.

He was raised in Gosport, Alabama during a time when blacks were being hung, mistreated and abused for many different reasons. At that time, the majority of white people thought themselves to be a superior race to blacks, and the mistreatment was the expression of this belief in white supremacy.

My grandfather was fortunate in some ways. His parents loved him deeply and upon their death, Mr. Arthur Sr. and Mrs. Florence Laffitte left him several acres of land. I was shocked to learn this. Like many others, I didn't know blacks were allowed to own land or property, especially during the time when they were being hung for minor infractions.

My grandfather met and married my grandmother, Ms. Lillie Bob Ely and together they raised ten children, seven boys and three girls. My mother, Jannie Mae Laffitte, was the fifth child of their union. She was born in August, 1942, in the state of Alabama.

My mother's parents were tenaciously strict with them. While growing up, the kids desperately wanted to attend school, but it wasn't economically feasible for their family. Their services were needed in the cotton fields, where they worked long days without pay. My mother told me: "I never picked a single cotton ball; daddy would be looking to see if we were working and I'd be standing straight up in the field and looking at everything except some cotton. Shit, I wasn't thinking about nobody's cotton and I sure in the hell wasn't going to pick none neither." Their dreams of going to school and learning how to read and write vanished, together with most of their hopes of being treated with dignity, respect and consideration by the southern whites who had no regard for them as human beings.

In those days, black girls weren't allowed to wear short pants in the south. It was an unwritten rule that was not in THE UNITED STATES CONSTITUTION. In Alabama, white people made the law up on the spot they were standing. Hearing those stories from my mother reminds me of the criticisms I hear now about other governments, and all the ill treatment of other women in those countries. Many people think African Americans' injustices occurred a thousand years ago, or that after 1865 everything magically became heaven on earth for blacks. In fact, most of these incidents took place in the 1960's.

My mother had a rebellious streak. She and her youngest sister, Reolar decided they were going to wear short pants in defiance of a nonexistent law. As they began their walk down a long, uneven, dusty road, several cars passed by carrying white occupants. My mother said, "White people saw us wearing short pants and were turning their heads on their necks like they were spinning tops, in total disbelief. Looking back at us like we were aliens, they came close to driving off the road. We just kept on walking, laughing at them." The white people couldn't believe those young black ladies defied them and broke their unlegislated law. They dared to express free choice and took a few very small steps toward freedom.

Can you imagine for over 200 years, African American women hadn't worn short pants in the south and here were two young ladies, not trying to be famous or draw any attention to themselves, just expressing their freedom? For a brief moment, they experienced what liberation felt like.

In private, my grandfather had to be strong, fierce and orderly, which his family never fully understood since he wasn't that way around the white folks. When my mother got older, she realized he was attempting to hide his anguish over his failure to protect his family from the ugliness they endured. He only wanted to protect his family like any man would, but he was confronted with being wrecked, both mentally and physically, simply because he was black. He couldn't figure out how to overcome, escape or evade the nightmare he had been born into. His thoughts were to find a way to make that horror in his life disappear, only it wasn't vanishing.

My grandfather, along with all of the demands of his family, had a serious drinking problem. He was attempting to drink himself out of his realities, as others had previously done. I imagine his pride was deteriorating every second of his life, although he never appeared to be broken or weak on the exterior. But when he was drunk, he took his frustrations, humiliation and diminished psyche out on his family, especially my grandmother.

In 1939, my father, Willie James Davis, was born in Claiborne, Alabama to Mr. Jake Davis and Mrs. Josie Williams Davis, a.k.a. Momma Joe. My father was the only child of this union. (His half-sister Georgia Mae was born ten years later.)

My father's refusal to accept the treatment and behavior white people displayed towards blacks in Alabama caused his family many problems. He never surrendered his soul to those who exhibited a blatant disrespect towards blacks. He believed those who practiced such behavior did not deserve to be respected, certainly not by him. His reluctance to submit to the physical and psychological abuse blacks were suffering caused his mother to worry about him more than she wanted to and she often feared for his life. You see, Momma Joe was born in 1905 in Claiborne, Alabama where she witnessed this terror most of her life. She knew my father was a prideful man and it scared her to death. He rebelled against authority figures at every turn, because the way most whites treated blacks was impossible for him to accept, regardless of his skin color. Instinctively, he knew they were wrong. The dignity he held for himself prevented him from ignoring what blacks routinely endured. To him, those experiences weren't illusions, but were surely real because blacks had been overwhelmed regularly with dehumanizing psychological subterfuges.

My mother's parents moved adjacent to my father's family when she was 12 years old. According to my mother, when my father was a young man he was a "roughneck", a bit wild, and disliked everything the state of Alabama stood for. However, even in his rebellious stage he managed to perfect the art of womanizing; he was considered a ladies' man. He was instantly attracted to my mother, but ran into an obstacle by the name of Arthur Laffitte Jr., who had forbidden her from dating anyone because he thought she was too young.

My mother's temperament was not that different from my father's. She lived a similar life of strife, but refused to succumb to the intense pressure blacks encountered every day of their lives. Instead, she stayed discreet, strong and dignified, never openly parading around her displeasures. She always remained immune to the lunacy that engulfed her. In spite of her mistreatment, and even though she was not afforded many of the privileges or civil liberties whites enjoyed in the United States, she took pride in herself and did her very best. Despite all the disparity she witnessed, she would tell me that all white people weren't nefarious, when I wanted badly to believe they were. That wisdom she shared with me revealed a quality about her that impressed me profoundly. She had within her the goodness not to judge all white people the way most of them had judged her.

The state of Alabama never let up on its efforts to defeat the spirit, will and determination of blacks. My father's refusal to submit to those ploys forced him to abandon his family in search of equality he thought existed somewhere other than Alabama. He wasn't far from being a dreamer, but what choices did black people have in a climate such as that? Should they have chosen to rebel and gotten themselves hung from a tree? How could that have helped their families? Blacks were facing this infection throughout the country. What other remedies were at their disposal? Should they have relied on **The Declaration of Independence**, where it states:

> *"We hold these truths to be self-evident, that all men are created equal, that they are endowed by their creator with certain unalienable rights, that among these are Life, Liberty, and the pursuit of Happiness. That to secure these rights, governments are instituted among men, deriving their just power from the consent of the governed, That whenever any form of government becomes destructive of these ends, it is the right of the people to alter or to abolish it, and to institute new government, laying its foundation on such principles and organizing its power in such form, as to them shall seem most likely to effect their safety, and happiness. Prudence, indeed, will dictate that governments long established should not be changed for light and transient causes; and accordingly all experience hath shown that mankind are more disposed to suffer, while evils are sufferable, than to right themselves by abolishing the forms to which they are accustomed. But when a long train of abuses and usurpations, pursuing invariably the same object evinces a design to reduce them under absolute despotism, it is their right, it is their future security."*

The Declaration of Independence didn't safeguard my father, grandfather or any blacks that came before them. It wasn't written to include blacks on any level. For more than two hundred years, blacks were treated inhumanely every day of their lives. No other race in America, with the exception of **THE NATIVE AMERICANS,** knows what it's like to be denied human rights for centuries at a time. Any human being denied basic civil liberties for that period of time would be affected psychologically in some manner.

YOU REAP WHAT YOU SOW

The Declaration of Independence

(Adopted in Congress July 4, 1776)

The Unanimous Declaration of the Thirteen United States of America

> *When, in the course of human events, it becomes necessary for one people to dissolve the political bands which have connected them with another, and to assume among the powers of the earth, the separate and equal station to which the laws of nature and of nature's God entitle them, a decent respect to the opinions of mankind requires that they should declare the causes which impel them to the separation.*

"We hold these **lies** to be **individually hidden** that all men are **originated dissimilar** that they are **deprived** by their creator with certain unalienable rights that among these are **death, enslavement** and the pursuit of **misery**."

That's how **The Declaration of Independence** read to blacks during those experiences. The truth America held to be self-evident, that all men are created equal, didn't apply to black people. The principal foundation of America, **The Declaration of Independence,** blatantly ignored African American civil rights. To this very day non-black Americans argue slavery wasn't that bad, but the people who say such a thing have neither suffered the devastation blacks were made to bear, nor have they experienced their human rights being obliterated for even one second of their entire existence on earth.

All American citizens have the right and power to elect whomever they choose based on the Constitution, and the power to make changes when those that have been chosen to serve the people fail them. The elected officials must serve the will of the people by administering the desire of the people, and by making every effort to protect and seek satisfaction for all citizens of the United States. Those elected officials should never lose sight of their duties; to ensure the best interest of the people is always first.

Do these dreams exist? Are they real or are they an illusion? My father was certainly a dreamer! Neither **The Declaration of Independence** nor **The Constitution of the United States of America** protected blacks from horrific experiences, as history will forever demonstrate. The Amendments to the Constitution of the United States are said to protect the rights of the people against an abusive government, but it is clear that these Amendments have not applied equally to all citizens.

How could my grandfather, an uneducated man, gain the respect of his family when he couldn't find any relief in the United States Constitution? He had no answers to protect himself against a powerful institution with no moral compass, an institution that never intended to treat him or any other black person as the equal of whites. Many blacks, through all that madness, managed to keep their heads held high, while others stood by, mentally feeble because they weren't able to dodge the debilitating tactics that paralyzed them.

Americans' strategy throughout the country was to make African Americans feel their lives were worthless and to dehumanize them until they were broken in every way. America wanted the world to view blacks as it had, as **HUMAN DEFECTS**. It didn't matter what methods were used to accomplish this end just as long as blacks became submissive to the commands of White Americans and believed themselves to be useless varmints along the way.

Blacks were almost helpless and had it not been for their ancestors' strength before them, it certainly would have been hopeless. They were compelled to rely on the very people that were terrorizing them. They needed to convince white people that their behavior towards blacks was immoral to say the least. How distorted was that?

Many blacks openly questioned what they had done to deserve the abuse they encountered, believing America's behavior towards them was somehow justified because they were Africans, which was false and repugnant. There also were those who knew better and consistently resisted America's efforts to dehumanize them. They understood their lives were just as valuable, priceless and worth living as all the other human beings on earth, certainly exemplary enough to fight and die for as so many had done. Many of them were gallant warriors with tremendous pride, courage and strength. Brave men and women endlessly protested to combat those injustices they suffered at the hands of people declaring themselves **PATRIOTIC CHRISTIANS,** "Christians" doing what God surely would not.

Many blacks never lost their faith, but continued to fight and help each other expose America's insidious behavior for the world to see. They illuminated America's demonic behavior, unmasking it as less beautiful than it attempted to present itself.

One of America's goals was to delude African Americans into despising themselves for being black, inciting them into believing they would be privileged enough to be loved as a people if only they weren't black. If they weren't black, they would be respected and treated as decent human beings. If they weren't black, their lives would be so magical. But because they were black they were treated as less than dogs; simply because of the color of their skin they had to be penalized.

Many whites were lawless and permitted to do anything they pleased, which included hanging African Americans from trees without fear of punishment. They were the police, judge, jury and executioners. They had no worries in the world for their misbehaviors.

Many blacks started to wish they had been born white, believing that life for them would have been torture-free. The more uneducated African Americans were, the easier it was to control, steer and drive them right over the cliff.

In most cases, when blacks talk about those experiences they're told to "stop crying, that was the past, get over it already. **You people** act like we're the ones who done that to your people." The truth of the matter is that many of them were responsible and continue to be. What I find most amazing is that many of the blacks that actually experienced those awful encounters are still living today, so when blacks are told to "just get over it already" that's ridiculous! I have yet to hear someone tell the Jewish people to "just get over" the experience their people had with Hitler. African Americans have a right to their history, just as other races have a right to theirs. African Americans have a legitimate grievance with America!

CONSTITUTION OF THE UNITED STATES AMENDMENTS

AMENDMENT 1

Restrictions on Powers of Congress

SECTION 1: Congress shall make no law respecting an establishment of religion, or prohibiting the free exercise thereof; or abridging the freedom of speech, or of the press; or the right of the people peaceably to assemble, and to petition the government for a redress of grievances.

Proposed September 25, 1789; ratified December 15, 1791.

The First Amendment of the Constitution guarantees the freedom of speech, but this guarantee is not extended to African Americans. America shouts at the top of its lungs the evils of other governments and expects African Americans to keep their mouth shut and do as they are told while they are being disrespected. Blacks are taught they should love America as white people love it, while experiencing a completely different existence. Blacks are told they must recognize and celebrate together with the rest of America its national holidays for the very men that abused, denied, mistreated and refused them every human right known to mankind.

Starting in 1789 with George Washington, John Adams and Thomas Jefferson, all the way through Dwight Eisenhower in 1961, African Americans lived in turmoil. To this day, many white people consider the Presidents decent human beings, because under their rule they never had to suffer as blacks did. It's easy to understand why whites honor their memories, because they were not denied civil liberties by any of them. However, it truly seems illogical for blacks to feel as many white people do. Explain the psychology of this hypocrisy!

How was it possible to overcome this hurdle when many blacks believed the government was the only thing that could save them from the very harm it was inflicting on them? Is believing in such a thing itself a sign of insanity? Many blacks learned the importance of finagling, masking, and disguising their true feelings in order to have the slightest chance of survival. They inhaled and exhaled white people's evils daily. Whoever stood up against their abuses was labeled a troublemaker, instigator or rabble-rouser. How is it possible for the abusers to start calling the abused the troublemaker, instigator or rabble-rouser? How demented is that logic? It happened and it continues to happen. This is classic bullshit!!

AMERICA'S CONDUCT

African Americans started to despise each other openly. They literally started to hate themselves for the life they were forced to live by America's founding fathers. They couldn't figure out how to save themselves from the hell they were subjected to. The answers were inside them, but they just weren't able to unravel this mystery. All they had to do was continue to fight, because GOD had already given them all the answers to all things from birth. They only needed to look within self - introspection.

For America, everything was working as planned within the rural towns and inner cities. They had successfully divided and conquered black people. It was a complete psychological catastrophe, igniting total chaos, hatred and many other illnesses blacks inflicted on themselves.

Disorderly Conduct

In Gosport, Alabama my maternal family was one of the only black families that owned a television set. Many blacks in town came over to watch when they weren't laboring in the cotton fields. My grandmother Lillie had several ways of making extra money for herself and one way was to charge everyone that came by for the sole purpose of watching TV. The charge was fifty cents **per episode**, her children included.

As people found their way to her doorstep, my father and his cousin Joe were often leading the pack, and TV wasn't the only thing they were interested in. My father made every attempt to court my mother on his visits there, but my grandfather stayed true to his declaration. It wasn't going to happen on his watch, or so he thought.

Martha, my mother's oldest sister, was allowed to date; in fact, she was already dating Joe at the time. Although they were permitted to date, it wasn't always as smooth as they liked. My grandfather didn't always tolerate them going out. He had several conditions, which varied depending on how he felt. They had to take my mother with them on their dates as a chaperone, in addition to buying him a half pint of liquor. My parents took complete advantage of those opportunities at Joe's expense. In spite of my grandfather's wishes that they not date, they were doing so secretly. Their hoax went on for some time.

Growing up for my mother and her siblings was extremely hard. They all truly thought their father was a mean, cruel, hostile and unpleasant human being. They didn't understand he tried his absolute best to be the perfect father to them all, but the criteria for being a great father for black men living under those conditions were impossible to fulfill honorably. First, he had to overcome the hurdles no other African American man had conquered in America.

Not being respected as a human being, that was easily **STRIKE ONE AGAINST HIM.**

SECOND, he had to show his family he was capable as a man, father, and human being of keeping them from harm's way, but that was a task neither he nor any other black man could perform for their families. They stood by and watched for many years as Black Activists who fought, marched, and protested against the injustices they encountered during the 1940's, 50's, and 60's were beaten, killed, abused and imprisoned for the simplest allegation of wrongdoings. All those courageous men and women who stood up for what they believed in suffered because of it. America was teaching African Americans what obedience looked and felt like first hand.

AMERICA'S CONDUCT

Arthur Laffitte Jr., wasn't alone in his inability to stop America in its tracks. He didn't possess the antidote to cure America of its savagery. His family had been exposed to an abundance of brutalities. Psychologically, it was too late to save them from that exposure - it had already been planted in America's soil and they would be forever traumatized. America had annihilated their psyche. That was easily **STRIKE TWO AGAINST HIM**.

THIRD, he had to learn how to respect himself. That was nearly hopeless, since he had absorbed all the disrespect, abuses and degradation throughout his life. Where were the lessons for him to learn this characteristic?

In black societies, there are two different worlds and various beliefs. Some have found it easier to attack each other and blame one another for the wreckage of black people. In the inner cities, many people haven't bought into the claims that America has truly changed its conduct, practices and control of African American interactions in today's society. Many black politicians have attempted to persuade their people that all is well in America, and they scorn and look down on those who reject this premise. In the inner city, black people have some realities of their own that are far different and contrary to those falsehoods the black politicians attempt to shove down their throats. Blacks who act this way toward other blacks do it to impress upon whites that they're different from those thugs, that they get it and have overcome.

All the material things in the world could never make up for one's pride, dignity and self-worth. Many black people cherished their lives and paid a heavy price for African Americans to hold their heads up with honor. Why should blacks pretend all is well when it's not? Black people aren't responsible for the criminal acts that took place against them.

That was **CHECKMATE**, and easily **STRIKE THREE** against my grandfather, along with every other black man in America. In his defense, society wasn't controlling only him; America had its grip on all the black communities throughout the union, as it has for centuries.

My grandfather's children lost faith in him because he, like those that came before him, hadn't solved the mystery of changing America's behavior towards them. My mother and her siblings felt it was his responsibility to protect them from being worked like slaves, not taking into account that America had to be responsible for its own crimes and shortcomings. Why should he have carried the blame for America's actions? My grandfather was innocent in this entire ordeal.

America was super-sophisticated in planting seeds in African American minds that only men with power were to be respected. And who had all the power? This didn't have to be expressed to them verbally; they had a clear vision of what respect looked like through direct encounters. That image alone disqualified the majority of black men, since black women rarely witnessed African American men being respected, and the ones that demanded respect were usually killed. Like any other human-being trapped in bondage, my mother and her siblings wanted to be saved. They saw their father as their last hope and savior. So when he failed them over and over they didn't empathize with him.

They saw glimpses of power in other African American men, strength and bravery in Malcolm X, James Brown, Mr. Muhammad Ali and Dr. Martin L. King Jr. These men all dared to stand up for black people's dignity.

Malcolm Little was born in Omaha, Nebraska, in 1925. Some Klan members killed his father when he was a young child. His mother would eventually move to the state of Michigan and fight a losing battle to keep her sanity, which ended in hospitalization. Malcolm took to the streets and mastered all the ugliness in them. That sent him to prison where he was introduced to Islam. Later he became a distinguished, intellectual super-brain, the likes of which America had never seen. Once released from prison Malcolm discarded his last name replacing it with the letter "X", because for many blacks their last names are those of the white people who once owned their ancestors. The Nation of Islam wanted no part of that side of history, so they gave their last names back happily.

Malcolm became a critical thinker, and was able to comprehend quite well all of the sophisticated tricks white people were trying on the uneducated. It was extremely difficult for them to get anything past him intellectually. When they tried, he fired back with flames of truth that did not sit well with them, nor with some black folks, as crazy as that might sound. There were blacks that ran to white people's rescue when a black person insulted any of them. They were used to dealing with passive acceptance and non-resisters. Malcolm was a breath of fresh air for blacks. He didn't hesitate to say the things they were afraid to, and he said them loud enough for everyone to hear. Many white people couldn't stand the sight of him. How dare he stand up and be a man when they were breaking blacks down in bunches? Many blacks disliked him even more than white people did. They thought he was starting more trouble for them. How crazy was that? Here blacks were being hung in trees by whites, and they were thinking, Malcolm was going to make things worse because he wanted to stop them, <u>BY ANY MEANS NECESSARY.</u> He was a strong man who had blossomed from the gutters of Detroit into a genuine man of righteousness and equality for all.

Brother Malcolm left the Nation of Islam, and started his own organization, "Afro-American Unity." Not long after his separation from the Nation of Islam he was killed in New York's Audubon Ballroom, shot multiple times, allegedly by black folks. Go figure!

James Brown was an entrepreneur, songwriter, and the baddest man in the entire music industry. He was able to tap into black people's soulful spirit and made them remember they had been descendants of Kings and Queens of Africa. He was also able to push black people across the finish line when so many of them had started to crawl on their knees. While white people continued to strip away at the fabric of their inner core, <u>James Brown sang at the top of his lungs, "SAY IT LOUD, I'M BLACK AND I'M PROUD!"</u>

Whenever blacks heard that song, their spirits were high and it made them feel they could make it out of the hellhole they were stuck in. He will always be the Godfather of Soul and his music will forever stand the test of time. "SAY IT LOUD, I'M BLACK AND I'M PROUD!!"

Mr. Muhammad Ali is the greatest boxer of all time. I am not qualified to write about the greatness of Mr. Ali, or describe with accuracy the depth of his contributions to the black movement here in America. However, I am compelled to write about his nobility. Mr. Muhammad Ali was heaven-sent to black people from God, to demonstrate what courageousness looked like in human form and how it is to be worn. Mr. Ali was the example of what one man can do if he believes with his heart, faith and determination that he is unstoppable if he puts forth the effort to be better in every endeavor, small or large. He was clearly a different kind of man; it was obvious for all to see. He refused to fight a war in Vietnam because of his religious beliefs, and was sentenced to 5 years as a draft evader.

He was willing to give up his crown, fame and material gains for black people. He showed them they possessed a conscience and backbone and that they needed to find theirs. He refused to fight for a country that was hanging blacks in trees, denying them their civil rights as human beings, yet still expecting them to love this country and do as white people told them. This was complete insanity. Mr. Muhammad Ali took a stand and rejected their command to die for a cause that didn't represent black people's interest and he won. **The United States Supreme Court** would eventually overturn his conviction. He never served one day in prison - he awaited the court's decision out on bail.

After being stripped of his championship title for several years, he returned to the ring taking names and kicking ass like he was born to do. The unfortunate man who fell victim to Muhammad Ali greatness was Big George Foreman. God saw it fit to sit the Greatest back in his throne and he wore the crown like a fitting King!!

Dr. Martin L. King Jr. was a civil rights activist, among many other things. He and his associates were on the battlefront wherever there were injustices toward human beings. One day in particular Dr. King was arrested for a non-violent protest in Birmingham, Alabama. While Dr. King sat in jail, he wrote a letter to his critics who had opposed his actions. Here's what he wrote to them.

LARRY DAVIS

April 16, 1963
Birmingham, Alabama

My dear fellow Clergymen;

While confined here in the Birmingham City Jail, I came across your recent statement calling my present activities "unwise and untimely." Seldom do I pause to answer criticism of my work and ideas… but since I feel that you are men of genuine good-will and that your criticisms are sincerely set forth, I want to try to answer your statement in what I hope will be patient and reasonable terms.

You may well ask, "Why direct action? Why sit-ins, marches, and so forth? Isn't negotiation a better path?" You are quite right in calling for negotiation. Indeed, this is the very purpose of direct action. Nonviolent direct action seeks to create such a crisis and foster such a tension that a community which has constantly refused to negotiate is forced to confront the issue. It seeks so to dramatize the issue that it can no longer be ignored. My citing the creation of tension as part of the work of the nonviolent resister may sound rather shocking. But I must confess that I am not afraid of the word "tension." I have earnestly opposed violent tension, but there is a type of constructive, nonviolent tension which is necessary for growth. Just as Socrates felt that it was necessary to create a tension in the mind so that individuals could arise from the bondage of myths and half-truths to the unfettered realm of creative analysis and objective appraisal, so we must see the need for nonviolent <u>gadflies</u> to create the kind of tension in society that will help men rise from the dark depths of prejudice and racism to the majestic height of understanding and brotherhood. The purpose of our direct action program is to create a situation so crisis packed that it will <u>inevitably</u> open the door to negotiation. I therefore <u>concur</u> with you in your call for negotiation. Too long has our beloved Southland been bogged down in a tragic effort to live in monologue rather than dialogue.

One of the basic points in your statement is that the action that I and my associates have taken in Birmingham is untimely. Some have asked: "Why didn't you give the new city administration time to act?" The only answer that I can give to this query is that the new Birmingham administration must be prodded about as much as the outgoing one, before it will act. We are sadly mistaken if we feel that the election of Albert Boutwell as mayor will bring the *millennium* to Birmingham. While Mr. Boutwell is a much gentler person than Mr. Connor, they are both segregationists, dedicated to maintenance of the *status quo*. I have hope that Mr. Boutwell will be reasonable enough to see the futility of massive resistance to desegregation…My friends, I must say to you that we have not made a single gain in civil rights without determined legal and nonviolent pressure. *Lamentably*, it is an historical fact that privileged groups seldom give up their privileges voluntarily. Individuals may see the moral light and voluntarily give up their unjust posture, but as Reinhold Niebuhr has reminded us, groups tend to be more immoral than individuals.

We know through painful experience that freedom is never voluntarily given by the oppressor; it must be demanded by the oppressed. Frankly, I have yet to engage in a direct action campaign that was "well timed" in view of those who have not suffered unduly from the disease of segregation. For years now I have heard the word "Wait!" It rings in the ear of every Negro with piercing familiarity. This "Wait!" has almost always meant "Never." We must come to see, with one of our distinguished jurists, that "justice too long delayed is justice denied."

We have waited for more than 340 years for our constitutional and God given rights. The nations of Asia and Africa are moving with jet like speed toward gaining political independence; but we still creep at a horse and buggy pace toward gaining a cup of coffee at a lunch counter. Perhaps it is easy for those who have never felt the stinging darts of segregation to say, "Wait." But when you have seen vicious mobs lynch your mothers and fathers at will and drown your sister and brothers at whim; when you have seen hate filled policemen curse, kick, and even kill your black brothers and sisters; when you see the vast majority of your twenty million Negro brothers smothering in an airtight cage of poverty in the midst of an affluent society; when you suddenly find your tongue twisted and your speech stammering as you seek to explain to your six year old daughter why she can't go to the public amusement park that has just been advertised on television, and see tears welling up in her eyes when she is told that fun town is closed to colored children, and see her beginning to *distort* her personality by developing an unconscious bitterness toward white people; when you have to concoct an answer for a five year old son who is asking, "Daddy, why do white people treat colored people so mean?"; when you take a cross country drive and find it necessary to sleep night after night in the uncomfortable corners of your automobile because no motel will accept you; when you are *humiliated day in and day out by nagging signs reading "white" and "colored"; when your first name becomes "nigger," your middle name becomes "boy," (however old you **are**) and your last name becomes "John," and your wife and mother are never given the respected title "Mrs."; when you are harried by day and haunted by night by the fact that you are a Negro, living constantly at tiptoe stance, never quite knowing what to expect next, and are plagued with inner fears and outer resentments; when you are forever fighting a degenerating sense of "nobodiness"-- then you will understand why we find it difficult to wait. There comes a time when the cup of endurance runs over, and men are no longer willing to be plunged into the abyss of despair. I hope, sirs, you can understand our legitimate and unavoidable impatience*

- **Martin Luther King, Jr., letter from a Birmingham Jail.**

Dr. King described the awful condition African Americans faced day and night in Alabama. If as a child my mother felt her father was powerless to protect them, what chance did my father have to succeed as her partner in life? They weren't fully conscious of the challenges America had in store for them, yet they were willing to push forward believing freedom, justice, and equality for all were right around the corner.

SUPERMAN was needed to decode the hypnotic state many African Americans were unaware they were in. African American men weren't even playing on the same mental field as White American Psychologists. Blacks had lost the psychological battle centuries ago, but they continued to battle them as best they could. **"SAY IT LOUD. I'M BLACK AND I'M PROUD"** was in order at that time in history thanks to the **GODFATHER OF SOUL!!**

In the beginning, my father was also seeing another young lady at the same time he was dating my mother. This young lady was pregnant with his child, but aborted it without his knowledge. He got quite upset over that, which led to them breaking up. He and my mother became closer after that incident. As time went on my father decided to ask my mother to marry him, and she said **YES!!** A few months later, they got married and moved in with his mother, Momma Joe, and his half-sister, Georgia Mae. One month later, she was pregnant with my eldest brother, James E. Davis.

My paternal family worked for a white man in Claiborne, Alabama named Willie Deer. In the 1940's, 50's, and 60's, African Americans still worked for white families, like the good ole days of Abraham Lincoln. Willie Deer wanted my mother to work in the cotton fields with my father while she was pregnant, but my father told her she didn't have to work. Willie Deer became fed up with my father's disobedience and told Momma Joe that my father was meddling, and that my mother still had to work in the fields despite being pregnant. Momma Joe told my father to listen to Willie Deer, and when he didn't, she told my mother she still had to work in the fields.

That didn't sit well with my father. He got into it with his mother about telling his wife she had to work. She didn't even work for her own father, but Willie Deer wanted to be somebody's master. He tried to push the issue but ran into stiff resistance.

AMENDMENT XIII

SLAVERY

SECTION 1: Neither slavery nor involuntary servitude, except as a punishment for crime whereof the party shall have been duly convicted, shall exist within the United States, nor any place subject to their jurisdiction.

SECTION 2: Congress shall have power to enforce this article by appropriate legislation.

Proposed January 31, 1865; ratified December 6, 1865; certified December 1865.

The 13th Amendment banned slavery in 1865, but Willie Deer and my parents' encounters were in the 1960's. How do you explain this mentality? Willie Deer and my father constantly fought over Willie Deer's attempts to put my mother to work and my father's unhappiness with his pay. He was working six days a week for a $20.00 grocery trade check each week, which meant at the end of the week he could go to the store and buy $20.00 worth of groceries. He was never paid in currency, yet he continued to work since it provided his family with food. One day he decided he would take all the cotton they had picked for himself. That was his way of saying fuck Willie Deer. He went to jail of course, but he stayed rebellious.

Willie Deer couldn't take it anymore and said to him, "If you can't listen I'm going to take your car away from you. Go and get it, and park it down by the stones." He drove an off-white 1954 5-speed Ford Falcon. He thought Willie Deer was joking with him; he had to be thinking that. He went on about his business; after he got off work, he found out quickly Willie Deer wasn't joking at all. As he tried to get into his car, Willie Deer tried to block him. He pushed right past him, so Willie Deer pulled out his shotgun and threatened to kill him if he took off in the car.

In the state of Alabama, African Americans were going to be tamed one way or another. **IMAGINE THAT!!**

Momma Joe saw Willie Deer with a shotgun in his hands, arguing with her son. She jumped between him and the car. Willie Deer ordered him to get out!!

My father shouted at his mother to "get the hell out of the way." She moved and he pulled off with his tires smoking and fire jumping off the rubber as he headed for Mobile, Alabama.

Willie Deer rushed to a phone to call his brother-in-law, a police officer in Purdue Hill, to warn him that my father was heading his way. When he answered the phone Willie Deer told him what had just happened, and to stop my father. The brother-in-law said, "He already passed by and the tires on his car weren't even touching the ground." He was flying. My mother said, "It normally takes an hour and a half to get to Mobile from Claiborne, but your father made it there in twenty minutes. He was flying, jack."

My father and Willie Deer continued to fight. Willie Deer told Momma Joe, W.J. can't come back to Claiborne. (W.J., which stands for Willie James, is one of my father's aka's) How was it possible for one man to make such a statement? Who was he, GOD? He knew the laws didn't apply to him and that he was judge, jury and executioner. A white man once again blatantly ignored the Declaration of Independence.

We hold these truths to be self-evident that all men are created equal, that they are endowed by their Creator with certain unalienable rights that among these are life, liberty and the pursuit of happiness. That to secure these rights, governments are instituted among men, deriving their just powers from the consent of the governed, that whenever any form of government becomes destructive of these ends, it is the right of the people to alter or to abolish it, and to institute new government laying its foundation on such principles and organizing its powers in such form as to them shall seem most likely to affect their safety and happiness.

My father came back to Claiborne and told my mother it was best for them to leave Alabama, so my mother and the baby eventually moved back home with her parents. Two months later, in February, 1961, my oldest brother, James, died of crib death.

My father couldn't stomach Alabama any longer, and decided to search for equality somewhere else in the union. He told my mother he would send back for her when he got situated. When he left Alabama heading for California he escaped one prison infrastructure, but ran directly into the confinements of California's restraints.

AMERICA'S CONDUCT

America had its bases covered in each state. In some states, they practiced overt racism. In other states, they practiced covert racism, but all their agendas were the same - keeping African Americans controlled and oppressed.

Discombobulated

My father arrived in California looking for respect, something that had eluded him in Alabama. For some reason he believed he could find it outside of Alabama. In his mind he couldn't believe all human beings acted the way most white people were acting in Alabama towards black people. He desperately wanted to meet peace, freedom, and tranquility.

He found a house on the east side of South Central Los Angeles. Three months later he had gotten himself situated enough to send for my mother. When she arrived in California it was a new world for her. She was amazed at what she saw. One of the first things that struck her was how whites and blacks were interacting with one another, far different from anything she had seen before in her young life. The lights and highways, together with not being compelled to address white men with "Yes Sir" or "No Sir" if she chose not to, all of this was unreal to her, and she loved every second of it. She didn't know such a world existed where black people could have the space to recapture their pride, dignity and dreams, to overcome the pains they had suffered back south. To her, California afforded all those possibilities. To put it mildly she was overwhelmed. She always felt African Americans were their own worst enemies and her opinion hasn't changed to this very day. She would say, "Black people make me sick; they're always snitching on each other to white people."

However, my father didn't share in her blissfulness. He blamed whites for all of African Americans' setbacks. He developed a sickness he couldn't overcome - revenge, stubbornness and an inability to be open minded. Everything had to be his way or no way at all. He became the very person he had run away from.

Once my parents settled in they decided to start their family. Bobby was the second child, born in 1961. He was an unconventional child, yet gifted in his own way. I never quite understood his calling in life. He was a mystery that took some figuring out. He would become known as Boxco.

Debra was the third child, born in 1962. She was a handful, independent in thought. She never cared what people thought about her. She did as she pleased. I didn't like that about her for a long time, but as I grew older I viewed it as a tremendous strength of hers.

I was the fourth child, born in 1964. The best way to describe myself is to say I am my father's child. I was his twin in many ways.

Shenette was the fifth child, born in 1966. She was the princess of our family. She was the light that illuminated everything around us. She was my parents' pride and joy.

AMERICA'S CONDUCT

My parent's journey together was truly a roller coaster ride. It was a very complex, perplexing and difficult relationship to say the least. It was a puzzle I couldn't solve at the time, but I finally was able to understand their problems with clarity.

As far back as I can recall my parents always seemed to be at odds with one another over something small, but there were loving moments in between their struggles. I truly believe they loved each other with all their hearts, but never understood how to effectively communicate their love for one another. They were distracted, bombarded and misguided by social injustices that kept them disorganized, mentally and emotionally.

America's mismanagement of its citizens is the primary cause for all the misbehavior in our society; that is what my father believed.

Times were always difficult for us financially. My father worked odd jobs; one in particular was a job at Jack's Rent in Santa Monica. He would put on his outfit and be on his way to do what he thought was expected of him, but he never looked comfortable doing it. I loved seeing him go to work. He also hustled on the side. He, like my uncles, loved women, alcohol and conflict. Even with all those crippling addictions he managed to squeeze out every ounce of effort within himself for us.

My mother would disagree, but what I've learnt is that everyone views love differently. I know my father's love for his children was real and strong. He was never able to discover his dream of being respected the way he thought a man should be. He had become identical to my grandfather in his conduct without realizing what he had turned into.

I was too young to recognize what he was experiencing, but my intuition was intact and functioning well. It hadn't been diluted with poisons, so I was on point with my instincts about my father's anguish. He was self-destructing right before our eyes.

The very first home I can recall us living in was located on Gage and Converse, right off Compton Ave. I was quite young, maybe four years old or younger. Our home was a one-story, small, two bedrooms, one bath, living room and dining room, front and back yard. To me, it was nice.

There were many children in the neighborhood that were our ages, Hispanics and Blacks, as well as all my cousins. No white children were to be found anywhere in that area. In fact, at that time I hadn't ever personally seen a white child.

Most of my mother's siblings had also come to California. Her brother, Uncle Ray Lee, the eldest of all her siblings, is the lion of the bunch. Out of all my uncles he's the only one that we all call Uncle. If we attempted to call him Ray Lee he'd say,

"What you call me?" Uncle Ray Lee! "That's what I thought you said." However, we called all the rest of our uncles by their first names.

Arthur III and Willie Bob passed away before we ever got the chance to meet them. Sam was full of life; he loved women, music, drinking and parties. California seemed like it wasn't his fit. Sam was homesick it appeared. He always looked unhappy to me. He was a real country man, Alabamian through and through.

Leonard was my favorite uncle. He came out here from Alabama and didn't miss a beat. He was the life of everyone's party; he drank so much seeing him sober would have been unusual. He was able to navigate his way through hell and back with a fifth of Vodka in one hand and a fifth of Jamie O Eight in the other. He lived each day of his life like it was his last. I loved that about him. He loved drinking; he drank so much that I didn't understand how he was capable of driving a car in that condition. We could hear him coming to our house long before he made it there. He drove like a maniac, extremely irresponsibly. The tires on his car sounded louder than a roaring lion and smoked like burning wood in a winter fireplace. He'd be completely disoriented and it amazed us all how he was able to make it to our house without being pulled over by the police. There is no way the police could have missed him. He was driving completely incoherently - it just didn't make any sense. He drove a shining black 1968 Lincoln Continental with red interior, suicide doors and big, pretty whitewall tires.

Ed is my mother's favorite brother. I found that out the hard way. He was real quiet and sneaky. Ed is the closest of our uncles to us. He made it his business to be around family as much as possible when he wasn't working. He works as a carpenter for rich white people in Beverly Hills and Santa Monica.

Ben is the player of all my uncles. Women don't stand a chance with him. He is the slickest, coolest and smoothest of all my uncles. He loves women's vulnerability and their need to be loved. He has no mercy on their hearts. He makes them bleed money, so to speak. He loves women's affection, money, drinking, clothes and cars, all of America's intoxicating distractions. He also works in construction and carpentry. He is the baby of the bunch; he didn't miss a step in his upbringing, because he was the most daring and outgoing of them all. California was sprinkled with Ben in all corners of its existence. He was the opposite of a country man - a full-blooded city slick, sleek, smooth, glossy, clever, tricky, crafty, creative, sharp, suave and urban. His gift was to play women like children played marbles. I could be wrong, but I never thought he took delight in those games. However, he played the part of a professional slayer, so I credit him with an A+ for sticking to his guns, in addition to driving a beautiful, money green 1968 Mustang.

Martha and Joe traveled out to California together as well. She was the princess of the family, carrying herself with grace and assurance. I liked those qualities about her. She was very motherly and genuinely loving. They were rolling in money; Joe was his own boss, a self-made carpenter. He was able to build houses and fix anything that was broken. I admire him profoundly. He contracted work out to all my uncles, Ben, Ed, Sam, Leonard and Uncle Ray Lee, together with many more of my family members.

Reolar, the youngest girl, was like Martha Stewart. She could cook and was quite refined. She was blessed to have a good husband, Norman Cotton, who provided everything she could possibly desire. She kept an elegant home in perfect taste.

Martha and Joe had four children, John, Anise, Robert, and Lonzo McDaniel. Reolar and Norman had four children, Terry, Sandra, Randy, and Cal, but Cal was still in Alabama living with my grandmother, Lillie at the time.

All three of our families lived less than a block away from each other, so we spent plenty of time together. In all their gathering together, it seemed our family had found in each other all that my father had been in search of for himself, love, pride, freedom, respect, happiness and self-worth.

It was beautiful for us kids to be amongst them during those times, because we had the chance at a young age to experience pure love. They were truly happy that they had liberated themselves from Alabama. They played all the latest records, B.B. King, Bobby Blue Bland, Joe Tex, James Brown, Spinners, Aretha Franklin, Gladys Knight, Isley Brothers, Whispers, Four Tops, Al Green, Marvin Gaye and the Dramatics. You name it; it got played in their gatherings.

They drank and reminisced about their experiences in Alabama, mimicking the whites they had worked for and how they were told to do something, and the manner they were told to do it. They'd be laughing up a storm. They also appeared to be safe from harm's way. It was as if they all knew they had barely escaped death. But one thing they hadn't evaded was their alcohol addiction. That was just as bad as all the other experiences they had to face each day. Life for blacks was hard, for reasons whites in America never had to go through personally. It's easy to understand why most of them care not to empathize with black experiences.

No matter how long the night was, the next morning meant everyone had to face reality. They all knew they had boundaries they couldn't cross even in their newly discovered world. They would quickly align themselves within their boundaries, until their next drink; then and only then would their dreams become reality.

Sometimes dark clouds would hover over our home and my parents would start in on each other over something that really didn't have anything to do with anything. Those were the ugliest times for us because we loved our parents and we never wanted to see them fight over anything. We were too young to understand any of that stuff. All we knew was we loved them both to death.

There were joyous experiences as well. My parents oftentimes had company over, and played their music during social gatherings. My mother enjoyed seeing me dance. It never failed, when they all got together she would say, "Larry, you feel like dancing for Momma?" I would without pause respond, "Yes." I loved to emulate James Brown, and she loved seeing me do it. I thought that James Brown was spectacular, even at that young age. I have never seen anyone other than Michael Jackson come close to his talents.

I'd get dressed up with one of my throwaway shirts, so I could rip all the buttons off it when I went into my act. I'd come into the room, cape and all, with a broomstick for my microphone. Once my mother played the record she wanted me to dance to there was no stopping me. I got down!! She would be so excited to see my little feet shuffling, she'd be screaming "Get it Poppa Cat, get it! That's my baby!!"

When I saw how happy my dancing made her feel, I wanted to dance for her every time she asked me to. I loved to see her with joy in her heart. She would be radiant as ever, a beautiful black woman. She often struggled and fought with my father, so times like those were always special occasions.

Some of the fun times were when my father would tease my sister, Debra. We had two African masks in our home that scared Debra to death. They lay atop our fire place. Debra was especially scared of the masks at night when all the lights were out. The eyes in the mask would shine, and Debra would get hysterical just at the sight of them. She would go completely insane and we would laugh ourselves silly. That was one of the funniest things ever.

We never knew what made her feel so afraid of those things. She never conquered her fears of them as a child. My parents finally got rid of them and Debra slept peacefully.

AMERICA'S CONDUCT

Deterioration

It was time for me to take my first steps outside the comforts of my mother's protection, so she enrolled me into pre-school. Bobby and Debra were already in elementary school. Shenette was still being safeguarded from society's hypnotics.

My family was the only people I had ever been around. I had no idea what to expect outside of their shelter; it was a task for my mother to get me to understand what that transition was all about.

I remember not wanting to part from her company. That was my hysterical moment, like Debra's hysteria with those African masks. It took some adjusting, but I finally got comfortable enough that she was able to leave me without the fear of me losing my mind because she wasn't there with me.

I can honestly say I was still at that time sinless in thought and conduct. Pure and innocent as every child is when it comes into the world. Society's influences hadn't penetrated my way of thinking.

Once I settled in it wasn't all that awful. All the children played with clay and we made prints of our hands and feet, and painted pictures of whatever came to mind. It was a lot of fun, yet the best time of the day was when my mother came back to pick me up. I loved her so much; I never wanted her to be out of my sight. When I became much older she told me, "I couldn't go to the bathroom unless I took you with me, because you would have had a fit if I tried to leave you with anybody else." Of course, I didn't recall any of those incidents.

My pre-school experiences were short lived. We moved again to the East Side of Los Angeles on 90th street, between Compton Ave and Maie. This particular area was completely different from where we had lived before. This location was lived in by all of society's castoffs, gangsters, pimps, thugs, thieves, hustlers, players, robbers, and murderers. Every conceivable character one could imagine resided there.

Our next door neighbors were the Norwoods, a nice family. The parents, Mr. and Mrs. Norwood, were older, cordial, social and generous to everyone. They had two sons who were their total opposite, Thomas Norwood and Jake Norwood. Everyone knew Thomas as Tom Tom. He was much older than I was, maybe 12 years old. Jake was known as Shaky Jake. He was maybe 19 or older, I'm not really sure but I do know he was a grown man. Shaky Jake was a jack of all trades. He was always into something outrageous. He was one of the respected thugs in the neighborhood. He had already been to prison, something I had no idea even existed.

I remember him so well because he was dating this lady named Connie Red. She was finer than utopia. Connie Red was of a light complexion, with little freckles in her face. Her body was flawless; she was 5'2 and beautiful. She had full size lips and light brown eyes. She wore a little Afro that was sandy red, and she was hot for life.

I always wondered to myself how in the hell was Shaky Jake able to get her? That was before I was old enough to know there are many reasons women connect with men who other people would never think deserve them. Shaky Jake was always moving about, slick and fast. I learned much later he had plenty of women, and Connie Red was one of them in his game.

Tom Tom had discovered his crash dummy in me, the new kid on the block. He wasn't able to get anyone else to try his stunts until I showed up for duty. He talked me into holding a rope tied to the back of his mini bike. I had a pair of Street King Skates, which were black padded rubber and high cut. The wheels on them were a cheap piece of thin steel, and when I was being pulled down the street at a million miles an hour fire, sparks and flames would shoot up from the hot blazing wheels. I held on for dear life, wobbling along the way. If I had let go I would've certainly harmed myself badly, so I held on and chanced a heart attack. Either way it was a frightening experience.

It took some doing, but after falling many times I finally learned how to control my balance. The art to it was avoiding all the little objects in the street that caused me to stumble while being pulled or dragged down the street. I broke even on the challenges of avoiding collisions while trying to stay on my feet most of the time, but I never truly conquered them as I would have liked.

By this time my father had just about given up on anything constructive happening for African Americans. He was arrested for a crime he didn't commit which made him even more furious. He told the police he wasn't responsible for the charges he had been arrested on, but nobody believed him.

In this country the police are almost always believed to have done their job well and fairly, so when someone in custody says they're innocent, many white people just refuse to believe this could be so.

My mother went to the Los Angeles County Jail to visit him. When she put in a pass to see him and another man came down pretending to be my father, my mother immediately got up and informed the deputy that this man who came down wasn't her husband. They investigated and released my father later that night. He refused to sit down for five minutes with his family. He always had to be somewhere other than home, and he would take me with him most of the places he went. I loved going any and everywhere with him. I loved my father with all my heart. Everyone greeted him as Slick Willie. They would say; "Slick Willie, what's up?

AMERICA'S CONDUCT

Whatcha know good baby?" "Hey Slick Willie, buy me a drink!!" He would respond most of the time saying; "I ain't doing no good." It seemed like the entire city was intoxicated or wanted to be inebriated. Many African Americans were drinking themselves into their own paradise.

Many in the Black communities appeared to have conceded defeat and literally given up on their aspirations of ever overcoming their oppression. They didn't seem to be motivated to fight for the unity, peace, love, joy, respect, happiness, freedom, tranquility, dignity and the right to be treated as human beings as the generation before them had.

I saw no traces of any efforts from black people to follow in the footsteps of the people who had fought so hard to accomplish greatness for our people all those years earlier. The only freedom, pride, respect, and dignity I witnessed them fighting for came in can, cup or bottle. Many blacks had stopped caring about their lives and the lives of others; it became evident in their conduct. They learned to embrace all the things that weren't helpful to their growth in this society. Self-destruction, exploitation, and manipulation of each other were the calls of the day. Many blacks had developed an immune system that rejected empathy and consideration for one another. They didn't care who they had crushed in the process. What kind of power or influences could possibly exist in a society that would cause an entire race of people to destroy itself the way African Americans were? Everywhere you looked, somebody was giving a party. Blacks in bunches were having the time of their lives, unconsciously celebrating failure, not even remotely concerned with learning how to read, write, or help better the conditions of African Americans. Neither education nor constructive activities were even thought of, let alone discussed.

Fights would break out for the silliest of reasons. Somebody stepped on someone else's shoes - that in itself was looked at in the black community as disrespect and a reason for a beat down. Many blacks' mental state had declined to inconsequential pettiness. It was frightening, but the reality of it all was that even the blacks in California had learned, as many other blacks had throughout the country, it was easier to give up than to challenge themselves to overcome the misconception about their potential as human beings, than to try to change the climate America had created for them to fail in. They were more than capable of overcoming any obstacles that stood before them, if they had given it the same amount of effort as they had destroying one another. Instead they chose to quit, and found every excuse in the book to justify doing so.

It was time for us to check into the new school and this time around the little princess Shenette, would join us. My mother checked us into Russell Elementary School. Russell reflected the community I described earlier. Children of all ages were acting like juvenile delinquents. I met a lot of kids, but my closest friends were the Thomases. They lived right off Compton Ave and Firestone, across the street from Charles Drew Junior High School. Larry, James, Willie, Danny, Frank, and Kathy, the sole sister of the Thomases. Danny, Willie and I used to hang out together. Their brothers were much older and were doing their own thing most of the time, except when they would escort us to school on their way to school. James and Larry went to Drew Junior High and Frank and Kathy went to Fremont High. It was truly ridiculous that little kids needed to be escorted to school. We were being safeguarded from our own people. But as crazy as it was, this was viewed as normal; it was a reality. You either lived with it or got ate up by it.

When I went over to the Thomas's house, Danny, Willie and I snuck off into their back yard to smoke cigarettes. I don't know where those urges came from, I suspected we emulated the grownups. It was a must-try because they made it look so good. Their sister Kathy caught us every single time we tried it. We never knew how she busted us until one day she couldn't stand it any longer and told us how stupid we were.

Every time I went over to their house, we found our way to the back yard. They had a wooden fence with loose nails in the boards. We lifted one of the boards up and twisted and turned it until there was a space between the fence and their neighbors' fence to hide in. Once we squeezed in, we thought we were hiding from the world. We set fire to our cigarettes and smoked ourselves dizzy.

Without a moment's notice, Kathy flew out of their house and ordered us out of our hideout. She told us one day; "Y'all back there smoking, like y'all starting a fire. It's a cloud of smoke coming up from the fence. I see y'all every time y'all go back there. Don't do it again or I'm going to tell your mother, Larry." We never thought about the smoke rising up, we were only concerned with concealing our bodies from being seen. We never gave thought to hiding the smoke signals which were the evidence that got us busted each and every time.

The Thomases were a close family. They had a reputation around the neighborhood for being united. If you messed with one of them it was known you had to deal with the entire family. Everybody's family was telling their children the same things at home; protect their siblings with all their might from any outsiders.

The streets were littered with attitudes of people seeking to be respected by way of violence against one another. I truly believe many African Americans chose to define themselves and their status in this society based solely on how tough they thought they could become or how rough they were able to fool others into believing they were, inciting many innocent-minded people to travel down the same path, wasting their energy and talents on unnecessary, unproductive, self-destructive causes while destroying their own people in the process. In their hearts it wasn't truly their intention; they just didn't know any better.

AMERICA'S CONDUCT

Frank Thomas, the oldest brother, was a gang member of the East Side Crips. He used to dress up all the time in his 501 pants, bumper jacket, black high top biscuit shoes, ace deuce hat with a black hair net covering it with stick matches laced in the band of his hat. I didn't know what to make of it, but I thought it was stylish.

Russell Elementary was the testing ground for young hearts. Instead of young kids going to school to get an education, they were going to find out if they were tough enough to survive amongst the bullies. I remember this underground tunnel below the crosswalk, directly across the street from Russell. You could either cross above the tunnel at the light, or walk through the tunnel to get to the other side of the street. Those who chose to walk through the tunnel knew they took the chance of being beaten up by the older kids from the Jr. High School who awaited their victims each day. If they showed any signs of fear or weakness they would be devoured. These bullies could pick up on people's fears like professional sniffer dogs.

It was astonishing to witness children evolve full predatory instincts at that age. It was as if we were in the jungles hunting for food to survive and the food we hunted was each other. These children were mentally aware and capable of plotting sophisticated schemes with ease.

These same abilities could've been used toward something much more productive with the same effort, but they weren't. Why was that? What would cause a race of people to constantly and consistently harm themselves in this way? Why hadn't society stopped this madness?

This is a learnt behavior. Where had African Americans learned to behave in this manner? I was eight years old in an environment where the choices were either to walk under the crosswalk or above it. If I walked underneath it, I would be looked at as brave and not afraid, but would still be confronted each day to make sure I hadn't slipped through the cracks.

I chose the path I would take for the rest of my life in a society that was so full of hate. The choice was quite easy for me to make. I chose survival, a decision I thought to be brave and courageous. I decided that I would take on the bullies if confronted, because to me there weren't any other choices. I had no understanding of the consequences for the direction I had chosen for myself. I became another casualty of the pressures of courage.

I studied all the bullies in the neighborhood. I mastered their skills and noticed how many of them needed assistance when they confronted someone they viewed as weak. I learned how to fight by watching how hard the winners of each battle fought. How bad the competitors want to win and how determined they are, that is the difference between succeeding or failing in any competition. I made my mind up; I would never give up no matter what I engaged myself in. The last man standing would always be declared the winner, the champ!! I intended to be the last man standing in everything I did. I learned the skills of fighting and became exceptional at it.

My parents continued their journey together, searching for ways to grow stronger and survive the conditions that were close to unbearable. My father had released himself from any responsibilities. He did as he pleased, whenever he pleased. Happiness escaped him; he wanted so badly to be in control of his life, but was never able to find what he was in search of in the places he looked.

He hadn't searched deeply enough within himself to discover the treasure of richness that was stored inside his being. His children loved him to death. He only needed to find the courage within himself to keep looking until he discovered God had given him all that he would ever need on this earth. He had within him the ability to know all things, but he would have to work for those answers without the fear of failure. Instead he continued down the wrong path, looking for something that wasn't there. Greatness was standing right before him - his family.

My father wanted to put a pond with big goldfish in our yard. This was unthinkable in the ghetto. We lived in a small house with two bedrooms and a decent side yard, right on the main street of Maie Avenue, next to an alley. Cars and people would travel by our house from sunup to sundown. My father asked Joe to help him build the pond. It didn't take them any time to build. When they were finished it was truly a beautiful pond with all types of giant exotic fish in it. They also built a water fall in it, so water would shoot up from it while the fish swam. It was the neighborhood attraction; everybody came by to see it all the time. At night it would light up so people were able to see the fish in the black of night. They also installed electricity into the water to prevent anyone from stealing the fish while we were asleep or away. Many people thought we had money because of the pond, but we were more broke than the poorest human being on earth.

It didn't take long before someone attempted to steal the fish. It was a dark quiet night; you could tell something wasn't right. It felt like that to me every single night. If you looked out the window, it felt like somebody was watching you look at them. The entire neighborhood was expecting somebody to commit a crime on their property; it was scandalous. In that area Jesus himself didn't stand a chance. We were asleep, but out of nowhere we heard a man screaming at the top of his lungs. We all jumped up and I recall my father telling us to go back to bed. He said "I bet he won't stick his hand in another pond." Needless to say there weren't any other attempts made to steal our fish. Word spread around about those electric forces circulating through the pond's water.

My father started to display his frustration openly. He was always playing with his rifles, and one in particular was a Thirty Aught Six (30.06) rifle with a scope attached to it. My father would practice his marksmanship in front of the world, by lining up rolls of cans on the railroad tracks and knocking them down one at a time. He taught me how to hold a gun, and how to look through the scope and line up the cross hairs on the target. I loved my father so much, words could never express the depth of that emotion I felt for him.

Things for my mother and him started to deteriorate. My mother had her own friends on the block, the Holmes family, Kathy and Richard. They used to party together all the time. My mother loved alcohol just as much as my father and uncles. In fact my mother was more of the gangster. She was fearless. She knew all the bookies and she went to all the gambling shacks to shoot dice and play horses. They even gambled at our house. Now that was a sight to see, being that she was a country woman and all. Seeing my mother around all those thugs, people would've thought a child would be worried about his mother. I never had that concern for her; I used to be frightened that she was going to hurt one of them. When she got drunk she said things out her mouth that would make even the Pope raise an eyebrow, and she backed every word of it up with action.

Kathy and Richard had three children; Yvonne, who was much older, along with Monica and Reggie who were my age. Monica and Debra were good friends, and that alone kept our parents close.

My father wanted my mother to stop going out with her friends while he continued to do as he pleased, but she never gave in to his demands. She did as she pleased as well, and they fought openly in front of us over her unwillingness to give up her freedom to be herself.

We lost our minds when they fought. We ran out of the house into the middle of the street late at night attracting more attention than the fish in the pond. We noticed that when they fought and we ran out the house, they would stop fighting, so the first hint of a fight about to ignite we headed for the street without any hesitation. They would stop long enough to round us all back up and take us back into the house.

I can recall also the police coming out to our house but never taking anyone to jail after they had beaten each other half to death. They would make one of them leave the house until they cooled off. Every time it would be my father. America tolerated blacks beating on one another back then, just as it had when my grandfather was beating my grandmother. That is a learnt behavior. It was society's mismanagement of its citizens. Things got worse for them and they eventually separated. My mother didn't miss a beat; she kept her dukes up and did her absolute best to take care of us.

My father, to his credit, stayed in our lives, as well as in my mother's life. He loved her; he just didn't know how to love her respectfully. He came to the realization that she wasn't willing to give up control of her life to any human being, and he wasn't willing to stop trying to rule her life. Their battles with each other were about my father trying to make my mother become submissive, the very thing he refused to become. He wasn't aware he was attempting to deny her the freedom he was in search of. She stood her ground. To this day I haven't met any woman that comes close to being half of who she is.

All the kids used to do some of the craziest things together for fun. We would jump off the roofs of neighbors' homes onto mattresses on the ground, turning flips along the way. One day in particular, Tyrone, Andrew, Annette and I, together with other children, were all playing in the alley. There was this one house that had a garage door that wouldn't close no matter what we did to it, so we swung on it like we were Olympians. Well, that practice vanished quickly for me. As I swung on the rod it gave way and the door closed. I came crashing to the ground and my mouth hit the cement with tremendous force. I busted my lips and chipped my left front tooth. I ran home crying like I had been beaten by a pack of children. My mother took me to the dentist, and I got a silver cap put over my front tooth and it's been in my mouth ever since.

All kinds of tragedies were happening around there. Tom Tom had been hit on his mini bike by a car and he broke every bone in his body. He was lying in a full body cast in a hospital bed for months. The family brought him home and all the kids would be outside playing and he would be in his front yard in the hospital bed getting some fresh air. He looked terrible. Frank Thomas was killed by a security guard at a W.L.C.A.C. dance, shot in the back jumping a fence.

That was the beginning of the end of my experiences there, with the exception of meeting my grandparents. My grandfather decided to come out to California to live. When he got to California he came by our house first. I looked at him and thought he was taller than a telephone post. He dressed like a farmer all the time in his Khaki suits with the buttons always buttoned up to the top, and he walked with a cane. He dressed just like the Crips, but he was close to sixty years old, so there would be no mistaking him for a gang member. It was clear he was the leader of my entire family; I saw that in the way his children responded to him. He immediately took over all of his children's rights.

He had these sayings that we never heard anyone say before. If he asked me to do something, and I didn't move immediately, he would say "Larry, are you going, or do you want me to go for you?" If he saw somebody doing something he thought was strange, he'd say "I never seen such a thang before in my life, what that boy doing?" If he heard a baby cry, he would say, "What are you laughing for?" or if he thought you were trying to stand up to him, he'd say; "I'm gonna put my cane around your neck." My favorite two were when he thought you didn't understand him. He'd say; "Let's go back!!!" Or when he had gotten upset about something, he'd say; "By golly, I'm telling you." I was standing in the presence of a man that had endured great suffering and survived it, a man who possessed the courage to continue to live. He was responsible for helping to bring other lives into this world to achieve the dreams he wasn't able to see yet, and gave other generations of his family the opportunities to be a part of those dreams when they manifest themselves. I loved my grandfather to death!!

Not too long afterwards my grandmother and Cal came to California. My grandmother was a little lady with long, straight, silky black hair. She walked with a walker and was the most gracious woman I had ever seen or met. Cal guarded her like she was going to be attacked by Jaws. Cal looked at us like we were strange and we looked at her the same way. This southern thing was a bit too much for me to handle. Cal was one hundred percent country. She was the true representative of what life was like for anybody that lived in the south during the time black people were treated unfairly.

We laughed at Cal until we almost died every time we saw her, and she didn't care what we thought about her. Cal never wore any shoes in Alabama and she brought that same habit with her to California. She would be fully dressed with no shoes to be found on her feet. We tried for the longest time to get her to wear shoes, but she used to try to prove to us she didn't need them by walking over glass. It took us awhile to convince her to put on shoes. I'm happy to say she does wear shoes today, reluctantly.

Destroyed

We moved across the tracks to our new location on 92nd and Croesus. That neighborhood was a carbon copy of the area we had just moved from with one exception; two rival gangs shared the same area. The Jordan Down Project Crips were a black and Hispanic gang located inside the Jordan Down Projects. Then directly on 92nd street was the 92nd Street Bishops, a Blood gang.

I thought both groups were together, because they associated with each other, and called one another Young Bloods. I hadn't heard the term cuzz. Cuzz is a term the Crips use to identify their association with one another. I was really too young to understand all of their intricacies, but all that would change a couple years later when I had an encounter with the 92nd Street Blood Gang. That experience distinguished for me the difference between the two groups.

We lived in a two bedroom house, the front house on a two-house lot. The back house neighbors were straight up thugs; they were all brothers who ran with the Crips and Bloods. Greg was dark-skinned, 5'7, maybe 130 pounds, skinny, dirty, greasy, nappy headed, and funkier than a hundred skunks. Robert was also dark-skinned, a bit more weight than Greg, and shared the same habits. He was also filthy, smoked weed and drank Ripple all day long. Bruce I presumed to be the oldest of the three. He stood 6'1, a strong, overweight 270 pounds. He was a little more stylish than his brothers. One of many differences between them was he was light-skinned with a bushy unkempt beard. He wore a large Afro, straight from the motherland.

They had two younger brothers who were around my age. I can't recall their names, however, they all shared the same convictions - they didn't have any regard for society's rules and regulations. They took anything that wasn't nailed down. The younger two lived with their parents further up the street; their parents were junkyard dealers.

Many people in Watts were completely defiant of all society's laws in one form or another, since it was apparent America had a separate set of rules and laws for black people. Most of them lived their lives as they saw fit and oftentimes ignored society's rules.

Greg, Robert and Bruce were hoodlums and didn't hide it from anyone. They took pride in not being tamed or controlled as many African Americans had been. When you look at all the challenges that black people have had to endure, can you explain why so many blacks have continuously refused to abide by a system that only claims it is fair and just for all?

AMERICA'S CONDUCT

It appeared blacks were making a statement for everyone to see, that they refused to be manipulated into believing they were happy, satisfied, fulfilled, or free. Life for them wasn't kind or equal, not by the wildest stretch of anyone's imagination. They became resisters and stayed true to that calling. Greg and his brothers owned those little tiny cars called Mazda, with the motor in the back of the car where the trunk is usually located for storage, and the trunk was in the front of the car where the motor is usually located. They were the very first people I had ever seen with low riding cars.

They fixed on their cars every day, repairing the hydraulics and changing strokes, and all of the problems that come with low riding cars. Their cars were always pristine, the paint, the interior, and the rims stayed immaculate. They had those rims called moon rims, all shined up like brand new shining quarters, which made their cars stand out even more. They took care of their cars better than they did themselves. On the weekends, together with their homeboys, who also owned Mazdas, they caravanned throughout the inner city, showing off their cars while making them hop off the ground.

To me, it didn't make any sense for anyone to do something like that to a perfectly drivable car, yet I found it to be genius of them to have understood those skills of altering something someone else had crafted so flawlessly. I also thought the way white people had turned blacks against themselves was equally cunning, because black people were born perfect, and many of them refused to believe so. And somewhere in black people's history many of them stopped wanting to be black. It was sad.

I recall during the summer of 1972 on a beautiful hot sunny Los Angeles day, how so many African Americans got together for the Watts Festival at Will Rogers Park that was held every year. It was the roughest, toughest, coolest and most suave men and women in L.A. who met up to show off their skills, whatever they may have been. Who had the biggest muscles, or who was the baddest, or the most powerful within the city. It was a sight to see.

My friends and I were always amazed at how so many blacks could assemble together; I remember reading about a statute in Virginia during slavery in 1669 that prohibited the gathering of five males or more at any time. Alabama also had slave codes; Jim Crow Laws prohibited the gathering of five males or more, yet there at the Watts Festival there were well over a thousand Africans, most prowling around aimlessly while others had their specific purposes.

I roamed around there trying to discover my own experiences; it was always a sea of Crips, Bloods, and Black Panther Activists, together with innocent citizens that were there just to see the black movie stars and singers who rode on the back of the cars traveling down Central Ave. It was a convention equal to the hippies' movements during the 60's; the only difference was this was Watts Festival. It was a Ghetto Concert of Rebellion and lawlessness; it seemed like the entire community was there with all sorts of flavor, style, attitude and struggles.

Many people were in despair and hadn't even recognized they were at such a low point in their lives, since suffering and struggles seemed so normal. People were smoking weed and angel dust, drinking liquor, taking pills, and shooting heroin around the clock, attempting to run away from the grip America had on their psych, a stranglehold that was suffocating their airways. And there I was, learning how to misbehave in the midst of something much too seasoned for me to understand at that time.

I always loved to see all the black celebrities that rode in the back of the cars down Central Ave. When I was much older I used to reminisce about how crazy I thought those people were for taking the risk to come back to the inner city, but it became clear to me that they themselves were also at some point in their lives in the same predicament as the rest of the blacks in the inner city. America didn't trust them either. No matter how successful they were financially, they were still black, and American policies were clear - destroy all that was black in some shape, fashion or form. It literally was an accomplishment to have survived around there each and every day, but seeing these people only showed us we too could succeed if we learned how to unite our power, strength and wisdom. Together we could accomplish anything we desired, but tons of black people's blinders stayed on around the clock, being defiant, which I truly understood.

The singers and actors were living proof we could succeed. Yet I'm sure it didn't register that way with those that felt trapped. They wanted everyone to feel as they had, like there wasn't any sense in trying to change their lives, nothing was ever going to change for them. They felt that those who tried to find a better way or submitted to America's injustices toward them were equally demented, and not worthy of being called real Africans. They were deemed "sellouts". The only way to fight the injustices was for everybody to suffer together, and to give up on themselves. In the inner city that's called staying down or true to the game. How crazy is that?

It felt so good to be in the presence of so much power, strength, love, bravery, cowardice, foolishness, weakness, genius, consciousness, flaws, faith, wickedness, stupidity, betrayal, deceit, trust, winners, losers, hopes, distrust, perfection, hopelessness, loyalty, pros and cons.

African Americans possess the abilities to be all things. They just need to know and understand who they are and discover within themselves their purpose in life, then go out and conquer it. Everyone is not the same and can't do all of the same things. It's extremely critical that each person separately discover, learn, trust in their own ability and believe whole-heartedly that they are capable of accomplishing whatever is in their hearts.

AMERICA'S CONDUCT

I can honestly say no matter how negative African Americans may have behaved, I have always felt privileged to have been born black. I also understand how black people are justified in rejecting the lies that have been imposed on them, and I will always tip my hat to all of those that have fought for black people's rights even when the government tells black people which black person is good or which one isn't. We have always recognized our own leaders.

Robert, Greg, and Bruce thrived on those congregations. They were set mentally on doing as they pleased. For them, they were free and didn't care what the consequences of their actions were. Anyone that knew them understood they loved themselves enough not to ever surrender their souls the way many African Americans already had.

One day, Bruce was so bold it was truly hard to believe. My mother had washed a load of clothes, together with my father's white apple hat. The hat was made out of this thick netted cotton material. She took the clothes outside in the back yard and hung them on the clothesline so that they could dry. Remember our back yard was their front yard. Bruce decided he was going to steal my father's hat. My mother noticed the hat was missing and here comes Bruce one day passing by the window of our house dressed to impress, wearing my father's hat. He acted as if the hat was his, and worth all the gold in Africa. Around there, anything thought to be of any value was subjected to being taken or stolen by those in need. That was the majority of the people in our neighborhood.

Bruce was laid back, but confident in his foolishness. He always tried to act like he didn't care, but that day he faced a man that felt the same way. It was an early morning weekend. Bruce and his friend always gathered together in our back yard and their front yard drinking, smoking weed, playing music, fixing their cars, just having fun all the time. We were all up that morning. Pops had never seen Bruce wear this type of hat before.

Bruce walked past our house wearing what my father believed to be his hat sitting on top of his head. My father confronted him about the hat, and Bruce swore that the hat was his and refused to give it back. Initially they exchanged words. I don't know exactly what was said, however, I wanted to see the outcome of that engagement. W.J. eventually got his hat back. I loved everything about my father; he was definitely my hero in spite of all his failures in this society.

We were surrounded by those types of characters up and down the street. I met some kids on my street that were outrageous. I started to play with them every day. They were the worst children any parents could ever dream of having. Selecting well-behaved friends in this society was impossible. I lived in a neighborhood full of delinquents. Everyone around us was identical in conduct and mischief.

I thought this was how life was supposed to be; only the strong survived. I had just left Russell Elementary School, where I had to fight older kids just to make it on the school grounds each day. I've openly admitted not being America's golden child as a youth, and based on how African Americans were and still continue to be treated in this country I can honestly say I don't think I could've ever been. Yet, I can assure you I wasn't premeditatedly spiteful.

These children's minds thought of ways to get ahead all the time. In my mind I just wanted to be a child, but I constantly fought to survive amongst my peers. Because of that I learned how to be aggressive and dominant when I had to be, and I would for many years to follow.

One day my "friends" and I were playing football in the dirt in front of my parents' house. There wasn't any grass whatsoever. We played in the streets, in the dirt anywhere we could. I was just about to run the ball in for a touchdown, but those scandalous, witty children had concocted a scheme to rob me for my silver cap in my mouth. Of course I didn't know anything about their plan. As I got near the end zone out of nowhere all the kids, including my teammates tackled me down to the ground and started throwing dirt into my eyes and pulling at my silver cap. They thought my silver cap was their ticket to paradise.

I was kicking, punching and swinging on any and everybody that stood before me. Fighting with outsiders wasn't a problem for me; I had mastered that skill at Russell Elementary. When they recognized that I could fight and wasn't scared, they acted like they were all playing around, but really they thought the cap came off.

I told my mother about it and recall her saying, "Those kids' parents told them to do that shit, thinking that thing was worth some money."

It didn't stop there. Across the street was a youngster my age, who went by the name Stuff. He had a problem with siphoning gasoline out of people's cars for absolutely no reason whatsoever. The boy was eight years old carrying on like that. I watched him walk around with a white ten gallon empty bucket, and a cut-off piece of water hose in his hand. The sun shone as bright as a forest fire, but that didn't stop him from stealing. He didn't care who saw him. He would stick the hose down anybody's gas tank and suck on that hose until gas spilled from the hose into the bucket.

I thought that was magical, so I asked him how was he able to do that? Curiosity was about to kill the cat, and make its way to killing the little boy's path to peace and harmony within himself. <u>MINES!!</u>

He told me, "Suck on the water hose until you feel the gas coming out. Right before the gas comes out put the hose into the bucket and let it fill the bucket up."

In hindsight, it was ridiculous for a young child that age to be standing there with the knowledge to teach another child how to siphon gasoline out of cars when in reality they should've been innocent children behaving accordingly.

I really didn't understand his instructions, but I was listening as best I could. He asked me if I wanted to try it. Of course I responded yeah, like any follower would.

There were some wrecked cars in a vacant lot directly across the street from where we lived. In broad day light we went and tried this experiment for myself. I stuck the water hose down one of the wrecked car's gas tank then sucked on the water hose until the inside of my mouth was filled with gasoline; that said a lot about my listening skills. I spit the gas out of my mouth thinking I was about to die, it was the nastiest thing I had ever tasted in my young life, and Stuff laughed so hard he was nearly crying.

One would think that I would've given up on this exercise, but I didn't. I kept trying until finally I succeeded, and gas spilled out of the water hose into the bucket. It looked like the gas wasn't going to ever stop running out of the water hose into the bucket. I felt like I had won the lottery for being witty.

We carried the bucket of gas to his back yard. Stuff, lived next door to the vacant lot. He went inside his parents' house for something while I stood in his back yard in disbelief all that gas had come out of a car's gas tank.

I had a book of matches in my pocket, since I was still occasionally leaving smoke signals in the air. Something led me to throw a lit match in the bucket of gas. I don't remember what it was that led me to do it, because I hadn't started a fire before. When I tossed the match into the bucket, fire jumped up so high it scared me nearly to death. I ran across the street to my parents' house faster than my father drove away from Willie Deer in Alabama. The entire back yard was engulfed in fire. My mother came outside to ask me what had happened over there. "I don't know," I immediately lied, because I knew she would whoop my ass far worse than that fire burning across the street, if and when she found out I had started it. My ass would be equally engulfed in flames.

I knew instinctively what I had done was wrong, but the pressures to fit in with my surroundings were so overbearing, what choice did I have? The choices between right and wrong didn't seem difficult to make since most of the people around me were always doing wrong, making wrong appear to be normal. It wasn't just African Americans engaging in wrongdoings. White Americans were as well, while constantly telling blacks their conduct in society was unacceptable, and that they were uncivilized people. However, every time you looked around, there they were leading the pack in abnormal behavior and getting away with it.

The fire department responded to the fire, along with the police. The neighbors had seen me flee the scene and sent the police straight to our house. When the policeman saw how young I was the first thing he asked me was if I had started that fire. I don't know if he believed I had or not. I told him yeah, but it was an accident, that I didn't know gasoline could catch on fire. I really hadn't known. He told me not to be playing around with matches and if he came back out there again he wouldn't have any other choice but to take me to jail.

Today you're not allowed to whoop your children, but I knew I needed my ass whipped for all the stupid things I was doing. My mother tried her best to save me from the allure of the street glitters, but those influences were much more powerful than her whippings in her efforts to detour me.

Then, across the street was another family of brothers, whose names I can't recall. They were grown men who were supposedly the toughest dudes in the neighborhood. What was funny to me about them was they were the shortest dudes on the block. The rumors were they were killers, but for whatever reason I never took them seriously. They stood around in their yard with their shirts off looking up and down the street like they dared anyone to challenge their authority that I hadn't been made aware of. I thought they were crazy - not street crazy, but medically insane crazy.

Right around the corner next to the neighborhood store was this dude named Monkey-Man. He lived directly next to the store where everyone in the community went for their necessities. Monkey-Man was frightening; he was approximately 20 or 21 years old. He stood 6'2, and weighed about 230 pounds, 20 inch arms, 52 inch chest, full shabby unkempt beard, and nappy-headed, like he never combed his hair. He always wore overalls with no shirt, no shoes on his feet. He never spoke to anyone that I saw. He just stared at people while they walked up and down the street. He did the same thing, paced up and down the street like he was lost.

People use to say if he caught any children going to the store he would kidnap them. They didn't have to tell me twice; every time I saw Monkey-Man I went in the opposite direction without hesitation. I was convinced Monkey-Man was everything people had said he was without a shred of evidence to back up their accusations.

My mother use to send us to the store for her cigarettes. She had to write us a note with her signature on it saying she sent us because it was illegal to sell cigarettes to minors. On my routes there I oftentimes saw Monkey-Man standing in the alley next to the store. I wouldn't go anywhere near that store until he left, and if he stood there too long I went back to tell my mother Monkey-Man was standing in the alley. She wasn't scared or intimidated by him. The cigarettes were more powerful than even the influences that had led me to the streets, so she would walk me back around there to get her cigarettes. Neither Monkey-Man nor Superman was going to stop her from satisfying the urges those cigarettes gave her. Monkey-Man had reason to fear her more than she did him. <u>Nicotine is King!!</u>

For whatever reason my journey led me inside the Jordan Down Projects, where I met a youngster named Puppet along with his brothers whose names I can't recall. In addition to them were Lester, Stacey, Monte and Henry just to name a few. We started our friendship off being mischievous. Inside the projects is a junkyard. We used to jump over the fence to roam through the place aimlessly, looking for anything we could get our hands on. I believe the adrenalin is what drew us to do it. Once inside we never took anything, since we would've had problems getting stuff back over the fence. Sometimes we got discovered, and had to run for our lives, we all believed.

The employees there would chase us screaming and hollering, "Come here you little bad motha fuckas." We ran like lost foreigners, in different directions, not knowing where we were going, causing us to panic thinking we all would be caught. But we found opportunities to scale the fence without being apprehended. Once we all made it out safely we gathered around to talk about how close that was, and how we weren't going to do it again, because it was too close for our comfort.

But the very next day we found ourselves doing it all over again, running through the junk yard like wild animals. It became a game to us; after a while we sat around betting that the workers inside couldn't catch us, and they never did.

My mother tried hard to steer us all in the right direction the best that she could, and honestly I don't see where she went wrong in raising me. I made all the choices contrary to the advice and wisdoms she gave me. Oftentimes a child doesn't know how wise their parents are until it's too late, or until they have children of their own. Then and only then will they be able to see and understand how wise, understanding and thoughtful their parents were then and now, and how much their parents truly cared for and loved them, which they weren't able to fully recognize at the time.

The girls stayed on course with doing well; however, Bobby and I were sucked in by society's influences, along with an abundance of Black Americans, and we went right over the cliff with the rest of the Black Zombies.

Even though we had moved out of Russell Elementary School District, we still continued to walk to Russell until my mother could transfer us to 92nd Street Elementary. One morning she woke us all up, Bobby, Debra, Shenette and I, to get us ready for picture day at Russell. This is a day when all the children get their picture taken with all their classmates and individually. Before we left she gave Bobby the envelope with all the money inside for each of our picture purchases.

My mother had taught us to stand up for ourselves and the importance of sticking together with one another, and to never allow other children to put their hands on any of us. She said to us, "If ya'll can't whoop the kids ya'll are fighting, or if anyone is too big for ya'll, pick something up and knock them upside the head with it." She was serious and we took her serious. Society structure was corroded, dissolved and destroyed long before my mother came into the world; she knew what kind of society we were living in and the measures it took to survive in it. Even while many others went through life pretending all evils had vanished into thin air, she refused to pretend, as my father hadn't in Alabama.

Bobby put the envelope in his pocket and we headed to school. It was a routine day; we were all walking close together when we noticed this black man walking towards us. He must've known it was picture day for Russell's students, plus, we were dressed up. We knew this situation wasn't good. Bobby told us to come closer, "Come on walk faster!!" as we attempted to walk away from this man. It was to no avail; he picked up his pace and headed directly towards us. Once he approached us, he asked us if we had any money. We said, "No!" Bobby was ten, Debra nine, Shenette six, and I was eight. This man was grown; he had a switchblade in his hand, threatening us while patting our pockets. We continued to deny having any money, and he didn't find any until he was about to let us continue on to school. When he saw the envelope in Bobby's back pocket he asked him, "What is that?" Bobby said, "Nothing!" The robber told him to give it to him. I thought at the time Bobby was more concerned with my mother being upset over the money being taken. He also tried to protect us from harm's way at such a young age; I thought that was truly brave of him. When the man got the envelope he acted as if he had hit the jackpot. He smiled like it was his favorite gift at Christmastime. He took off running in one direction and we went on to school. I couldn't believe this man was taking money from children. What state of mind do you think he was in to prey on children so young? What was going on in the world that would make him pull out a switchblade on some children? First he was much too big for us to fight, plus he had a knife. Those two factors prevented us from picking up all those rocks on the train tracks, where Washington Park is now located, and lord knows there were thousands of them lying around.

When we made it back to the house, we told our mother what had happened, and she was upset naturally, not at us but at the person that had the audacity to steal from her children. My mother was a warrior. She didn't believe in allowing us to be scared of anything in society. She just tried to protect us from being swallowed up by the evils of it.

When my father got home she told him what had happened. He wanted to find this man that day. He walked with us to school for the next week pretending not to be with us telling us to point the man out if and when we saw him. My father carried a straight razor on him. He said "I betcha he won't take nothing else from nobody else's children when I finish with his motha fucken ass." I was hoping we never saw the man again, so my father would walk with us to school every morning. I loved my father to death. He always struck me as being independent, a ruler, and I always felt safe around him because I knew he loved us aside from his turmoil in society. I never once judged my father by society's standards of what a good father is supposed to be. My father to me was the perfect father who had endured extreme circumstances.

I saw and felt his heartache, but his love for us he could never hide. We were unable to find the man that had robbed us. I was glad we never did.

Bobby was more than we could handle around the house. He was also a bully. He practiced all his tactics on Debra, Shenette, and me. I wouldn't fight Bobby for a long time, for reasons I didn't completely understand for many years. I wasn't afraid of him, because I had a mean streak in me as well. I really believe I was expected to be his little brother, and the oldest brother is supposed to be the leader, so I wasn't supposed to beat up my older brother, was I? He was smart; he never gave me a chance to outgrow him. He always reminded me I was his little brother. I literally thought of him in the highest esteem.

My mother finally checked us into 92nd Street Elementary School. It was much like Russell Elementary. Many kids at 92nd were tough, roguish, and unscrupulous, yet, unaware that anything was wrong with them; this behavior was accepted as being normal. "Only the strongest survived" literally meant just that.

Bobby was ten years old. He discovered fast that he wouldn't be able to intimidate those kids as he had us. Bobby was the king of our house for sure. The first signs he was breakable, which I thought was impossible, came when a rumor got started in the neighborhood that he couldn't go to school because some other kids didn't like him. They said he was going to get beat up the next day if he went to school. I couldn't believe that. I knew we had to fight together if there was going to be any fighting. I didn't have any problems with that and I was sure Bobby didn't either.

I'll never forget one boy in particular named Lee Andrews. He was the king of 92nd Street Elementary School, meaning nobody at the school could beat him up. He was charismatic, fierce and strong, and led by example. I thought he was more than just a bully, as bad as people said he was. I saw how fair he could be also. He would, on occasion, protect children that were unable to defend themselves from other bullies that hid from him. He was one of those kids that was just tough no matter the people around him. Without question he would have qualified as one of the toughest.

Every morning before school Lee Andrews and his sidekicks stood in front of the side entrance gate, taking money from the kids as they passed through the gate. So we had to encounter him the next morning, one way or another. There wasn't any way around that.

Bobby, on the other hand, was our king and we believed in his abilities to stand up to anybody that challenged him or us; so that made for a clash of the Kings.

Lee was supposedly the one who started the rumor that Bobby couldn't come to school. Bobby knew about this rumor, but he didn't know we knew about it as well. The next morning we all were up getting ready for school, but Bobby was still in bed pretending to be sick. My mother said to him, "You weren't sick yesterday when you were outside playing all god damn day." Bobby didn't want to find out if the rumors were true or not. He continued to pretend he was sick, going as far as vomiting in the toilet bowl. He convinced her that he was ill. She told him he could stay in bed that morning. Where does a young child that age learn that kind of behavior?

I just couldn't believe my brother was scared of those kids. He would've without hesitation fired upside our heads without blinking an eye lid, but there he was frightened to fight those strangers. That didn't sit well with me. I told my mother that he wasn't sick, that some kids at school said "Bobby was going to get beat up if he came to school tomorrow." She went back into our room, got Bobby out of bed, and told him; "Get your ass out of that bed and take your ass to school. You better not let nobody put their god damn hands on you."

That was the longest walk we ever took to school; mind you the school was less than three hundred yards from our house. Bobby was walking slower than a snail crawls. Finally we made it to the side entrance gate where Lee Andrews and about nine of his hooligans were doing what they did every morning, pocket-checking randomly as the kids passed through the gate. When we went through the entrance they didn't say a word to us. We learned later that Lee Andrews didn't even know who Bobby was; the other kids were trying to scare him and succeeded in doing so.

I learned then that he would back down, yet we continued to allow him to be our leader. My mother on the other hand had a long talk with Bobby about allowing kids to bully him. There would come a time when she'd show him she wasn't playing or just talking.

I truly think Bobby suffered from my father's lack of attention towards him. My mother disagrees with me on this point, but my father was always harder on him than he was on me. My father wouldn't punish me for anything. He called me "Poppa Cat." I loved when he would say it too, "Hey Poppa Cat." I felt so loved by him. I had both the disciplinarian and the communicator and still I was pulled into the streets. Bobby got it from both barrels, mom and pop. My father always sat me down and talked to me about why I shouldn't do something and coached me on how to fool my mother when she called him to discipline me. I never saw him do any of those things with Bobby; he was always on Bobby's case about something.

Soon after that Bobby had an encounter with this boy named White Mike. Mike was this high yellow skinned kid who was around thirteen years old. He lived several houses down from us. White Mike was a gang member. He was from 92nd Street Bishops, along with his younger brother John and his cousin Willis who would later be known as Rosco.

Bobby had words with Mike over something, and Mike wanted to fight him, but Bobby didn't want to fight. They stood in our front yard pushing each other, saying things like, "You better not do it again," over and over. I stood there hoping Bobby would pop Mike in his mouth. I went in the house and told my mother "Bobby doesn't want to fight Mike. They're in the front yard and that Mike is pushing him, but Bobby won't hit him back."

My mother came outside and told Bobby, "You had better hit that boy back if he puts his hands on you." Mike hit Bobby again while my mother was standing there. Bobby still didn't hit him back. My mother started whooping Bobby's ass with a belt until he began fighting back. She told him, "I bet not ever hear about you being scared of any of these god damn kids around here you hear me, Bobby?" I never saw him act scared again until many years later.

My parents continued to have their problems. My father was upset with my mother because she refused to accept him disrespecting her. He had two children by this Mexican woman on 89th and Maie Street, a boy and a girl. My mother didn't ever overlook that circumstance fully. Maria Sanchez was the woman's name. My father would constantly be gone without a word as to his whereabouts, and my mother continued to go out with her friends.

One day we went out with my mother over to Kathy's eldest daughter's, Yvonne, who lived inside the Nickerson Garden Projects. When we got back to our house most of our furniture was gone. Only our beds along with a few other items were still in place. My mother immediately said "Your father took that stuff." They fought endlessly, yet she stood tall resisting his efforts to dominate her, and he never gave up his attempts to rule her.

I remember hearing my mother say to somebody that she went to Pomona, over to this black lady's house that was a friend of their friends, and she saw our furniture in her house. I also heard her one day say that was one of my father's ladies.

Their journey together was entangled by challenges and struggles. I recall being up late waiting on my mother to come home from going out one night, but she didn't come home. My father came by the house and waited for her as well. Later he told us she had been involved in an accident. She had been out with Kathy and Richard partying and drinking. Richard was driving his trash truck on the freeway, drunk as could be, and my mother fell out of the truck on the freeway while it was moving and split her head wide open. We were extremely happy to see her walk through the door. That accident slowed her down just a little. She still continued her journey and continued to stand tall through it all.

    I recall her saying the doctors said they didn't know how she had made it. They didn't know, Jannie Mae Laffitte-Davis is the toughest woman I've ever known.

Cloned

We moved again, back to the neighborhood where we had originally lived, but this time further up the street, 60th and Compton Avenue, into a four-unit apartment complex where my uncle Ben and his girlfriend Dot were living. They occupied apartment A. My Aunt Hessie and her husband Sammy, together with their three children, Derrick, Lisa and Seritha lived in apartment C. Hessie was Joe's sister and my father's first cousin. Her husband Sammy is the first cousin of the late David Ruffin, a well-known lead singer of the famed singing group called The Temptations. He told everyone he came in contact with this fact. Sammy looked just like him, which made it believable. However I never heard Sammy sing a note of music. My Uncle Ed's girlfriend Jean lived with her sister Passie in Apartment D and we lived in apartment B.

It had been close to six or seven years since we moved away from this area. I didn't remember anyone there, so it was a new beginning for us. This particular neighborhood was also full of its own characters; it was a little different from the communities we had just moved from. This area was a mixture of Blacks and Mexicans, whereas the other neighborhoods were predominantly African American.

In this community were mostly older men, i.e. ex-gang members of the Black Panthers, Slausons, Business Men, and the Outlaw Bloods whose members were black; however there was the Florence Thirteen that was a predominantly Mexican gang with black members. I hadn't seen or noticed any Crip gangs in this area at that time.

This location had not escaped whatever was taking place with most of the African Americans' psyches in America, I'm sure of that. Black history was repeating itself in each of their communities. African descendants were engaged in deceit, betrayal and manipulation towards each other. These things had occurred in Africa centuries before, as far back as the mid-1400's when the Portuguese natives were involved in the slave trades with African Kings on the continent of Africa. There African tribes fought wars against one another and those who fell victim to their nemesis were often captured and held captive, and exchanged with the visiting Portuguese for the commodities that Africans deemed worth the sacrifice of that which they had to exchange.

Here in America many Blacks deliberately abuse each other, emotionally and physically, then kill one another for things that at the end of the day are deemed senseless. Scores of African Americans are puppets here in America, and are exhibiting behavior similar to their ancestors. Blacks aren't even conscious this cycle actually exists. The mental sabotage that is occurring to African Americans in this country surely has hit its target and destroyed many brain cells. Once anyone becomes conscious that this illness is actively functioning within black people's daily lives, it would be criminal to stand by and watch.

My mother checked us into Lillian Elementary School. Lillian wasn't anything like Russell or 92nd Street Elementary Schools. Lillian was softer and much milder surroundings. It was tranquil, for those who were in search of such a thing. I on the other hand had been compromised, and I sought out conflict because after my experiences with the other children at the previous schools, I believed that was expected of me.

When a man is blessed to recognize his own race's pitfalls and finds the courage to step back and analyze the damage they have caused their own people and then continues in his destructive ways to further diminish his people's growth it has to be defined as psychotic. I am guilty in many ways of this behavior.

It didn't take us long to make new friends. Most of the children in this community were literally innocent in every way imaginable, children who didn't belong to any gang. Their parents, as far as I could tell, had raised them all to be decent. I myself at that time never contemplated joining any gangs, even though I had been raised around them. It just never occurred to me to become a member of any of them.

The children my age were not aggressive, nor did they practice any of the bullying tactics that I had come to master. They were in for a hellacious encounter with me. I didn't waste any time. I picked up where Lee Andrews and his hooligans left off at 92nd Street Elementary. I started another wave of self-hate and black destruction with a new generation of young, strong, talented African American children. That negative, destructive seed inside me was sprouting and grew wildly. I didn't have a clue I would become a contributor to the corrosion of other African Americans the way the Ku Klux Klan had been before my time. In my mind I was surviving amongst other fools, and those that weren't capable of standing up to the tyrants that confronted them deserved to be preyed upon. That's what I forced myself to believe even though deep in my heart I didn't feel that way. Hey, the show must go on, right?

At the age of ten I had been through some extraordinary experiences for someone my age. I still enjoyed my young life playing all the games and sports children grew up playing with each other. I was a handful for the children around there, including the twelve year old kids; I didn't spare any of them. My mind was set on dominance to prevent anyone from taking advantage of my siblings and me. Debra, Shenette and I started staying after school every day playing with other children. The playground director was Mrs. McGruder. She was a beautiful lady with a chocolate complexion, about 5'6' in height, and 160 pounds. She was exquisite, lovely and ravishing. Fluffy big ass, nice size breasts, straight-pressed midnight black hair. She was motherly to all the children and any man's dream for a woman. Mrs. McGruder was very serious about her job. She saw to it that all the children who stayed after school got fed and didn't leave the playground hungry.

In that area they had programs where most of the schools and recreational parks gave out after-school meals throughout the inner cities. I didn't miss any meals. I stood in those long lines like all the other hungry children and loved doing so.

The McGruder family was the first family we became friends with. Mrs. McGruder had four children. Tommy was the eldest of the four. He rarely came outside. When he did, he sat in a chair in their front yard. He never socialized with anyone outside his immediate family. When he was much older he became known for being cut out of the side of their house, because he had gotten so big he could no longer walk or fit through the door. Ellis was the second-born; he was my age. Ellis, who everyone called L.A., was different from the crew of men I started to hang out with. Ellis was a skinny kid with a large Afro, light brown complexion, and taller than I was. I was probably 5'0 tall, so he had to have been 5'3 in height and weighed approximately eighty pounds. We were best friends in our own non-committal sort of way. We were definitely opposites. I was an untamed child and he was mild-mannered, yet we were always together. One day Ellis and I were at the playground slap boxing. Most of the kids in the neighborhood played liked that. We either thought of ourselves as Muhammad Ali or Bruce Lee; we were always engaged in some kind of physical combat.

L.A. hit me in my nose and it started to bleed. L.A. was scared to death that I was going to beat him up. He ran saying "I'm sorry." I wasn't upset at all, I was shouting to him, "Man stop running, I'm not trippin on you." I knew Ellis wasn't trying to hurt me nor was I trying to hurt him. He slipped a punch in on me. I was more shocked by that than anything else.

Pearlo was Mrs. McGruder's eldest daughter. She was the spitting image of Mrs. McGruder, but she was a full-fledged tomboy. She played football, basketball, baseball, and soccer. All the sports the boys engaged in, she was in, and played better in each of them than many of the boys. We accepted her as a girl who could play like a guy, and we never mistreated her or a better way to put it, she never allowed us to disrespect her. Then there was the youngest, Audrey. She was the same age as Shenette, a little cutie. I saw her years later and all of her innocence was gone, she was fully active in the game and hunting down men like nobody's calling.

My brother Bobby would stay after school sometimes. He had begun to hang out with the Mexican gang Florence 13. He dressed like them and began acting and talking as they did. He was a Black Hispanic on his way down a path he would never recover from. This was the time when we started to hear the name Boxco.

My sister, Debra Denise Davis or Deborah would spell her name a variety of ways. I thought it to be spelled Deborah; that's how my mother spelled it on her birth certificate. But Deborah started changing and so did the spelling of her name.

Debra was always an independent young lady who I loved very much. She would scream up a storm when Mr. Boxco went on his prowl around the house. Debra was seeking her own space in her young life early on. She grew up always wanting to be around boys and she had this huge butt for a girl her age. Back then having a big ass got you ridiculed. The kids would point at Debra saying, "Look at that girl's big ole butt!" Didn't a single word from those kids affect Debra's actions in the slightest. She was confident in herself. I never saw one day of her life where she felt ashamed of what she looked like to others. She would swing her butt for the world to see and kept the line moving straight ahead.

Shenette was getting older. She was eight and still beautiful as ever. I was overprotective of her, and I seldom allowed outsiders to get close to her. I was her protector, and I took that responsibility quite seriously.

We played after school on the playground with all the other kids in the neighborhood. We played checkers, caroms, kickball, and all sorts of games. Many of the young boys there liked Shenette, and they always wanted to play with her, but I was impervious. Getting through me was close to impossible.

One day Shenette and this girl named Yvonne were at school on the mats, where there are these rings that the little kids swing around on. I believe it was no more than eight rings you could swing around while not allowing your feet to hit the ground. Wherever Shenette played, all the little boys on the playground came over to play with her, but I wasn't having any of that. I could be clear across the playground and still keep one eye on Shenette at all times. As the boys made their move towards her I made mine. I would come flying across the playground "Ya'll better leave my sister alone, I ain't playin' ya'll." They would respond "Larry we're just playing with her, we're not messing with her." The kids were innocent and sincerely didn't mean any harm, but I wasn't accepting any part of my mother's instructions being ignored. "Ya'll better leave my sister alone I ain't playing with ya'll." You could hear the kids talking underneath their breath saying, "I don't like Larry, and he's messing things up. I hope somebody beat him up." I would respond out loud, making sure they heard every word I spoke. "Why don't you do it you little punk."

Shenette would just stand there, not really knowing if I was protecting her or destroying her childhood experiences. Nevertheless she rarely played with other children around me unless they were family.

I remember one day I still laugh about to this day. I always suspected Yvonne to be jealous of Shenette, although they became friends. Yvonne was very unattractive and too big for her age. She looked much older than she really was, eight to be exact; but she could easily be mistaken for thirteen or fourteen years old. Yvonne and many other girls thought Shenette believed herself to be pretty, but she never looked at herself that way. She was a little child who just desired to play and have fun with whomever. All those other thoughts were going on in those other children's minds. I caught myself knowing what everybody else was thinking, and acted on what I believed them to be thinking.

I knew Yvonne didn't like Shenette, you could see it every time she came around. Shenette probably never noticed it, because she just wanted to play with all the girls and didn't think those little girls were capable of such pettiness. But they were and I was on top of it for her. I'd pretend like I was engaged in something else, but all the time I kept my eyes on Yvonne. She would be circling around Shenette like she was waiting to get on the rings, even though she could get on at any time, somewhere Shenette wasn't. I stood there watching Yvonne, saying to myself jump on the rings girl, before I beat your ass.

Shenette wasn't afraid of any of the girls. She had dealt with Boxco, so she surely wasn't scared of anyone else. One thing he taught us all was brutality, so if it came our way soft we were capable of devouring it. There wasn't anyone on the playground like Boxco, not even close.

Yvonne moved in on Shenette, conspicuously to me and said to her "I was next on the rings." Shenette responded "No you weren't." Yvonne said, "Yes I was." I didn't allow that charade to go on for one minute. I knew what time it was. I ran over there and popped Yvonne right in her mouth as hard as I could. I hit her like she was a boy. I told her "You better not put your hands on my sister, ole ugly girl." You know how kids are when they're expressing something they truly believe to be the truth, they don't care what comes out of their mouth and whatever it is many times it'll be the truth. I held my dukes up and told her, "You better leave Shenette alone. You must think I'm playing with you." There I was a young boy, throwing down on a girl. Back then in 1974 it wasn't a big deal to see boys and girls fighting one another. It was common and oftentimes the girls were the bullies. Yvonne lived directly across the street from the school. She had an older brother named Richard Hunter and three sisters, Janice, Carolyn and Ally Mae. Two of her sisters were gang members from the street gang Pueblo Bishops, which was a tiny unit of apartments, the Projects. But I had fought my way up at Lillian and became the king of Lillian Elementary School. I tried to prove I was worthy of the title every chance I got.

Yvonne climbed the fence and ran home screaming and hollering like she was dying. I did hit her hard, and I didn't care at all. I wasn't going to run, I was neither scared of her brothers nor her sisters. I went to Shenette and told her to get on the bars. When it came to my sisters, I didn't play. Yvonne's eldest sister Janice came back with her. Janice was approximately 5'2 tall, and she weighed roughly 110 lbs. with brown eyes and a light brown complexion. She was beautiful as ever, a sexy, fine woman that I would've punched equally as hard if she thought for one minute I was going to approve of Yvonne disrespecting Shenette.

Janice said to me, "Larry you better stop putting your hands on my sister." Staring her dead in the eyes I said to her, "She better leave Shenette alone. She is jealous because Shenette is pretty and she's ugly."

She looked at me like what did you say! I told the truth; nobody had 24 hour surveillance on the situation the way that I had. I knew the truth. Janice walked away looking at me like this little boy is crazy. Unmoved by her stunt, I was quite serious. If Yvonne came close to acting out towards Shenette, I would've done it again and she knew it.

Bobby continued his dominance over us. He had this thing about being the first person to eat everything edible in the house. When my mother went grocery shopping and brought the food back home, he would immediately claim all the food he wanted to be his. He would say, "These are my cereals. These are my apples. This is my bacon, and ya'll bet not mess with them until I eat first."

We would look at him like he was crazy and immediately start eating everything we could get our hands on. We knew the consequences for doing so, which was being attacked by him. We were so used to his attacks that we preferred the food. My mother always left room for us to stand up to him, so she didn't interfere with his aggressions towards us unless it was absolutely necessary, which was most of the time.

One morning my sisters and I knew there wouldn't be enough cereal to go around. So that morning we got up earlier than normal to get a jump start on Boxco. We knew if he got to the kitchen first, he wouldn't leave us anything to eat and wouldn't think anything of it. When we made it to the kitchen, we sat quietly down at the kitchen table. I went to the cabinets to get the bowls for us. Debra or Shenette got the cereal, spoons and milk. We filled our bowls up to the brims. We thought we would outslick Bobby. While pouring the milk into the bowls we covered the top with our hands; holding down the cereal so Bobby wouldn't hear the Rice Krispies Cereal popping as advertised. Right when we thought the coast was clear, I was about to fill my mouth up with the first scoop of cereal and out of nowhere, BANG!!! Boxco hit me right upside my head and hollered at the top of his lungs as if he was going crazy, "Didn't I tell ya'll not to eat my cereal!!!?" Without pause we started hollering for my mother. "Momma!" Debra wouldn't stop hollering. You would have thought the house was on fire. "Debra, these are not your cereals." She didn't want to part ways with her bowl; those hunger pains we experienced were atrocious.

Boxco had no sympathy - we got what he left over. My mother came into the kitchen and commenced to whooping his ass with anything in her reach. Bobby stood there saying "I didn't do nothing momma, they're lying." We'd still be hollering hoping my mother had enough sympathy for us that she would beat him to death.

When my mother got through whooping him, she said to me, "Larry you better start standing up to Bobby, I'm not going to always come to help you."

I had no intention of standing up to that fool; mom had done a good enough job of that for me. As for eating, Boxco was always full, you can bet that!!

Even though I didn't fight my brother I could whoop most of the other kids around me. I grew up acknowledging that Boxco was my big brother and in my strange way of thinking, I always wanted him to be my big brother and never challenged his seniority over me, even at the expense of my personal suffering.

Even after my mother and father separated, Pops came by as he pleased, and often stayed with us still. I can tell you that my mother didn't miss a beat. She wasn't one of those women that sat at home worrying about when her husband was coming home, SHIT!!! Jannie Mae would make sure we were fed and told us she'd be back in a little while, then instructed Bobby to watch over us. For us that was like leaving your children in the care of a lunatic.

My father sometimes came by and saw that my mother was gone and asked us, "Where did ya'll momma go?" All of us would hunch our shoulders simultaneously, then say; "I don't know." Shenette would be holding on to Debra, pops wouldn't waste any time seeking Shenette's company. He would say "Come here Blump! Blump!" That's the nickname he gave her. He picked her up and continued to question us about my mother's whereabouts. "Have ya'll been eating?" Sometimes we had, but sometimes we hadn't. Our family wasn't doing well financially; we were one of those families that received government aid. We used to get donated food from the school's program. Some families were able to give extra canned goods and other food items to the school, and the people in charge of this program would divide the food for the families that were in need. We qualified for that and we loved every bit of it. I remember we all would be happy to get that box of food.

To this very day I'm still grateful to those that had the compassion to be so thoughtful for those families that were in need, and grateful to my mother for her ability to find avenues that kept us afloat in a divided, hateful and evil society towards African Americans. She had the strength and courage not to give up when many people would've understood if she had. My father didn't want my mother doing anything outside the house, not unless it was with him or family. He was southern, no matter how much he fought against it, and he believed in the traditional upbringing of most southern men towards women. Some of those traditional ways were women should obey their husbands' every wish and for a while my mother was submissive in that way. But she broke out of that traditional role of being passive and discovered her own life, her own way of existing. She loved her new-found freedom and refused to give it up to any man, including my father. She wasn't going to be treated inhumanely by whites or blacks. She found the courage to fight for her life and rights, one of the best things she ever did for herself.

My parents truly loved one another in spite of their struggles. The problem with most relationships is people are afraid to be themselves and oftentimes they pretend to be something or someone they're not. This causes them to become unfaithful, deceitful, and unhappy, so it becomes difficult to continue this act and the anxiety from faking eventually spills over in their very existence.

Surely her children loved her with all their heart, and my mother found the courage to love herself the way God made her. If the people in her life couldn't accept her as she was, she was willing to find someone who would. I had to learn that lesson.

Bobby started to act out, not just towards us either. He became rebellious in every way. He started smoking weed and angel dust, sniffing glue, all sorts of things that were odd for him to even have considered. Although he was hard and aggressive towards us he has always been intelligent, smart and witty.

My mother knew Bobby was bright, so she went out of her way to make sure he had all the things he needed in school where he excelled. When she learned about his conduct she was devastated; she couldn't believe he was throwing away his future. My mother never showed it outwardly. She tried her best to correct the path he had been traveling down. She whooped his ass until it was clear that wouldn't help any longer. The streets had captured her son.

Because of Bobby's conduct we started getting our asses whooped more. She refused to allow the same things to happen to us. Those were some serious, but funny times for us when we got into any trouble. When we managed to find trouble and make no mistake about it, trouble we were in search of, she used to tell us "Go outside and find me some switches to whoop ya'll asses."

We sat there like she wasn't talking to any of us. Outside in our yard were trees everywhere, so finding switches came easy. When we didn't come back into the house fast enough she would come outside looking for us saying, "That's all right. I'll be here when ya'll decide to come back inside." In one hand she'd be holding an extension cord clearly implying; find the switches like I told ya'll to or I have what I need right here; letting us see the extension cord dangling.

I would always try to be slick. I got the thin switches, thinking they would break easier than the bigger ones, but they didn't. The skinny ones were the most deadly of them all, because they stung and never broke. The bigger ones always broke, but the thought of getting whooped with a tree branch always overrode good sense.

Mom saw I was becoming more and more unruly as well, but drugs weren't my problem. I was becoming curious about the nightlife; it always intrigued me why a bunch of grown men liked to hang out at night. Life for many of the men around there was truly meaningless and their actions spoke volumes.

I started staying out, lying to my mother about my whereabouts, telling her that I was over to a friend house, and I forgot what time it was - stuff that was stupid.

She never bought any of my lies. She would ground me for days on end, but that never worked. She did her very best to save us from harm's way just as her father had attempted to do for them. But my path was to be fulfilled, so I went astray from the direction my mother was pointing me.

When she got completely exhausted from putting up with my unruliness, she would call my father. She'd say "WJ, Larry is acting up; he's beating up all these kids at school and taking their money. You need to come talk to him." Pops would come over and that would be a joy to me. This would be the time my father and I could have auditioned for a role in a Hollywood movie. I knew how he would make his entrance before he got there. He would come through the door, "Where is that boy?"

My siblings and I would be in our room. We shared a bedroom with two bunk beds, one for Bobby and me, and one for Debra and Shenette. They would be in the room waiting on my father to come whoop me or so they always thought. They'd begin with "Ooh, daddy is going to whoop your butt when he gets over here." I would always respond, "No he ain't." They'd be laughing at me when out of nowhere my father would bust through the door all dramatic and say, "Where's that boy at?" My siblings would say, "Hi daddy, hi daddy." "Come here, Larry bring your ass over here. Your mother told me you've been acting up. Take your ass to your momma's room. Jannie Mae, where's that belt?"

My mother would be looking at me like you made me do it while at the same time handing him what looked like a whip. All along she knew my father wasn't going to touch me. That was her way of getting him to come over so they could become intimate. How about that?

I was used as bait for my minor violations, but violations nonetheless. She still however was going to touch me up after he left or sometimes while he was still there. While in my mother's room, Pops would say, "Hey Poppa Cat, are you takin' money from those kids at school?" I wouldn't know what to say to that question. I didn't know if he'd approve of it or not so I just trusted he would understand and I told him the truth, "Yeah." He said, "Get over here." With me standing right next to him, he'd holler, "Don't have me keep coming over here to whoop your ass, if I have to come back over here again you're not going to like it, you hear me Larry?"

He'd be yelling this pretending like he was whooping me, but he'd be hitting the bed with the belt, instructing me to holler. I acted like I was being killed in there. "Okay daddy, ooh! ooh! aaw! aaw! daddy! daddy! okay daddy! aaw! daddy! daddy! I ain't goin' to do it no more I promise daddy, please, please, please daddy, please daddy, daddy, please I ain't goin' do it no more!!!!"

Before leaving the room my father would say, "Put some spit in your eyes and get the hell out of here. Your momma is gonna whoop your ass if you keep acting up, you know that don't you?" "Yeah." I would shoot pass Moms as fast as I could, because I knew she'd be right there when I came out to see if I really got disciplined. She was always skeptical about whether I was truly being punished, so I would never look her directly in her eyes when I came running out of her room.

No matter how slick children think they are with their parents, they never really deceive them the way they think they do. I knew I couldn't fool her, but that never stopped me from trying since the outcome would be the same anyway. Weeks later, after you thought you got away with something, she'd be whooping me for something I just did, then she'd remind me, "Don't you ever lie to me, last week you thought you got away with that shit you did, I was just tired. I ain't tired now. This is for last week and the week before that, don't you ever lie to me." So I made it worse by even trying.

My father would stay the night with my mother, and we would all be happy that he did, until bedtime. Once we all went to bed, Debra and the other two would start in on me. "Ha ha you got a whooping, daddy whooped your butt!" "No he didn't." "Yeah he did." "No he didn't." "You are lying." "No I'm not, daddy didn't touch me he was hitting the bed." They would all jump up knock on their door. Pops and Moms would be attending to their duties, but my sisters and brother didn't care. "What do ya'll want?" "Momma, Larry said daddy didn't whoop him." "Get ya'll assess back in that goddamn room, and don't knock on this door again." It was my turn to tease them when they came back into the room. "I told ya'll daddy didn't whoop me." They didn't care what instructions they were just given; they wanted me punished. They all ran right back out there crying, "Momma, Larry said daddy didn't whoop him." My mother would come shooting out of her room swatting anything in her path, "Come here Larry." I'm the only one in the bed following her previous instructions while everyone else had totally disregarded them. "Get your ass down here right now." I'd take my time - this was no auditioning. With Moms this was the real McCoy ass-whooping. "So your daddy didn't whoop your ass huh? Run in there and tell them this, run in there and tell them this Larry!!!"

When I went back into the room I was defeated, wasn't no lying about that ass-whooping. They witnessed it firsthand. I got back in bed and they all said in harmony, "You got a whooping that time." After they had been reassured of this fact we'd all fall asleep.

The next morning Pops got up and called me, "Poppa Cat come here. Your momma whooped your little ass huh?" "Yeah." "That's what you get for running your mouth. Next time keep it closed."

My father had gotten sick. Drinking was taking its toll on him and his liver. He had this rare disease where all of his organs got hard and he was hospitalized. We kids didn't know how serious it was and to this day I don't know if my mother knew how serious it was. I assumed that she did. We started visiting him often in Martin Luther King Hospital; he looked strong, healthy and radiant to me. His smile was always bright when he walked towards us. He would light up, as we would when we saw him. I loved my father and I never saw any faults in him.

He would continue to go in and out of the hospital while we lived in our new location. One day we were over to my Aunt Reolar's house. My father and Uncle Norman, Reolar's husband, were into it over something; I had no idea what it was. Later on when I got older, my mother told us a story about my aunt and my father, so I assume now that confrontation was over the story my mother shared with us.

Norman is close to 5'6, 5'7 or so, 230 lbs. and my father was close to 5'7, 5'8 and 150 lbs. As I stood there watching them argue, I noticed in my father's right hand that his fingers were laced with razor blades encouraging Norman to come closer. I assume Norman saw the razor blades in his hand and declined to move forward. I assure you that Norman never backed down then or later in life, but that day it wasn't a good day to be brave.

One day when we all came back from school my mother sat on the couch as we walked through the door. She told us all to sit down she had something to tell us. I wasn't ready or prepared to hear what she had to say. She told us, "Your father passed away today." I didn't know what she meant by passed away. I don't remember if I asked her, but later she said he had died. It was unbelievable to me. At that time I never knew anybody that had died. I heard about my friends, Danny's brother, Frank, but I didn't know death personally.

My father was gone from my life in the first ten years; I was devastated. My life would never be the same from that day forth. My father was the very first human being I knew that had actually died. There would never be any more auditioning, no more Poppa Cats, no more visiting with him at his house, or with his friends, no more holding his hand while walking down the street, no more fear of him walking through the door after my mother had called him to discipline me, no more fights with my mother and he, no more guidance in life, no more bright smiles, no more WJ's or Slick Willie's, no more lessons in life from him, no more anything. He was no longer here on earth with us. My father was gone. He had passed away.

We never talked about my father's death openly and I didn't know how any of my siblings took it, or how it affected them. But Bobby began smoking cigarettes, which my mother didn't approve of. I recall her making him eat a pack of cigarettes to stop him from smoking.

As for me, my father's death killed me inside and my mother knew it. She kept me close to her. She knew that my heart wasn't strong enough to beat on its own. I needed her guardianship. I loved my father so much, it's impossible to express with words.

My mother made all the funeral arrangements. He was buried in Alabama next to his father's grave. My entire family in California planned to drive out there. That was an experience within itself for a ten year old. All of my uncles, aunts, and cousins rolled out there in mobile homes, cars and trucks. Once we arrived in Alabama, I immediately recognized the difference. To say it was just different than L.A. would be a gross understatement. It was 1974. Immediately anyone that wasn't from the south would notice they had played a completely different game there; racism was thick and prevalent for all to see. The difference was like night and day from how California operated. Most of the people back south thought people from California lived close or next door to all the Hollywood Stars that they saw on television. My father's sister Georgia Mae's children would ask us "Have ya'll seen Michael Jackson?" We told them those people lived in a different part of the city, a part we could not go into.

Alabama was a different world for my siblings and me. Alabama for me, even at the age of ten, was just too much to bear. The state of Alabama is a beautiful state. The air was so fresh and clean, it was like breathing in pure oxygen and drinking clean cold ice water - quite refreshing.

My grandmother Momma Joe, together with her daughter, children and mother, all lived in the same home. Their home was like all the pictures I saw of many African American southerners on television - run down, but inside an abundance of love, harmony, and joy that they all shared with each other.

My great-grandmother Kissiah Williams was bed-resting. She was extremely old. They all took great care of her and I remember thinking to myself when my mother got older I prayed we would take care of her the way they took care of my great-grandmother.

Before the funeral my cousin showed us around Alabama. It is a beautiful state I must admit. They took us to the cotton field where my mother and father once picked cotton. They showed us where the cotton got processed, and the place Willie Deer owned. Alabama was just a beautiful sight. My grandmother Momma Joe told us stories about my father when he was young. We enjoyed hearing her tell stories; it was as if you were at the place she was describing.

We met many people back there that were kin to us in one form or another. It's almost impossible to keep up with how everyone is kin in the south.

Before the funeral I started acting up a little; I didn't like how most of the blacks back there were still submissive towards whites. Everywhere you went blacks still were saying, Yes saah! No saah! to white people. It didn't seem nor sound right to me.

My grandmother's friends came by to meet us. Momma Joe would say that's WJ's son right there, referring to me as she spoke to some white people. They would say, "You WJ's son?" I responded, "Yeah." "He acts just like him. WJ could've shitted that boy out."

My mother told my grandma, "That one right there," referring to me, "is something else," meaning that I have my father's ways.

Momma Joe was so loving and beautiful. I wasn't raised around her, but she, like my grandfather, was strong, firm and authoritative. You would never mistake who was in charge when you were in her presence.

She saw that I had my father's ways, and she knew I wasn't a country boy. I had my father's blood running through me. I heard people say that's little WJ all over again. I took that to mean I wasn't going to take nobody's shit.

I wanted to see the outhouses I had seen on TV. My grandmother and family had a toilet inside their home and an outhouse in the back yard. It was something that just blew my mind. I couldn't believe my mother lived like that when she was younger. African Americans are mighty strong, I concluded.

My grandmother's back yard was gigantic. The children in the south have plenty of room to play with one another without the fear of being shot by other black children if they chose to hang out at home in their football field size yard. I was impressed - it really blew my mind.

If it was possible to erase the racism from the roots of Alabama, they'd have a state of fresh harmony forever because Alabama is such a beautiful landscape. It was spacious and tranquil back there. I could easily see how people could fall in love with the south, but the disrespect towards African Americans was still prevalent. George Wallace was still the governor of Alabama at the time, and I recall my Aunt Georgia Mae had pointed out the governor's mansion one day when we were driving down the road. She said, "That's where George Wallace lives." I didn't have a clue who she was referring to at that time, but when I got older, I read about how racist he was. He was like the king of the Klansmen, and ran Alabama with an iron fist, bar none.

It was time for the funeral. My mother had gotten us all ready. She handled us and the death of my father the way he would've expected her to. She showed us she loved him by the way she buried him with respect and dignity. I will never forget how special and beautiful my mother is. It was a transparent, still but breezy morning. I remember feeling like I was floating in mid-air while standing on my feet, but my mind had drifted off into another galaxy while everyone started gathering together to bury my father.

I still hadn't really understood the magnitude of what was happening, until it was time to bury him. Once we arrived at the church where he was being eulogized there were so many people it was unbelievable.

My father was in the casket right in front of us. He looked at peace; he looked as if he was just resting. I didn't understand why my father had to leave, but he had finally gained his freedom through the journey of death.

I sat in my mother's lap, still in disbelief that my father was dead. I swear when it came time for everybody to walk up and view his body, the process started to register to me. That was it. It was all over for our relationship as father and son.

When we were in Los Angeles, my mother and I went to view his body while she made arrangements leading up to the funeral. I had been fine, and hadn't acted out, but I was destroyed eternally. When I walked up to his casket inside that church something inside changed. I went completely demented. I can't really describe my behavior accurately; all I remember was that I temporarily was inconsolable.

My mother did her best to calm me down. I was so hurt. I was literally heartbroken my father was gone. We went to the burial ground where we laid him next to his father. Once they started shoveling dirt onto his grave I understood full well he wasn't ever going to come back to us physically.

Everybody went back to my grandmother's house where everyone talked about him and how he looked since they had last seen him, and how different all of my mother's siblings looked since they left Alabama.

Back south, at the time we were there, all of the stores closed early. I can't remember the exact time, but I do remember they had to go purchase liquor from people that were bootlegging it out of their homes. So a lot of us went out with my family members to get them something to drink. When we arrived to the house that was selling the liquor, of course everybody knew each other, so they all stood out there socializing with one another. Also standing out there was this young lady named Lisa. It was dark back south, and when it got dark it was midnight black. You couldn't see your hands in front of your face without light. Therefore people left the car lights on while everyone stood outside conversing. While we stood out there I heard someone say "Girl you better go over there and meet your brothers and sisters." I looked up and saw this girl we had seen at the funeral and at my grandmother's home but nobody said anything about her being our sister. I guess she wasn't going to let us leave before we knew that was her father also.

Lisa stood there looking scared and confused, debating if she should come forward or not. There was no doubt she was our sister. She looked just like my father and my eldest sister Debra, big butt and all. Lisa's eyes were like my father's, hazel brown.

I thought that was funny, you know how children are when they find out they're sharing the same parent from different families? Well, Lisa claimed our father the same as we had. It didn't bother me; I was watching my mother, because I don't know if she knew anything about Lisa already or not. It didn't appear that she had. She was more concerned for our well-being.

I had acted out something terrible, and I for sure bore watching. Debra was looking at Lisa in disbelief that she was our sister. Debra was 12 years old, so Lisa was around fifteen years old, at least I presumed as much. I walked over to Lisa and said "Hi" to her. I wanted any and everything connected or associated to my father around me. I didn't care if it was a tree he had planted out there when he was a child, I was all for it.

I loved my father more than I could ever express in words. If I remember correctly, my mother urged the rest of my siblings to introduce themselves too.

My grandmother's side of the family already knew of Lisa. She was a native of Alabama. A few years later we found out Lisa had been killed in a car crash. My mother was upset about her being buried next to my father's grave, I do remember that.

When it came time for us to leave, we all said our good-byes and how much we enjoyed one another and we were on our way back to sunny California. We had brought my father back to his roots so he could rest his soul and spirit in the very place he despised. His mother's love for him overpowered all that he felt was wrong in Alabama, so his spirit hovers throughout the south.

I knew that I would miss all that fresh, clean and refreshing air that the South had to offer. However, my journey was in California. We passed through Mississippi and Louisiana, and fueled up in Texas. I told you how we traveled there - when we pulled over it looked like we had come to take over the town. We were jumping out of mobile homes, trucks and cars.

As I was walking toward the inside of the store with my mother this little white boy, who couldn't have been more than six years old, began running toward us, pointing his finger at us, screaming to his father, "Daddy, daddy, daddy, look at all those niggers, look at all those niggers."

I couldn't believe it. I had heard the stories my mother and father had talked about, but I hadn't ever experienced racism firsthand until then. Without hesitation I started after his little ass with every intention to whoop his ass. I knew this would be easily the fastest ass whooping I ever gave any child, plus my father was just buried. I didn't care how old he was, I was going to teach him human decency, something his parents had failed to teach him. He was about to learn it from me the same way many white southerners had taught African Americans when they misbehaved according to them. This was called correcting during slavery. I was about to correct the little white boy's conduct.

I immediately gave chase after him, and my mother ran after me and grabbed me by the arm and said to me, "Get your ass back in that truck!" I never saw my mother that intense. She was serious and she had a look of such concern on her face I knew there would be no challenging her authority. That was clear as the air in Alabama. She knew the consequences of my actions would be dire if I had carried them out as planned.

The boy's father didn't flutter, blink nor waver as he looked at all of us. He was assured we weren't crazy, surely we could see this boy was white. Little did he know it was a few people riding with us that would've carved his ass inside out, but my mother took the lead on the situation. I know one thing, I didn't grow up in the south, so I didn't get to see nor experience all those African people being hung in trees, raped, killed for looking at white women or for whistling at them or for just being black. So I was far from being afraid of the little boy or his father. Whatever mission I would've been sent on, his ass would've been fried chicken. Whites didn't scare me; I was more afraid of black people.

My mother lived through that era, so she knew the realities of the situation we were in. She rounded everyone up and told them to stop further up the road to fuel up. She also knew if I had caught the boy we would've suffered far greater. Once we got inside the mobile home truck, she never once said a word to me or did she scold me for my reaction to what the little white boy had said. I had a right to be treated with respect and decency and she wasn't going to make me feel like I'd done anything wrong.

My mother is a dynamic woman and consistently stayed on me about doing right, but I had too much of my father in me and the streets had already gobbled me up.

Retardation

We made it back safely to California, THE LAND OF THE FREE AND THE HOME OF THE BRAVE. Immediately my mother sent us back to school. Everything that I had been exposed to was entirely too much for me to handle; school was the last place I wanted to be. My father's death left a gaping hole left in my chest. I knew life would never be the same for me again. I missed him so much, and there wasn't a day that went by that I didn't think of him.

My existence on Earth had just begun 10 years earlier. My brain was still in the stages of curiosity and there I was internally empty, distraught and uninterested in participating in many of the activities around me. I continued to admire my mother because she showed us a great deal of calmness and strength. She was our SUPER-WOMAN. However, clandestinely, I continued to ignore her guidance and wisdom.

School for me became recreational and I had no interest in academics. I wasn't one of those children who liked math, reading, language or spelling. I hated all of those subjects and oftentimes expressed as much. Whenever the teacher called me up to the chalkboard to solve a math problem or to read a paragraph from a book, the other students looked on with anticipation of me failing in my duties, like stumbling over words as I read, or getting a math problem wrong. I would be so frightened that I was going to embarrass myself; I'd literally be shaking like a wet dog internally. Those who made the fatal mistake of getting up there not knowing how to read or solve the problems given to them would be welcomed with a loud outburst of laughter from most of the children in the classroom. I was going to avoid that humiliation by all means. In the past when I had attempted to work on the problems I would lose focus for whatever reason, and I was unable to pronounce words correctly. So each time I was chosen to stand up I thought it would be better for me to act belligerent so the teacher would never want to call me to the chalkboard again. But that didn't work with Ms. Berry. She stuck with me to the end.

My mother tried her best to get us through the tragedy of my father's death. Bobby, Debra, Shenette and I never talked about his death; we just kept on living. I didn't know how it affected them nor did they know how it affected me, but my mother knew I had been mentally wounded.

She, being her spectacular self, put me in the school band, where I had a choice of playing any instrument I chose. I chose to play the trumpet because of Louis Armstrong, the famous trumpet player. I saw him on TV shows playing a lot, and I knew how everyone marveled at his mastery of that particular instrument. So I figured I would get people to be amazed at me in the same way, if only I could learn how to play as he had. He was African American and it didn't seem as if he was treated with the same contempt as most of the black people were in the inner city.

Ellis and Pearlo decided that they also would join me in the band. Pearlo played the clarinet, and Ellis played the trumpet. I was allowed to bring the trumpet home each night to practice but other things distracted me, like playing hopscotch, marbles and jump rope. All sorts of games with my siblings, cousins and friends were much more alluring. I never became as good as Mr. Armstrong. However, I did learn how to play the trumpet well enough to be invited to perform at the Hollywood Bowl with the rest of my band mates. When we arrived there I was trembling like a man caught in a freezing blizzard. I managed to get through our performance missing every note; I was shook up! Because there were so many of us playing at the same time my follies went unnoticed. At one point during our performance I stopped blowing into the horn altogether and Milly Vanillied my way through to the end, pretending to be playing with everyone else while not playing a single note. As soon as that experience was over, so was my trumpet career.

My cousin, Big John, was massive. At age 17 he stood 6'1" in height, weighed 180 pounds with 17-inch arms, an enormous chest, a large afro and brown eyes. Most of the women that entered his presence were captivated by his charm. He also was one of the most persuasive, smoothest-talking dudes I have ever been around. One thing was certain - any man who left his woman around Big John would be doing so at his own risk.

Big John was a street-savvy thug who ran with The East Side Crips. This was my first opportunity to actually meet some of these dudes. I thought they were ghetto stars. They carried themselves with a tremendous amount of dignity and self-esteem, and they surely didn't lack confidence. They were strong and admirable. They were staking their claims on the City of Los Angeles County and truly believed they were a force to be reckoned with. They also acted as if they were all biological brothers, something I personally found rich and attractive. Looking back on it now illustrates to me how easily the strong can be taken advantage of. Mighty as they were in strength and muscles, economically they were completely weak and without vigor. They just hadn't noticed it because they were in search of what all black men wanted in their lives, to be left the fuck alone by white people. However, America wasn't going to spare them, so all of their struggles continued forward.

Big John started coming by our house regularly to take me places after my father's death. Being around him I started seeing a lot of things I wouldn't normally have been exposed to. I recall one day in particular when Big John, Lonzo and I were going over to my cousin Terry's house. As we walked along some railroad tracks, we ran into a dude Big John had some history with. From the look of their conversation, it wasn't pleasant, and before we knew it, the dude Big John was talking to fell to the ground in excruciating pain. We thought nothing of it and went on about our business.

A couple months later, Big John was walking home, down the street from where he lived. He had completely forgotten about the incident he had with that dude on the railroad tracks. He wasn't paying attention and he allowed a car to pull up alongside. Before he realized what was happening, he walked into a hail of bullets and was hit several times. I couldn't believe it - everything that could possibly go wrong in my life was occurring repeatedly. I was sad the person I most respected in the place of my father was now fighting for his life. I wanted to be just like him. His behavior wasn't the worst I saw in this society; in fact it was mild in comparison to how most white people in America had carried on for centuries. I wanted him to live. He had to pull through.

My entire family went to the hospital to see him and the doctors told his parents, Martha and Joe, that if it wasn't for his huge muscles he wouldn't have made it. A few days after his surgery they allowed us to visit with him. He was all wrapped up looking like a mummy, but when we walked in to see him he had a gigantic smile on his face. I knew then he would be fine.

Finally one day I had the chance to see the leader of The East Side Crips, Raymond Washington, who stood 5'9 inches in height, 210 lbs., built like boxer Mike Tyson. Raymond Washington started out belonging to a gang called The Avenues. The Avenues weren't Crips or Bloods; they were a neighborhood gang like the Slausons, Businessmen, and Farmers.

Raymond was too young to be amongst the older members so he was a Baby Avenue, which he was not too happy about. He thought that status was beneath him and wanted to be a part of the older crew. The leader of Avenues was a man named Big Craig Munson who stood 6'3 in height, 230 lbs. with 22-23 inch arms. He was bigger and rougher than all the Avenues and many others in the Los Angeles area. Raymond was determined to move up the ladder, wherever that was. It surely wasn't going to be next to Big Craig Munson.

Raymond ran around brutally beating the younger members of the Baby Avenues without mercy. Craig warned Raymond many times to stop acting like a bully but Raymond didn't listen, so finally Craig was compelled to make an example out of him. Craig kicked Raymond out of the gang.

Raymond didn't take being kicked out of the gang lightly. In anger, he vowed to start his own gang. He began recruiting members into his newly discovered love, The East Side Crips.

In 1969 they started with eighteen members at Fremont High School in the City of Los Angeles, on 76th Street between San Pedro and Avalon. The first men to Crip walk on the East Side of Los Angeles were Raymond Washington, Alton

Jones, Big Paul, Pookie, Sleepy, Psycho Michael, Mack Thomas, Terry Simmons, Lil Danny, Avis, Vertis Swan, Bull Dog, Number One, Caldell, Lil John, Iky, Mad Dog and L.C.Butler and others.

Immediately after their meeting they all went to Leo's Surplus on 88th and Broadway to buy Ace Deuce hats, which became one of their signature trademarks. Raymond instructed them that they were going to recruit other members, and that they had to be tough and hardcore to holler East Side Crips out of their mouths. In addition, members would be initiated into the gang by running down a line with Crip members lined up on both sides, fighting their way through to the end as the other members beat them half to death. Now wasn't that something? The things we do to prove our love and loyalties to one another in the inner city. **CRIPPING AIN'T NEVER BEEN EASY.**

Raymond didn't hesitate to let everyone know he was now a Crip. He painted the walls everywhere he went – **"Chitty, chitty, bang, bang, nothing but a Crip thang. Crips don't die they multiply."**

The Crips grew in number, which was fine with Raymond because he wanted to prove to Big Craig Munson that his gang would be bigger and rougher than the Avenues could ever be. Soon the Black Panther Party members took notice of the Crips and their swagger. They approached Raymond, and asked him to convert the Crips into Black Panther members. Raymond told them emphatically, "No!" **CRIPS DON'T DIE THEY MULTIPLY. CHITTY, CHITTY, BANG, BANG, NOTHING BUT A CRIP THANG!!!**

Raymond wanted to spread the Crips throughout Los Angeles' East, West, and South sides. They all had heard about a dude name Big Tookie from a gang that called themselves The Al Capone's. In 1971, the Crips set up a meeting with Big Tookie and his homeboys at Sportsman Park. When they met, the Crips thought that Big Tookie was Crip material and recruited him into the Crips. That's how Big Tookie became The Godfather of the West Side Crips.

Not long after he started The Crips, Raymond was sent to California Youth Authority and Big Alton stepped in to take his place. In addition to Raymond and Big Alton, I was also fortunate enough to meet Baby Alton. Baby Alton was shorter than most of the Crips, but he was just as ambitious as any of them. He stood 5'7 inches in height, with light brown skin, 17" inch arms and a huge chest. He struck me as being someone who loved his homeboys dearly and would do almost anything to protect them. He was self-assured and cool as they came. Like Big John, women were out of their element when in his presence. I could tell he believed in every fiber of what The Crips stood for. I saw strength, determination and conviction in his style. He always looked after me as if I was his little brother and to this day, I respect him as I did when I was a young child. He also recruited Big John. They met at Fremont High School, and they were the best of friends. When you saw one you for sure would see the other. Together they began their journey, although they had no idea where it would take them.

I have always considered myself fortunate to have been brought up by these men at such a young age. I understood later what I had fallen in love with, The East Side Crips. To me they were brave men that looked out for everybody in our community. Many people say that's crazy, but where I come from it seemed crazier for black people to continue to believe that white people would save them from their hardships, to constantly beg them for the things the so-called black leaders would have us believe we already received, such as freedom and equality. For those that claim such a thing, what does that make them? **Say it, don't be scared.**

While Raymond was away in jail, some of the original Crips began to move away to different parts of Los Angeles County. Big Bull Dog moved to Hoover Street and started The Hoover Crips. Mack Thomas moved to Compton and started The Compton Crips. From these men came every other set, on both sides of L.A., East and West, and throughout the United States. Their cousins, brothers, friends and nephews, their uncles, aunts, sisters, girlfriends, mothers, and fathers all became a part of the Crip establishment. That is where Crips come from. UNCUT!!!

In addition to the original eighteen Crip members, there were four Crippletts, Jackie Todd, Pam Todd, Crip Connie, and Tanya Wright (aka Tiny). They were just as Crippish as the men, and they represented all that the men did but from a woman's perspective. The Cripstletts would do anything for the Crips, because like most of the people that encountered them, they found them quite captivating. The Crips moved in lockstep; if one of them got involved in something, they all were involved. If one of them was hurt, all of them felt the pain. Anywhere they went, they took control of the event and everything surrounding it. It was what white people had always done - take everything, but I liked it more when The Crips did it. It didn't dawn on me they were taking more from their own people than even they realized.

The gains blacks claimed they had made with white people hadn't appeared in the inner city, where blacks continued to be treated like shit. As The Crips picked up momentum, surely Raymond and Tookie were aware of J. Edgar Hoover's track record against all black movements in The United States. They were about to take on a power that hadn't experienced a single setback at the hands of a black organization. What would make The Crips any different from those other organizations that came along before them?

J. Edgar Hoover was born in 1895. He started his career with the Bureau in 1919 when America was engaged in World War I. Two years earlier President Wilson had proclaimed **"The world must be made safe for democracy"** while his administration kept African Americans at the bottom of America's humility list.

LARRY DAVIS

In 1918, when the United States Supreme Court approved draft laws, J. Edgar Hoover worried that blacks wouldn't be loyal to the causes of The United States, because of how they were being treated. Now to me, J. Edgar Hoover was being honest about his suspicions of black people, because like anybody with common sense he instinctively knew that people treated as bad as blacks were in America could not be trusted to support the country.

Can you imagine being asked to sacrifice your life for someone who had abused you your entire life? Would you be willing to do that? Hoover was right on point with his concerns, because many blacks held ill feelings towards America, then and now. Because of this, Hoover made it his business to have all black organizations investigated starting with the Civil Rights Movements.

Here again was another example of debasement of black people. How on Earth could the abused be considered the victimizer? America didn't trust blacks to fight for them because it was abusing them, so that was cause to investigate them. I guess the logic here was to flush out those who had the good sense to be unwilling to die. Only those who had been broken and didn't know any better, those who were inclined to surrender their lives as instructed were ideal for America. How crazy was that psychology?

Blacks had a legitimate reason to refuse to relinquish their lives in the draft, if that was their choice. However it was difficult for J. Edgar Hoover to acknowledge blacks as human beings so he had to label them as traitors for refusing to be drafted. **WOW!** He didn't believe they all had good cause to say to the government **HELL NAW,** we aren't fighting until we get what we are entitled to equality, respect, and real freedom as you all have had all of your lives.

The country didn't need any distractions from black people crying about their civil rights. That decision would be made for them once the country's leaders decided that they were entitled to such a thing. In the meantime they needed to behave themselves and continue to dangle from the nearest trees. Hoover recruited African Americans he knew would turn on their people as informants. He dispatched them across the country to report on black ministers and anyone else that had something to say in defiance of America's agenda.

J. Edgar Hoover needed to penetrate the black organizations and get accurate intelligence about how they were thinking. He started with the **NAACP,** a group that advocated racial equality. I guess that wasn't a good thing for blacks to be engaging in while the country was at war. I'm guessing they were supposed to just accept their mistreatment and keep their mouths shut, and just do what they were told when the government asked them to go to war.

After reading "Racial Matters 1960-1972" by Kenneth O'Reilly I understood why my mother made that statement about black people always informing on each other. Scores of black people knew they should have been ashamed of themselves for helping the Bureau destroy the black movements, but they weren't. They wanted to be looked upon as being different, i.e. "I'm not like the other ones, boss, and I'll help you destroy them despite the fact that you don't care anything about me either."

In 1919, Hoover went after Marcus Garvey, the founder of the Universal Negro Improvement Association (UNIA). Garvey talked openly about black people going back to Africa. I was surprised to read that black people hadn't killed him themselves for wanting them to be free. In the end, Hoover took him down and sent him to prison for defrauding black people out of their money for his Black Star Steamship Line.

J. Edgar Hoover didn't stop there; in fact he was just getting started. Hoover went down the line infiltrating and dismantling all black organizations he knew to exist, until they became skeletons of themselves. All these black organizations felt his might, the movements for African Americans Civil Liberties that started with the Abolitionist Movement in 1830 to 1860.

1. 1937 Southern Negro Youth Congress
2. The Civil Rights Congress - CRC 1946 had 10,000 members
3. NAACP to this day doesn't resemble its original self, does it?
4. National Urban League
5. Southern Conference For Human Welfare
6. Congress of Industrial Organizations C10 Political Action Committee PAC
7. Progressive Democratic Party PDP
8. Montgomery Improvement Association MIA
9. Southern Christian Leadership Conference SCLC
10. The Women's Political Council WPC 1955?
11. The Tuskegee Civic Association TCA 1958 Gomillion v. Lightfoot
12. Student Non-Violent Coordinating Committee SNCC 1966
13. Congress of Racial Equality CORE
14. Leadership Conference on Civil Rights LCCR 1964
15. Mississippi Freedom Democratic Party MEDP

16. Nation of Islam: Most black leaders were forbidden to associate with the likes of Minister Louis Farrakhan, the leader of the Nation of Islam. Black leaders caught associating with him were ostracized by many white people. So most of them ran away from him faster than an African Cheetah, scared to death that America would continue to punish them, for association with him has not been approved. In the inner city many blacks think that the government doesn't have anything to take from them, so it cannot control their behavior. They do what they want until the government catches them in an unlawful situation, and punishes them for being disobedient. But one thing is for sure, they love men like Minister Farrakhan, and the government could never sway them in an opposite direction. Many people in the inner city ask questions like "What has Mr. Farrakhan done to cause America to hate him as much as it does?" Then you look at his conduct and all you see is him informing African Americans that America is mistreating, deceiving, and abusing their mental facilities and they need to be more conscious of what's going on in their lives. **THE TRUTH shouldn't disqualify him from telling us these things. Should it?** What about our rights under the First Amendment?

AMENDMENT I

Restrictions on Powers of Congress

SECTION 1: Congress shall make no law respecting an establishment of religion, or prohibiting the free exercise thereof; or abridging the freedom of speech, or of the press; or the right of the people peaceably to assemble, and to petition the government for a redress of grievances.

Proposed September 25, 1789; ratified December 15, 1791.

1. US: that movement was killed in a fire bombing ordered by the Mayor of Philadelphia who was a black man. He suspected one of the US members, who was allegedly a fugitive, was holed up in one of the apartments, so extreme measures were called for. Several people died as a result of this foolishness. Black people will never fail to amaze you, you can count on that.

2. The Black Panther Party: Surely Raymond and Tookie heard about how the FBI brutally enforced their powers on their organization. Were they truly conscious of what they were about to undertake? The Black Panther Party was being dismantled by J. Edgar Hoover at the very time the Crips were expanding and seeking respect from any and all. Raymond, Big Tookie, and the Crips had their hands full and steep mountains to climb, a battle like they had never seen before. May God be with them, because as it stood he surely hadn't been with the other groups before them.

AMERICA'S CONDUCT

Being part of the Crips was, for many of us, a true insight of power, growth, dignity, and unification. The Crips were intoxicating to be around. They had their own style that was quite distinct from any other group in Los Angeles. Crips were immediately recognizable, whether they were together in a group or alone. An abundance of people saw them as being their own big extended family.

They had their own individual distinctions that made them who they were. Scores of them dressed in clothes that identified them as Crips such as:

- Wearing overalls with no shirts underneath showing off their muscles.
- Ace deuce hats with hair nets covering them with stick matches in the hat band, shaped in a pyramid.
- Blue rags hanging out of their left back pockets
- Long chain earrings with crosses on the end of them down to their shoulders

There wasn't any mistaking them. They were surely Crips. Most were superb fighters and the ones that weren't would fight fiercely for their dignity, honor and respect.

I loved the Crips. I loved watching them all stand around and practice their whistling. They would whistle like chirping birds, and a sea of Crips would appear out of every opening of the earth, from all directions, following the sound of the whistle. When I got much older I realized the Crips were not just functioning on a whim - they had African history in their game. I read a story in a book called "America Is Me", by Kennell Jackson. It told of West Africans being caught and enslaved and put on a ship called Amistad. During this ordeal the captured Africans rebelled and killed the captain and three members of his crew. The leader of the captured Africans was a man named Cinque. Whenever he whistled, all the Africans from his tribe would come running to his aid. Raymond Washington was the Cinque of the East Side Crips. When he or any other member whistled they all came running.

I had found what I wasn't consciously looking for, a new family, one that wasn't going to take nobody's shit, especially white people's. However, I wasn't quite ready to fight down the Crip line of loyalty. I continued to be their mascot until I knew I could handle the pressure of being a man. I went to school with blue rags hanging out of my back pockets. Nobody at school knew I was hanging out with my cousin Big John and The East Side Crips, but they would find out soon enough.

I started fighting more and eventually I was suspended. I just didn't care anymore. I was tired of standing up in class saying, "I pledge allegiance to the flag of The United States of America, and to the Republic, for which it stands, one nation, under God, indivisible, with liberty and justice for all." In the inner city, many people just refused to believe those words meant anything for black people.

I wanted to be like Big John. I loved him through and through. He was what every kid, in all the neighborhoods, wanted to be. He had a low rider with color bar lights inside his car, and hydraulics that made it jump off the ground. He had the prettiest women, one in particular, Darlene. She was beautiful, with light brown skin, brown eyes, long black hair, the prettiest smile ever, a thin build, and self-worth like you wouldn't believe.

Big John was resourceful. I mean this literally. He could play the guitar, fix cars, tear down an entire motor in a car on his own, and put it back together. He could build houses, and he was an electrician, a carpenter, and a painter. He did it all; he was Joe's and Martha's son.

It was time for me to take my show on the road and off the school playground. In all the time I spent around the Crips, I had never witnessed them being opposed by any other gang or groups. They were a moving force without any opposition to be seen.

One summer day my cousins, Lonzo, Terry, and Darlene's brother Freeman and I went swimming at Roosevelt Park. There I was whistling away like the Crips, chirping my heartfelt devotion to their movement. There wasn't a Crip in sight. I wasn't whistling to attract any of them; I was really only practicing. I wanted to perfect their art of chirping. So, I continued my Crip call, along with throwing up the Crip sign which is the letter C. Suddenly, without warning, grown-ass men jumped over a fence that ran along the perimeter of the Park with a row of big tall green trees that stretch along the entire length of the fence. Terry, Lonzo, and Freeman all looked apprehensive. I didn't know what was wrong with them. I hadn't noticed these men approaching us. I was too busy admiring the Crips in my own private little world, as I continued to emulate their gestures. Soon it became clear why they were looking so afraid. These grown men were running towards us. I still didn't panic, I thought these men were Crips acknowledging the Crip whistle. I had no knowledge that the Crips had enemies. However, I started to feel that this wasn't a good thing that was occurring. Terry pretended to pick up paper in the grass but he was figured out because there wasn't any paper in sight. Lonzo and Freeman acted like they weren't with me, wandering about looking up in the sky like they were blind and couldn't see this entire scene was a mess. I was the youngest of the bunch, 10 years old, but I was the only one whistling when they approached us. It was four grown black men who directed all their questions to me, "You're a punk ass Crip?" I knew the answer to that question should be no, and I said it emphatically, **"No!** I ain't no Crip." Tears streamed down my face; here I was 10 years old, and being confronted by grown men in the most aggressive form. I knew then that the Crips had enemies and they weren't loved by the men standing before me. I continued saying that I wasn't a Crip, crying up a storm. You remember those fake spit tears my father used to tell me to put in my eyes after he gave me those make-believe whippings? These were no spit tears. These were the real McCoy, Nile River tears.

I didn't believe they intended to hurt us. More than anything I believed they were only trying to scare us, because we were kids. They told us to "Get the hell out of the park. If ya'll ain't out of here in 10 seconds we're going to kick ya'll asses." We were out in less than 5 seconds flat.

Immediately after that experience the crew started in on me, "Ahh you were crying, they scared you. I bet you ain't goin' be throwing up no more Crip signs or whistling no more."

Boy, were they ever wrong. I would grow up to become a mammoth of a Crip and loving every minute of it, with strong vocal cords to sound off the Crip whistle for the world to hear. **CRIP HERE !!**

I continued to hang out at my cousin's house. I wasn't fazed by my last encounter. The Crips were still my idols. I knew everyone would be at Big John's house lifting weights. They would have hundreds of pounds of weights scattered around. I enjoyed watching them talk shit to each other while competing to see who was the strongest, flexing their muscles against each other. I couldn't believe how big those dudes were. One day on the way there I stopped by the store to get some candy. I was riding a Huffy Dirt Bike, fixed up with mirrors, truck lights, radios and many other things to make the bike look like a show bike. When I stepped out of the store to continue on my journey, I walked into approximately seven or eight Pueblo Bishops Bloods. I attempted to grab my handlebars; mind you I had a blue rag in my back pocket. They surrounded me and threatened to jump me if I didn't let go of the handlebars. I told them, "I'm not giving up my bike." One of them said, "Stab his young ass." I still was 10 years old; ten wasn't a pleasant time for me. I let the bike go, ran up the street to my cousin's house, and told him that some dudes out of the projects took my bike. He said, "Why you let them take it?" I told him, "They had a knife." He and his homeboy went to the projects looking for my bike. He knew many of the Bloods inside the projects because he had once run with them, but they never found my bike.

I started to recognize that outside of my mother's house, people were retarded, meaning backward and under-developed, and I started to act just like them. I promised myself I wasn't going to take no more shit from nobody; I began carrying a switch blade.

My brother Boxco still was acting up as well. He went to juvenile hall for something - I can't recall what. My mother told us one day, "Your brother is in jail."

I remember feeling sad for him because all of our lives we hadn't been separated, ever. Now my big brother was gone. I used to ask my mother if we could go visit him. She told us no, because the juvenile administration don't allow siblings to visit, only parents. I still went along with my mother when she went to visit him. I just sat inside the car while she went in to see him. I couldn't wait for her to come out to tell what he had said, how he looked, how he was doing. I had a thousand questions for her about him. I missed him so much. He stayed gone for a few months and finally they let him out. One day we walked through the door and saw him. We all were happy to have our brother back home with us.

He had grown a lot; in fact he started to look a lot like our cousin Big John, at least muscle-wise. His chest was huge. And he started to have different friends and to dress like the Crips, wearing suspenders, khaki pants, sling shot undershirts, biscuit shoes and doing a dance called the Crip walk. He could dance just as well as I could. I was still a James Brown feet-shuffling king, so the Crip walk was tailor-made for my feet.

My experiences at school only grew worse. The kids started to detest me. They would stage fights with anyone they thought could whoop me. One day this new kid named Nathan Ness, who would become one of my best friends, moved to the neighborhood. He used to wear karate uniforms to school, wanting everyone to think he knew karate. For the kids this was their dream come true. They just had to figure out how they were going to set up the fight between us without me finding out they were behind it. They went behind my back and told him that I had said I could beat him up. Then they came and told me that he said he could beat me up. I played kickball, watching their every move. It didn't bother me how they went about setting up the fight. I wanted to fight him. I didn't like how he pretended to know karate in the first place, so they were doing me a favor. I saw that he was kicking his foot high in the air looking over in my direction as if he was inviting me to come and get my ass whooped if I wanted to. All the time I was playing kickball, I had been timing his kicks in my head. I was surely about to whoop Bruce Lee ass that day. When they were sure they had succeeded in their manipulation, the kids started promoting the fight. They told Nathan, "I bet you can't whoop Larry, he's the king of the school." He began bouncing around on his feet as if he was light as a feather, and at any moment he would float in the air. He told them, "He better not run up on me." That was more than enough for them; they sprinted that information back to me in record time. "Larry that boy over there said you better not run up on him, he's going to kick your ass."

As I approached him everyone gathered around us watching him work out. When anyone got too close to him, he sent roundhouse kicks over their heads. This was some real psychological shit going on with us children. I had his kick patterns down to the second. As soon as he tried that slow shit on me, I could grab his foot and beat his ass. Now they were telling me, "Larry, we don't think you can whoop him, he knows karate." My mother used to say to that, "I don't give a damn about somebody knowing karate, I know Karazy." When Nathan tried his kick I grabbed his foot stopped his kick and handled my business. To make a long story short I continued to remain the undisputed king until the day I graduated.

All my time in school wasn't spent being a delinquent. I played third base on the school's baseball team, and we were pretty good too. We played in a tournament where we defeated four of the best schools in our district to become champions. The team picture was placed on the Los Angeles Sentinel's front page depicting us as the champions. We were overjoyed to see ourselves in the newspapers.

My mother signed me up on a baseball team at Bethune Park where I would meet most of the people I'm writing about. At Bethune Park we played organized football, baseball, basketball, and every other sport you could think of and I was rather exceptional in each sport. In football, many of the square kids who thought they were going off to be professional stars never really wanted me to play with them. They claimed I played too rough, so I literally had to sit on the sidelines and watch them play until one of the teams lost a player for whatever reason. Then the teams were uneven and they would let me play, after they had me make a sworn declaration that I would not try to hurt them. Then, the minute someone snapped the ball I tried to take their heads off for being little punks. I didn't care if they let me play or not. I didn't want to play with them any more after they started acting like little girls. I began playing with the teenagers. My cousin Cal had a boyfriend named Jeffery Wright who was the best football player I had seen at that time. Growing up he was fierce and pernicious. He would ram his head and body into anybody that touched the ball, separating them from the ball the majority of the time. He played for Manuel Arts High School. On the weekend he would take many of us youngsters on the west side to play with his football partners. They thought I was too small until I duplicated Jeffery Wright collisions on them. Jeffery didn't look the part of someone who would break anyone up on the football field because he was 5'6 or 5'7, maybe 170 lbs. Quick and fast, he was vicious offensively and defensively I learned how to play football from him.

While at Lillian Elementary I continued on the wrong side of right and it didn't appear that anything could slow me down until I met a young lady named Artacelly, a Mexican girl I liked a lot. She was extremely pretty, and she captivated the animalistic side of me for whatever reason. When she was anywhere in my presence I was reluctant to act out. She would stand afar just looking at me. We were in all of the same classes and she moved her chair next to mine and asked me if I had a girlfriend. I told her no, and she said that she wanted to be my girlfriend. I told her, "I don't care," meaning I would like that. So it was a verbal contractual union, albeit we didn't know what a contractual agreement or union was.

She didn't think I was as bad or tough as I acted. She never hesitated to approach me to tell me to stop acting so crazy. She was cool. I walked her home every day after school. She lived in a predominantly Mexican neighborhood that didn't particularly like blacks. We were experiencing discrimination from every race here in America, but for whatever reason many people try to pretend that it doesn't exist any longer. Blacks were strong and hadn't been drugged out yet. I continued to walk her home whether they liked it or not.

Ms. Berry watched us the entire time we were together and figured she found the kryptonite to bring me down - Artacelly. Ms. Berry was on to something and used that information to keep me in my place. Whenever I came close to acting up she would instruct Artacelly to talk to me. It worked and allowed me to graduate, which for us didn't take much to accomplish because they graduated everyone. If you couldn't read, write, or spell it didn't matter, they still passed you. I was one of the ones that passed.

It was getting close to graduation for us. Ms. Berry, my favorite teacher in spite of her being white, never gave up on me no matter how rebellious I was. She never stopped trying; she saw the good in me that I didn't think existed. She told me, "Larry you're a smart kid you just have to believe in yourself. I know you're smarter than you act. When you go to your next school watch the company you keep around you. You can do anything you set your mind to."

What Ms. Berry was communicating to me was true for other kids, but what she didn't know was the black community had declared war on itself. We lived within a perimeter, and if we traveled outside it our lives were threatened, from other blacks and the police. Her advice wouldn't have done me a bit of good at Roosevelt Park, the store where my bike was taken or Russell Elementary School when my siblings and I got our school picture money taken. I had to fight for my life at the tender age of ten. Of course you're going to have those who say the choices I made were on me, completely ignoring the conduct of white America towards blacks. It's easy that way for them, because they know white people will punish them if they think about accusing them of any wrongdoing. Trust me, in the inner city, like James Brown, people say it loud while being Black and Proud. Outside, people continued to pretend all was well, but you couldn't pay those people to live in the inner city if their lives depended on it.

I decided I was going to take my show on the road, with every intention of keeping my pride and dignity, with my head held high. The ghetto was going to be our home; there would be no backpedaling for my family. The inner city was all we had, and we intended to make the most of it.

Times had gotten much harder for my mother. Being kids we never realized how our actions were affecting her; we were only concerned for ourselves. We didn't understand how to support her emotionally. We were still being nurtured and seeking her guidance and all that other stuff was grown-up doings, which oftentimes they didn't understand themselves. I'm sure my mother was hurt she wasn't able to fight for us as her father had fought for her when she was our age. She was learning how powerful America's hypnosis was on her children and the blacks in America. Black people were in a world of hurt and had been for centuries.

My mother was a strong woman during those difficult times for our family. She never quit on us or gave up hope that we could overcome those challenges. She was remarkable to me as a mother. We were too immature, so a lot of her problems were over our heads. She was now alone, to live the rest of her life in a state my father had brought her to. To him, California gave her the best chance to discover the dreams she had always wished for herself and now he was gone, never to see her dreams fulfilled. She had to survive in California without any professional skills. She wasn't working; my father was the crutch she had leaned on, and now it was all on her. Mrs. Davis would be tested to see what she was made of. We never saw her pause in her duties to take care of us.

For Christmas we wanted everything we could think of or saw on TV. She got us the things she could afford. She quickly told each of us, "There isn't any Santa Claus, I'm Santa Claus, and I'm broke, besides money doesn't grow on trees."

We learned to understand her struggles and managed to be content with what she got us - sometimes. One particular Christmas, most of the kids in the neighborhood were getting fiberglass skate boards, so I wanted one as well. My mother told me, "I'll see if I can afford it." "I'll see" is an expression that hardly ever bodes well for children. "I'll get it" is what we were hoping to hear. When Christmas came, we all got up to open our presents. I grabbed my gift that was obviously a skateboard, and damn near died when I found myself staring at a wooden skateboard. I knew when I went outside I would be ridiculed by the children because my skateboard was inferior to theirs. I fell to the floor in disgust. I never took the time to think about how hard it was on my mother. She had to take care of four children on her own and loved us with all of her heart and she had at least gone out and bought me a skateboard. I was inconsolable. She told me, "Larry I couldn't find the one you wanted, what's wrong with that skateboard?" I responded, "It's not fiberglass." She couldn't take any more of my whining. She went out to find me that particular type of skateboard that I had asked for. A lime green fiberglass skateboard is what she found and brought home. It saved me from being humiliated by the other children in the neighborhood.

In the inner city one thing that took place every single Christmas was that children let you know how poor they thought your family was based on the type of toys and gifts you received. They did so by examining all the things you got for Christmas then determining how expensive the items were.

The parents for the most part don't care about those things; they only want to do the very best they can for their children. But the children, oh, they cared immensely what the cost was, because if the product was cheap, then your family was considered poor. This caused enormous emotional pain and trauma, so much so it would cause some kids to rob and steal for these materialistic items in order to escape the pressures of being humiliated by their peers. Many parents aren't conscious of the degree of meanness children inflict on one another to make themselves feel superior to those that have less materially. The pain from such abuse in children's lives could be the difference in becoming a Crip, Blood, murderer, or burglars, depriving them of an opportunity to make a contribution to the growth of black people's advancements in society. The advertisers know full well most of society's inner city youth can't afford the things they flash on the TV screens. Those children beg their parents to get those things, and when they can't afford to buy them, the parents become trapped with a decision that haunts them night and day.

What do you think children want? They don't understand when they're young that these things aren't free, or at the very least outside the range of affordability. They only witness other children with those items, never taking into account that their parents aren't fortunate enough to afford those things. Happiness is what kids are in search of; unfortunately, it isn't in those gifts that they so badly desire. It's the happiness they witness, the smiles, the laughter, the temporary joy that's in the air. That's what the children want for Christmas, those things that are alluring in a place where misery resides, so they will throw a fit to attain it and parents go through life thinking it's the gifts that they want. But it's the continued humiliation in life that the children are trying to avoid at all costs. Being taunted, laughed at, or told that they're less than all the other children around them has a tremendous negative emotional effect, and no kid wants to feel that at any point. **WOW!!!**

Debra started dating boys. She went out with this dude named Clarence Nelson. He was my age and he was an athlete at a very young age. Football, baseball, and a track star, he did them all well. Growing up I saw people who could run fast but Clarence was a jet in a human body. He was cool and we got along well. Debra was different, I never tried to get into her business as much I did Shenette's.

Debra had a friend named Ali Mae, Yevonne's sister. She was a big ole country girl, not fat, but thick like Yevonne. She was also too big for her age, so to speak. She had a big ass like Debra and every chance I got I used to feel on it and run. She would say, "Larry you better stop." In my mind, I was saying you had better stop coming over here. For young boys, puberty sneaks up on us when we least expect it, and if no one ever sits down and explains what puberty is, it leaves a void in a young boy's understanding. It's a time when a young boy wants explanations about what's going on with his body, but more often than not he won't ask anyone. Here we were going through life not knowing we would ever have hair springing up in our groin area. My father died before he could talk to me about what all of this meant. When hair started to grow in my groin area, I was too scared to say anything to my mother about it, so I asked my brother and my cousin Terry, "Do ya'll have hair down there?" Each of them would say, "Yeah." I asked them to let me see, and we went to the back yard, showing each other that we had hair in our groin area, which made me feel much better. I didn't think anything weird was going on with me when I saw other boys my age were going through the same transformations and I told myself if I ever had a son I would be sure to talk to him about puberty as soon as I could, no matter his age.

Ali Mae started to expect me to feel on her ass when she came over, and I obliged her every chance I got. My penis started to get hard often so I knew that meant something special. I was ready for reproductive services. Ali Mae asked me had I ever kissed a girl. I had kissed Artacelly but I had never stuck my tongue down someone's mouth. Ali Mae said, "Let me see if you can kiss." She came towards me so we could kiss. She stuck her tongue down my throat; I had no idea she was going to stick her tongue down in my mouth. I tasted her tongue and it tasted like that gasoline I had years earlier. Immediately that was the end of my erection, and she escaped being my first conquest.

All kinds of crazy things continued to happen around us. This lady named Patty Hearst was kidnapped in Berkeley, California, allegedly by a group called The Symbionese Liberation Army. She was the heiress to the Hearst dynasty, linked to all newspapers using the name Chronicle and all magazines using Time or any subsidiary. So obviously, this circumstance created world news interest. One day we were in the house and heard gunshots. It sounded like somebody was shooting a machine gun. We heard sirens from police cars and fire trucks. There were helicopters flying in the sky, and smoke filled the sky with blackness. I and a few more kids on the block walked up the street to see what all the commotion was about. We lived on 60th and Compton Ave. The police believed Patty Hearst was being held inside one of the duplexes on 55th and Compton Ave. If she was inside one of them, she surely wouldn't have survived. The police burned down the entire complex, and killed many of the people that were inside. Rumors were that the people inside had a hidden tunnel and made their escape. This is the kind of shit children in my community had to deal with each and every day.

For my graduation I told my mother I wanted a blue suit and a pair of biscuits. She said that she'd try to get them. The word try didn't sit well with me, ever. She had bought my brother Boxco some so I knew that she knew what kind I wanted. She went out to purchase them when she came back I almost died. They resembled biscuits, but they weren't. Those shoes were square toe and had a high heel on them that looked like an Evil Knievel onramp with no space between the heel. I told her I wasn't going to wear them. She said; "Shit boy, you better put those God damn shoes on your feet and call them biscuits." I didn't wear them because they looked too deformed, so I wore another pair of shoes. I wanted to Crip walk right out of elementary school, like the East Side Crips. They were stylish and biscuits were one of the reasons why.

At graduation, Ms. Berry had one more conversation with me she said to me, "Larry you have a lot of potential to do some great things, but if you keep hanging out with the wrong crowd and your attitude doesn't change, you're going to end up in prison." She knew America wasn't going to tolerate disobedience and I had been full of it.

MS.BERRY THE FORTUNE TELLER!!

Submerged

My mother started dating a man named Jerry; he was military, in one of the Reserve Units. He stood 5'8, 180 lbs. with a dark brown complexion. In spite of being in the service, his heart was loyal only to alcohol. Most of the times I saw him, he was drinking some sort of liquor. Alcohol and black folks were connected at the hip. Why were so many African Americans staying intoxicated in a country that offered them a dream that Africa couldn't provide, at least according to scores of white people who had proclaimed they saved our ancestors from a life full of savagery by bringing them to America? I believe many blacks here in America were drowning themselves, drinking themselves away from their agony, torment and distress here in America. America was sucking the life out of black people, literally. I didn't see Jerry being a soldier on anyone's battlefield, but he was capable of killing a fifth of Gin Rummy.

He used to say to me, "Larry as soon as you get old enough I'm going to see if I can get you enlisted into the Army." I wasn't going to join any military branch. I felt like Mr. Muhammad Ali, why in the hell would I want to fight for a country that treated black people like the scum of the earth? And furthermore, why was a black man going out of his way to recruit young black men to die in war for a country that didn't care anything about his people? I heard many black people claim because our ancestors suffered and helped build this country, it's just as much ours as it is White America's. If this is the case, black people aren't any different than white people who took it away from the Native Americans. How is it possible for African Americans to just jump in front of the original owners of America's soil?

The only Army I was interested in enlisting in was the East Side Crips. My mother liked Jerry a lot, for whatever reason. I never cared what her reasons were as long as he didn't put his hands on her. He was allowed around her, but the minute he violated that trust he would've had to test his military skills in the inner city streets where we didn't care anything about anybody outside of our neighborhood. In spite of his training, we all thought we knew karazy!! I barely focused my attention on him; he was my mother's problem. One thing I liked about her relationship with him was she never permitted him to live with us. I wouldn't have been able to stomach that. As far as I was concerned this was still Pops' spot.

I never accepted any man she dated as a father figure in my life. Willie James Davis was literally my idol. I loved him with all of my heart and I intended to always remain loyal to him. One of my objections to allowing another man to take the place of my father was that most of the black men I was around acted like everything was fine and black people had found peace. But the Crips, Thugs and other resisters didn't adhere to those beliefs and refused to be brainwashed into thinking all was well.

One day Jerry was sitting on the couch in our living room where he thought he had it made. As I came walking through heading outside, he said to me, "Son, can you hand me that?" I don't remember what that was, but I do remember saying to him, "I'm not your motherfucking son and you're not my father." My mother was standing right there and she quickly told him, "Don't call him your son." The thing that was most shocking was that I used profanity, which she didn't allow us to use in her presence. When Jerry called me son she made an exception to her rule because she knew how I felt about my father. I wasn't going to ever allow another man to call me son. Jerry knew full well he wasn't my father. Because he was dating my mother he thought that he had to pretend he was willing to accept her children. He wanted to illustrate that point to her by using me to prove his commitment. HOWEVER I WAS THE WRONG CHILD TO TRY HIS GAME WITH. I wanted to make sure he never tried it again.

My mother gave me a look that expressed I violated her space with the profanity I used before her. My thing with Jerry was settled, but my mother wasn't going to allow me to get away with disrespecting her. I told her I was sorry for cursing and she forgave me and said, "Don't do it again."

Their relationship didn't last long, because my mother didn't respect men in my opinion. She was her own boss and most of the men that I knew or had been around thought women were beneath them. However, Mrs. Jannie Mae Laffitte Davis never wavered in her stance that she was just as capable as any man. There would be no submission with her. I loved to watch her give him, and any other man she met, a dose of reality, and they knew she would back up every single word she uttered. She wasn't weak by any means.

I enrolled in Edison Jr. High School, located on the east side of 65th and Hooper Ave. By this time I was running with a new crew of aspiring dreamers who thought being disruptive and unruly would gain us the respect we thought black people deserved in this society. We wanted so desperately to be treated different from how other blacks were being treated and most of the young minds believed gangbanging and Raymond Washington's ideals would get us there. We truly loved one another and watched over everybody in our area, as if it were a job. That was how we felt, like one big giant extended family.

Big Vince was a big dude for his age, and he always clowned around while having fun. He didn't take much of anything seriously unless it had something to do with us in a negative way, and then he found his serious side. He was claiming a gang in Los Angeles called the Kitchen Crip. He hadn't been anywhere near Kitchen Crip neighborhood, but he played the part as if he had. He wore blue rags down to the ground out of his back pockets, tied around his head; no one would've ever mistaken him for belonging to any gang except the Crips.

Mr. Low was from Kitchen Crip. Mr. Low followed behind Big Smokey who was the leader from Kitchen Crips. He ran with Big Wolf from 89th street Neighborhood Crips. Smokey lived next door to us with a young lady named Patricia White (aka Pat). I guess he made an impression on Mr. Low because he swore he was from Kitchen Crips and I never questioned it; he just popped up around there. He had gotten the name Mr. Low because he was the lowest form of a human-being that anyone would ever run across. Whatever shocked you about a human being, Mr. Low would be the person to do something even more startling. He went back and forth to jail for every crime you could imagine, but unlike many of the youngsters around there he was being sent off to placement. Placement is like one big house that housed juvenile delinquents. It was the closest thing to being on the streets with counselor supervision. If the people housed there behaved well enough they were given weekend passes to go home.

On many occasions we would be somewhere in our neighborhood standing around and out of nowhere we all would see Mr. Low running past us saying, "The police is chasing me." They were always trying to put him in one of the many cages that they have built for black people to live in. I would have run too. I sure as hell didn't blame him. **RUN MR. LOW RUN!**

Lil Kev could be described in several ways because he had so many different personalities. One day he would be quiet and mild-mannered, then on other days he would be outrageously wild and difficult to control. He was for sure our crash dummy when it came to smoking marijuana. We used to do this one particular experiment that I won't reveal. However, every single time we did it he would collapse, coming close to hitting the concrete with his head. Somebody would always be in position to catch him, but that wouldn't stop him from trying it over and over again. That in itself was evidence he was mentally imbalanced, and we were equally foolish, so each time he requested our assistance we gave it to him. I was the only one who saw the stupidity in that act and refused to follow suit, so I thought.

Jeffery Leon Reynolds, (aka Lil Will) was the purest definition of mentally insane, yet we loved him nevertheless. He had many problems but one in particular was he couldn't control his bowel movements. Whenever all of us went out together we would smell shit and thought that somebody may have stepped in dog shit. Every time this would happen, Lil Will would all of a sudden have to go home for something. It took us a little while to figure out that it wasn't any dog shit anyone had stepped in, it was him shitting on himself. Once we all knew it was him we teased him. He continued to pretend it wasn't him, and then go home and change pants, come back, thinking nobody would notice he had changed his pants. They called him Lil Will because he was willing to do anything. Had I known how far his willingness would extend, I would have run away from him as fast as Mr. Low had been running most of his life. He would become an informant for the F.B.I. and the local police department and would be the person who would take my life away.

Jack Jones (aka Nu Nu), was a gymnast and he thought of himself as a player. He had his eyes on my sister Shenette, but I quickly had him readjust those thoughts in another direction, because I was still overprotective of her. However, Jack moved from the neighborhood to the Pueblos, which were our sworn enemies. One night Jack and I were standing inside the Projects talking. I had my blue rag hanging out of my back pocket and Jack's mother's pistol in my waist band. For whatever reason, Jack asked me for the gun, something he had never done. The minute he took the gun back to his mother, Dr. Dirt, a notorious Blood and gang member, approached us, together with Killer Carl, (that name spoke for itself), Hard Times, Lil Kev, Peter Rabbit, and several more Pueblo Bishops. They asked where were we from. I immediately knew this was bullshit, because every single one of them knew I was from 6-Deuce. Dr. Dirt asked me, "What are you doing over here?" I replied, "Visiting my homeboy." To me that should've been the first sign that Jack had betrayed us. I used to actually go over to Peter Rabbit's and Lil Kev's house to smoke weed with them. Without them telling me I knew that was the last time I could openly come inside the Projects. So once again another piece of territory for black people had been made much smaller. So I took their approach as a declaration of war. It became the **MODUS OPERANDI.**

Troy, known as Lil C-Bone, was a little chubby kid who tried to hang out with us but was too young. He sat on the sidelines hoping to get called in to play with thug prodigies that we were, but like I had been years earlier, he was too young. It worked out for him years later. I wasn't shocked though; he was determined to holler Crip out of his mouth.

Big Erin was a reluctant member at first. He hung out with some of our foes, and he was a fighting machine. He had to be persuaded to come over to our side. He started out trippin, but he got his act together when he truly recognized we weren't playing any games. He was a few years older than the rest of us and started dating Big Vince's mother. Big Vince's mom was the original Ms. Cougar long before today's Cougars. We didn't think anything of it because, Big Vince didn't care, so who were we to be concerned with their business; after all it wasn't any of our mothers. I made it quite clear that he bet not had tried that shit with my mother. I wasn't turning either side of my cheeks.

Ricc Rocc was from 6-Deuce Neighborhood Crips. He was wild as they came. Lil Kev, was his younger brother. Ricc Rocc dressed with a thousand blue rags all over himself. Wherever he could put a rag it would be one placed there. He went around spraying his name and 6-Duece wherever he could find space. One day he got caught spraying on this man's property. The man told him if he caught him doing it again he would make him feel sorry he had. Ricc Rocc didn't take the man seriously and got caught spray painting on the man's wall again. The man beat him half to death, but it didn't stop him. He was determined to let everyone know who he was and where he was from. He continued spraying up the city, Big Ricc Rocc 6-Duece Crip.

T-Dog was just as quiet as Lil Kev, shy almost to suspicion, but he stayed ready to do some mischief on call. He always appeared to be uncomfortable around us. I wasn't close with him at all. One day he just vanished not leaving a trace of his whereabouts and nobody asked where he went we didn't miss him at all. (This isn't Big T-Dog from SD. I hadn't met him at that time.)

T-Tiger was quite curious about everything going on with us. He was hesitant to follow behind us because he lived several blocks away from where we all hung out. He tried his hardest to fit in with our crew but my homeboy, Big Sike, didn't like him for whatever his reasons were. Years later, T-Tiger was successful in hooking up with one of our extended cousin alliances, and from what I learned became their leader.

Michael Allen (aka Lil Mike) was my best friend. He was smooth, slick and cool. He wore a long process (a hair style from back in the day), tailor made clothes, and he loved to shoot dice and play women, although I found that difficult to believe seeing how he only had one girl, named Desiree. He really didn't like her as much as she thought he did. He tried with all his heart to be a Crip but it didn't fit his style. He was a self-professed player and women did in fact love him, but he was scared to death of women. I had to encourage him in that direction. I recall how we all would go out, girls would be all over him and he'd say to me, "Larry let's go, ain't nothing happening here." I knew he was scared to talk to the ladies. I'd say to him, "Cuzz, those girls like you, let's talk to them." He'd go crazy and say, "Nah, cuzz, let's go!", and we would pretend we had some serious business to attend to. I'd roll with him because he was my ace in the hole. We all would go out with blue rags tied on our heads and for some reason to me Lil Mike didn't belong with us. It wasn't because he didn't have any heart; he was just as brave as any one of us. It was mainly because he was my best friend and I couldn't stand to see anything happen to him. I used to tell him. "Cuzz, this ain't for you." He would argue with me telling me, "I know what I'm doing cuzz." He didn't even say hey cuzz right, it sounded like he was forcing it out and it came out all wrong. I was quite conscious that I was trying to save him from the dark side of the streets of L.A. I was always against him joining the Crips. He eventually honored my request. He continued to hang out with us every day, but after that he just wasn't a member of the Crips. However, he was an honorary member. I felt much better for him after his decision.

Alan Gibson was something else altogether. He was dating my sister Debra. He was an athlete at Bethune Park all of us played sports up there so we knew him from the park. He lived on the other side of Slauson, on 57th and Hooper, known as the Blood Stone Villains area. They were one of our rival gangs of course. We didn't trust him at all. We thought he was a spy for them. He assured us he wasn't, but to be sure we made him join the Crips and we walked with him to his house every single night so the Bloods could see him with us. We deliberately walked with him on the street where the Bloods hung out, with our blue rags visible for them to see, making sure they saw him with us.

The funny thing about that was all of us went to Edison Jr. High School together so we knew each other and weren't trying to kill each other at that time. We eventually made his house one of our hangout spots where we all would smoke weed and where I got the name Big LaLa, on one of those smoking weed nights. Like Mike, Alan wasn't cut out for the work, but he stayed on for the ride as long as he could, until his relationship with my sister ended. It didn't dawn on me until much later what segregationists we were at the tender ages of 12 and 13 years old. Black people were discriminating against each other and were proud of it. The Crips were on a course to being far worse than the Ku Klux Klan had ever been towards blacks, and they didn't have a clue that their journey would be so horrific until the smoke eventually cleared for them to see their ruins.

Dino, he was just there in the beginning. He hung out long enough to become a member but when he finally met the members of 62nd Street Crips, they hadn't ever seen him before and thought he was an adversary. Big Crumb threw him down a flight of stairs at Lil Oscar's house. Dino didn't run though, he stuck around so they let him stay.

Lil Caver was from 62nd Street Crips when his family moved on 59th and Hooper between Compton Ave. All of his brothers were senior members of the 6-Dueces. We hadn't met them yet but we had heard a lot about his brother, Big Quake, who had a reputation on the East Side as being one of the baddest dudes in the city. He was feared, so I couldn't wait to meet him. Lil Caver would deny it, but he was spoiled rotten. He would have a fit if we all didn't want to do something he wanted to do. He was playful, but not when it came to playing with him. Once it got to that point, and it did from time to time, he would get mad and want to fight everybody. We all laughed at him while running from him because we didn't want to fight him. We'd all be saying, "Cuzz, you're trippin," and he'd be swinging away. That was Mr. Caver who would later be known as Lil Quake. His other brothers were Kay Kay and Bruce, and both of them were street committed as well.

Then there was Dee, from Compton Grandee Crips. He was my next door neighbor. Pat, his sister, was dating Smokey. Dee and I were close. He was a little more advanced than the rest of us, because he was already thinking about different ways to make money. We were only out to have fun and gain respect. We hadn't focused on the importance of money; we were more interested in making sure we all were safe and not allowing anyone to disrespect what we stood for. Any money we came across we shared with each other. If somebody didn't have any money, we split what we had between everyone, making sure we all had the same amount. This was the crew that hung out each and every day.

It bothered me that everyone was from different gangs and we all lived in the area, so I started our own gang, The Bethune Park Crips. Everyone joined except Dee. He stayed representing the Grandee's Compton Crips. We now had our own identity. There was one problem, Bethune Park was once Slauson Park, and an old original gang on 62nd and Hooper Avenue, The Blood gang, Outlaws, hung out there along with ex-members of the Slausons.

We decided we had to convert them in order for them to take us seriously. Bethune Park had a history and they felt that the park should remain theirs - we disagreed. Because we were so young they thought they could run us over, but they underestimated our upbringing, especially mine from Russell, 92nd, and Lillian. I was ready to go on the offensive and we did just that.

We started by wearing our rags to the park, provoking them into challenging us, which didn't take long at all. They weren't punks by a long shot. To be honest they were much stronger than the crew I had assembled, but they were much weaker than the crew that was backing us. They would say to us, "You little motherfuckers better stop wearing that shit on ya'll heads up here." Not only did we ignore them, we made examples out of their older gang members by catching them without their strengths and having at them. We did battle with them on many occasions and won. But before we actually conquered the park we had to deal with the Sheriff Department which ran the park and sponsored the sports activities there. One sheriff in particular, Deputy Williams, was like a mentor to all of us. He was a black man who loved his community and the children in it. I can honestly say without any reservation that he never viewed us as gang members, nor did he ever act like the police with us. When he saw us doing wrong he always attempted to tell us to straighten our lives out. He would say, "All of ya'll are going to end up in jail if ya'll continue to act as y'all are." If one of us was on the football team and didn't show up for a game in time for the van to take off to Jordan High, where the entire league's games were played, he came and found us and took us to the game. He was always there for us, but we were heading in the opposite direction fast and he couldn't stop us no matter how hard he tried.

Before we completely took the park, Big Quake had to jump on board with us. Once he did, the fight was over faster than one could blink their eyelids. He was a bad man. He whooped ass from sunup until sundown. When he came home I got the chance to study his behavior. Bethune Park gave dances every weekend and he would come with several members of 6-Dueces. The Outlaws still hadn't fully accepted defeat. Marcus, Isaac, Big Dave, Double R, Dino, Player, Bird, Renae, and Bob and others tried to dig in so from time to time we still had to get down with them.

Quake would show up in an all blue khaki suit with an Ace Deuce hat, Romeo shoes, blue rag wrapped around his hands, riding a bike with Lil Oscar riding on the handle bars. Lil Oscar who was 5'6 maybe 120 lbs, dark complexion, would be dressed so that no one would mistake him for being anything other than a Crip.

Once the dance started they would take to the floor Crip walking. They were delightful with their feet and I was impressed beyond words how artful they were. With their feet they told a story of strife, struggle, sufferings, pride, dignity and determination. I literally understood what they were communicating with their feet. From that point forward I was committed to telling my story in the same manner, and became a storytelling champ with my own feet. I told the same story of pain, disappointment, betrayal, manipulation, deceit, joy, amazement and bewilderment. Every one of us learned how to communicate with our feet, Crip walking. I never stopped expressing what I saw and how I felt, and to this very day I continue to do so effectively.

At the dances, Big Quake and Lil Oscar, who were so magical with their feet, put on a display of Crip excellence that some of the Outlaw members couldn't stomach. They felt offended they had to stand there and watch this exhibition of art and witness the young ladies being mesmerized by their confidence. Out of nowhere they would confront Quake, and a sea of Crips would come to Quake's aid. But every time I was around him he would tell everybody to back up and tell whoever he was talking to, "We don't need everybody in our business. We can get down head up." This would be the first display of lighting and thunder. Quake would whoop ass with a touch of grace and a sprinkle of speed as well as power and an overdose of brutality. He wouldn't stop until his opponent was defeated both physically and mentally, leaving no doubt with them that they had made the wrong choice in challenging him. I wanted to be just like him and my cousin Big John in the streets of Los Angeles. They were my idols and I was determined to pattern myself after them.

Without truly being conscious of our achievement, we had failed to recognize that conquering territory belonging to other blacks only made our space in this society more restricted. But hey, the show must go on right? Although Quake was the king of the streets in my opinion, he ruled together with Big Bubble, Big Casper, Key Boss, Big Sadd, Big Lime and a few more members not worth mentioning because of their transgression. Everyone had their roles to play and Quake played his the way I intended to play mines, whooping ass along the way.

AMERICA'S CONDUCT

There was that familiarity staring me dead on, like my grandfather had to face and like many before me. I had chosen to run around the inner city destroying anyone that challenged us, accepting this as honorable. We hated each other the way white people hated blacks. This behavior was, to say the least, subconscious hypocrisy. After that encounter in Bethune Park, Big Quake and other 6-Dueces constantly flooded the park. The more they came to the park the more they saw an opportunity to recruit the rest of us. Lil Will, who had become known as Lil Bubble, converted. Lil Caver and Ricc Rocc were already members and they wanted me to join but I wanted my own gang so I held out for a while, until it was obvious to me we all were from the same set. So I decided to join the 6-Dueces and all the rest of my homies came along with me. We had to be initiated once again on 62nd and San Pedro. My life from that day forth would never be the same.

I was growing up too fast and I knew that instinctively. However, my mother never gave up on a decent future for me, whatever that was. She could see I had given up on myself without being conscious that I had. As far as I was concerned, I was doing all the things I thought were expected of me. I refused to be weak or allow anyone to disrespect me. I kept my head held high, and rejected the prejudices that I knew existed. I fought for my pride, dignity, and convictions. In my mind I didn't have a problem being black. In fact I loved that black people were so distinctively different from white people because I viewed white people's behavior as inexcusable. So I made it my business to let people know I loved who I was, even when they expressed we were worthless. And the Crips gave me the courage to keep my head held high and never allow anyone to tell me that I was beneath them. We felt like most white people did, i.e. that nobody was better than us. We were carrying on just as they were. I was going to find the respect my father and others weren't able to find, and I figured I would start seeking it in the streets. I saw how people respected the Crips; I witnessed how people feared them wherever they went. They demanded respect and received it. But what I hadn't noticed was it was all coming at the expense of black people. All the people we were getting respect from, and who were willing to die for respect, were black people. We were destroying our own people for it. I had become so blind I couldn't see how nonsensical I had become. Here I was, the third generation of my grandfather's offspring, and the condition for blacks was worse for us than it was for him. My generation had taken up arms against their own people. Where did this idea come from, and how was it possible for us to achieve this goal by destroying each other? We all had become poisonous towards each other and didn't care. The people we needed to respect us were putting us in jail, chasing us down the streets to place us in jail cells, beating us in substations to obtain coerced confessions, planting drugs, guns and fraudulent charges on us. We weren't able to get those people's respect, so we continued to pretend that we had, and told ourselves they ain't ever going to control us. Not only were we being controlled by them, we had become zombies for them, finishing what they had started in the south, by attacking each other.

My mother never acknowledged the fact that I was a gang member. No matter how much evidence she saw, she rejected the idea that I could be so stupid. All the signs were there for her to see. I wore blue rags on my head openly. I snuck and got my ear pierced. To this day I don't know how she found out about it. I tried to hide it every time I entered the house. I would put a beanie on my head covering my left ear lobe. She came up behind me and snatched the beanie off my head and asked me, "What's that in your ear? It better be something you glued on your ear lobe. I know goddamn well you didn't get your ear pierced. Girls are the only ones that get their ears pierced. Larry, you ain't no girl are you?"

Any reasonable person would have taken the earring out without hesitation, to prove to their mother they were indeed a young man, not a girl. But the Crips had my undivided attention and I knew they wore earrings and they weren't girls. They were men who didn't take any shit from anyone; this is what I wanted for myself. I wanted my mother to know I wouldn't submit as many other blacks had. I was willing to die in the streets for my pride, dignity and respect. Why couldn't she see that I was refusing to act like I was white? I didn't want to learn in school that Christopher Columbus discovered America, or how Africa was uncivilized. Most of the lessons in school were of how great white people were and how worthless we were as black people. I felt if I accepted their programming I would lose the determination that permitted black people to be strong. My way of standing up for myself was rejecting all that they felt I was supposed to be. The Crips didn't want any part of this foolishness. We wanted to be the complete opposite. Black people weren't capable of dehumanizing an entire race of people the way they were doing us, so the earring was going to stay. At that moment I didn't realize that I had chosen the streets over my mother's love for me. It wasn't that clear to me at the time, but years later I was able to recognize the impact of that decision.

My grandfather didn't know anything about the Crips, Bloods, or any other gangs. He wanted me to start working for him. This would be my firsthand experience, working with him just like my mother's siblings did when they were my age. He hadn't changed one bit.

His job consisted of going around to every supermarket in the area collecting all the aluminum cans, card board boxes, and copper wire. I didn't want any part of this job but no matter how awful I was in the streets, I never disrespected my elders. My mother wanted me to work so I could stay out of the streets. My grandfather paid $5.00 dollars a day. I was overjoyed with excitement about all of that money. Imagine that!!

What was so humiliating about the job for me was jumping inside the trash bins throughout the city, including sometimes in rival gang territory, where I wasn't supposed to be. I couldn't say anything to him about being a gang member. He would have said, "Larry what the hell is you talking about you're a Crip? Do the Crips pick up trash?" He would've wanted every single one of them to jump on the back of his 1972 white Ford pickup and stack those boxes to the sky. I did however love being around him. He would tell me the importance of working, and when I was moving too slow for him he'd say, "Larry are you going, or do you want me to go for you?"

I recall one day we were on Slauson and Compton Ave at the grocery store named Country Farms. I was suspended from school for something; I was always getting suspended for something stupid. I got in a trash bin to collect all the boxes inside, breaking the boxes down and throwing them out so my grandfather could place them in back of the truck. While I was bending down to fold the boxes I noticed that the kids in school were getting out early and coming towards the store. There wasn't a chance in hell they were going to miss me. I stayed as low as possible without causing my grandfather to wonder what was taking me so long to get out of the trash bin. When that didn't work he called to me, as if he knew I was ashamed to work in a trash bin. He didn't care who saw him in one, just point in the direction the boxes were and he would be certain to get them. He would see cardboard lying in the street and say to me, "Who's throwing that money in the street?" I wasn't going to get any passes from him. "Larry what are you doing?" I was caught, "Folding these boxes," I replied. "Come on, let's go. Ain't no more boxes in there." I jumped out of the trash can for the world to see and here came the kids. "Larry what's up, what are you doing in the trash can?" "Helping my grandfather," I replied. I couldn't wait for him to start the truck so we could disappear. He told me when we were leaving, "Larry you act like you're too embarrassed to make money." That was wisdom I didn't understand at the time. I was too busy worrying about earning my pride, dignity and respect out there in the streets.

Zombies

Roots: The Saga of an American Family, written by Alex Haley. All that I had ever learned about white people's atrocities against blacks came from my grandparents and parents. But when I actually watched the movie *Roots*, it was beyond anything I could have ever imagined. Our entire community had been summoned together to tune in to the movie. We were about to be taught a lesson in how white people carried out savagery successfully, and we didn't miss an episode.

For most of us it was our first educational insight into what actually happened to our ancestors and the suffering they endured. Most of us had no knowledge of what took place. It was truly a sad piece of commentary for many of us to watch. Schools throughout the entire district of Los Angeles County were vigilant on campuses. It was an unsettling time for a bunch of people.

An abundance of black people weren't able to hold their emotions in check. They wanted revenge on white people in the same manner as black people in the movie. Scores of people, no matter how many stories they had heard about African History, couldn't believe that white people could be so sadistic. But you had those that were fully aware of white people's conduct because they had lived, studied, researched, and learned and never were grouped with those that only heard.

Those that knew voiced their convictions on the others, who by that time were willing to jump over the cliff for one another as opposed to being tricked into jumping off at the deception of white people's manipulation. I recall people saying there was no way on earth that a human-being could be so ugly, egregious, flagrant, appalling and outrageous as white folks were in the movie *Roots*. But those people were wrong. White people represented that ugliness, and a heap of them continue to do so without any shame.

Watching *Roots* we witnessed white people systematically tear down Africans limb by limb, emotionally, physically, psychologically, spiritually and effortlessly, without a thought of anything being morally wrong with their behavior. They were successful in detaching many Africans from their true history, but not all of them forgot who they were, or where they came from. Those who chose to remember their history were brutally executed for daring to hold on to the smallest piece of knowledge of their true identities. Only the strong survive, and being here today is a testament to our people's determination to endure white people's cruelties.

This went on for centuries. White folks had to be certain Africans were successfully broken to assure their own safety. They knew if anyone had done to them what they were doing to Africans by no means would they have accepted it. Those who commit any act offensive toward America are demolished, but black people need to forget about what happened to them because it's in the past. Now how crazy is that? White people also knew that at some point some Africans weren't going to go for their abuses and would revolt. However they were going to be sure to minimize those revolts as best they could with as much savagery as they were able to dispense on Africans. The ones that had the slightest thoughts of rebelling would think twice after witnessing beatings, hangings, rapes, and outright murders of their people.

White folks had declared themselves the kings of the universe, or they wanted blacks to believe they were. To them blacks only had two choices in the matter - submit or die. They intended to carry out their plans to enslave black people whether they liked it or not, but there were Africans willing to die before they allowed themselves to become subjected to slavery. Watching this movie, many basically thought white people had lost their minds, but tons of white people call black people frightening. One of the things that struck me more than anything was that Africans assisted white people in pulling off this monstrous act against their own people.

How could white folks have been so persuasive in convincing Africans in Africa to enslave themselves for centuries? For me that was one of many revealing signs that African people had disdain for their own people and it has been passed down to our current generation of African American populations. It was truly shameful then, as it is now.

However, just like many of those slaves in the movie *Roots*, many of today's children and adults have no idea who their ancestors are beyond their parent's parents. I was fortunate to meet Momma Joe's mother Kissiah Williams, but that was the extent of my family tree. Most of us were just as ignorant as many of those slaves. We were running around in the United States thinking that we were free because in California they weren't beating us with whips or hanging us in trees. But they were stuffing our brains with misinformation in addition to jamming as many blacks as they could in prisons, sentencing them to hundreds of years for crimes that carry 2, 3, 4 or 5 years. They were getting away with this abuse of authority because so many blacks in this country somehow think they're different from those of us who refuse to accept that America has our best interest at heart. They side with those that are in power, even though if you see a system abusing its authority it is your responsibility to see justice done for everyone, to represent those that are less fortunate. Scores of black people don't equate prisons with <u>slavery</u> because they have been brainwashed into accepting that our behavior completely warrants us being enslaved. They forgive the white people's conduct and worship the ground they walk on, and detest their own people. How sick is that? White people have once again successfully tricked, deceived, and manipulated a whole host of black Zombies, especially black elected officials of the inner city ghettos. If it wasn't so sad it would be funny.

> **AMENDMENT XIII**
>
> Slavery
>
> SECTION. 1. Neither slavery nor involuntary servitude, except as a punishment for crime whereof the party shall have been duly convicted, shall exist within The United States, or any place subject to their jurisdiction.
>
> SECTION 2. Congress shall have power to enforce this article by appropriate legislation.
>
> Proposed January 31, 1865: ratified December 6, 1865; certified December 18, 1865.

Most of us were then and still are now, walking **Zombies**.

The children of Africa had a rich history of knowledge about who they were and from where their ancestors had descended. White people could never strip the truth away from the land of Africa; no matter how many beatings our people endured, the truth could never be altered. Because of the lessons the children of Africa had to attend both morning and evening, their knowledge of the Qur'an was something they had before they were allowed to graduate. We are blessed to have intact the true history of our African ancestors. Watching the movie and seeing the levels of information they had to absorb about their history, for me it was a totally different perspective of Africa's history. Knowledge is power.

I learned they were proud Muslims, which many of us in our modern day communities have no idea about. Because of all the negative stories we've heard in America's pseudo-educational institutions that Africans were Voodoo Doctors, idol worshippers, i.e. carved wooden and/or stone objects were seen as gods, we come away with a belief that the African people were primitive and underdeveloped. These stories were endless with unflattering things that were spread about black people, but to see it for ourselves was enlightening for many of us. Scores of us were walking dead, psychologically.

In the movie, Kunta Kinte was from the Mandingo Tribe. He was born in the year 1750, in the African country of Gambia, to the parents of Omoro, his father, and Binta his mother lived in the village of Juffure. What I found to be interesting was how their family was structured, and the support system they had in place to fully develop him and other young men in their village, preparing them to become accomplished men in their community.

They were taught to respect their elders no matter where they encountered them with the greeting "Kerabe," meaning "Do you have Peace." All the children respected the rules and laws of their parents and religion. As a child, Kunta Kinte went through all these stages to make his father proud, showing he was a capable man to carry their tradition further in the Mandingo Tribe. The tribe's elders would warn all of them to be attentive when they were out doing their required exercises for their village. They had known about the "Toubob" which meant the white man that had been running throughout Africa for centuries, kidnapping men, women, and children. They also were aware that they were being assisted by Slatee, which meant traitors to their own people, "Africans."

Once someone was captured, the Slatee would help the Toubob take them to the ships where they would be hoisted to the bottom of the ship's deck, naked, chained one next to the other, hundreds at a time. The Slatee, "Traitors," always thought they were doing a good deed for the Toubob until they stripped them naked along with the rest of the captured and chained them right along with the others. It's shameful how many black people don't respect history. Can you imagine the look on some people's faces if they knew what their punishment would be for all the transgressions they personally committed against our people? How many Slattee are amongst your community pretending to have your best interest at heart? In the inner city, we see them all the time and refuse to acknowledge anything that comes out of their mouths.

Kunta's father told him all the time when he was a young boy to always be careful and take someone with him whenever he went out to do the smallest of chores in and around the village. Kunta who had three younger brothers would convey these same lessons to his brother, Limin.

They were told awful stories about Toubobs that would frighten even the bravest of men. They didn't know exactly what was happening to all the people that were being taken from their homeland. They believed they were being eaten by Toubobs. That's what was being communicated throughout the villages. However, nobody really knew because no one had ever escaped out of bondage to report back to them about what was really happening to those that were snatched.

They weren't being eaten; however, they were being beaten, raped, killed, disfigured, hung, and worked literally to death. They had misinformation in the villages about Toubob's actual needs for their services but they weren't being used as delicacies.

I couldn't believe that a race of people would travel so far around the world to stuff millions of people in the bottom of ships lying naked in feces, vomit and urine for months at a time, then beat them until they were willing to submit into involuntary servitude for the rest of their lives. Then the abductors found it within themselves to call the very people they'd kidnapped and tortured lazy, but the reason they stole them was to work them against their will. What kind of psychological abuse would that fall under? Really how would America's most renowned psychologists analyze this behavior and the effects of such a thing on the abused? What would the diagnosis be? Wouldn't you want to know?

What gives a race of people the right to invade another country, take its citizens back to foreign land that wasn't even theirs to begin with, then force the people they've abducted to erase all their memories of who they were, and delete the history of where they came from. They not only wanted them to forget who they were, but they also didn't want them to learn the language, to read or write. In the land they would be enslaved in they would be forced to surrender their names and compelled to take their kidnappers' surnames. I would pay top dollar for the psychiatric evaluation on such behavior.

In the book *Roots*, Kunta Kinte's ancestors quoted the elders as saying, "Even worse than Toubob's money is that he lies for nothing and he cheats with methods, as naturally as he breathes. That's what gives him the advantage over us." As well as, "Toubob could never do this without help from our own people." In addition to that they would say, "For Toubob's money, we turn against our own kind." Also, "Greed and treason, these are the things Toubob has given us in exchange for those he has stolen away."

Kunta was forced to take that ship ride that he never thought would be in his future. He went out one morning to find a drum stock and never made it back to his village. He was taken from his mother, father and three brothers who depended on him for leadership and guidance. They would never see him again because of the selfishness and greed of some barbarians. And we're supposed to believe it when white people say we are an uncivilized race of people. How did the roles magically switch from their unjustified conduct towards black people in America to us as the people abusing white folks, when their conduct is documented for the world to see against us? Please somebody explain how America was so successful in pulling that switch off on us?

If Kunta Kinte could have sent a message back to Africa and his ancestors about what was really going on in America with those that were kidnapped, he would have screamed from the top of his lungs for everyone with a pair of legs to run for their lives because Toubobs were lunatics. It was far worse than any of them could have ever imagined.

From the start, there was going to be no misunderstanding about anyone being warriors except for the white men. Kunta Kinte was given the special treatment of abuse the entire time it took them to reach America's soil. Then he was sold as quickly as he stepped foot off the ship. Africans were lost in this foreign land, and those that were born in America during slavery despised those that were born in Africa, and openly displayed their dislike towards them when they arrived. How preposterous was that?

What I also learned from the movie and book was that many slaves did not accept these forced practices. Those who fought against slavery attempted to gather as many blacks as they could to revolt, but many times other blacks told their kidnappers what these warriors were up to, spoiling many plots to stand up for their rights as a human beings, to be returned to their land. The white man was simply genius, because many black people still hate themselves and their people today.

Retribution

After watching Roots, many of us saw white people the way Roots had depicted them. We were revengeful and set out to harm, destroy or cause as much havoc as possible towards them, be it physical, monetary or property value. It didn't matter to us.

Now that I was attending Edison Jr. High I was with many of my homeboys. Big Ed, Too Tall, Big Mark, Big C-Bone, Bam, Crazy Lar, Leroy, Big Vince, Darrell Wilson (aka) Dick Head, Boxco, Lil Kev, Ricc Rocc, Lil Caver (aka) Lil Quake, Lil Fluxx, Nat, Big Erin, Lil Mike, Lil Will (aka) Lil Bubble, Pounds, and many others. We were well represented.

However, the black students at Edison Jr. High were constantly fighting with the Mexican students, who were from Florence 13. It was mainly my neighborhood, the 6-Deuces, against them. For whatever reason, the Mexicans didn't like blacks. They had become the new Ku Klux Klan against the blacks. Every day after school we had riots with them. They all knew about Big Quake. He was like the lion to the hyenas in the jungle, no competition. When they saw him they knew that they would be in for a brutal ass-kicking. Big Quake was 6'0 tall, 190 lbs, and black as night with strong-textured hair. He was simply an African warrior. He always made us proud and helped us to hold our heads up high and believe we could win in anything. He battled them in a manner no one would believe unless they were actually there to witness it. God had blessed his hands and made his enemies respect and fear Big Quake. The security guards at Edison became familiar with Big Quake, and whenever they saw him near the school they would ask him to leave. But they never confronted the Mexican loiterers that circled the school daily. Quake never missed the festivities of war. As soon as we got started he was always the star of the battle. I can tell you, in all of my experiences in the ghetto's gutters, only a few men have impressed me with their warrior traits. Quake was at the top of the list.

The Crips had started to fall out with each other, both on the East and West. So Big Tookie called a meeting at Centinela Park. Raymond, Baby Alton, and many other original Crips attended the meeting. Big Tookie's objectives were to stop the fighting between the street gangs, but many Crips there felt that Big Took was the cause of most of the dissension amongst the Crips. Monkey Man, from West Side Underground Crips, pulled his pistol out on Big Took, and told him basically that he was the one who needed to change his conduct, because he was responsible for many of the problems. Raymond stood there without saying one word, permitting Monkey Man to make his case.

Before they were able to resolve their dispute, one of their adversaries surprised them all by opening fire, leaving the Crips as they were when they arrived

- in total disarray. From that point on, the Crips never recovered. They started to engage one another throughout the city of Los Angeles. My neighborhood fell out with 52nd Street Broadway Gangster Crips over some females, and it snowballed downhill. Hoovers, and Kitchens Crips, as well as Swans (which was a Blood gang), and many other black gangs were added to the list.

In school I continued to show a total disregard towards learning. I was running around with Lil Mike, gambling on campus and ditching school. One thing had changed for Lil Mike; with my help he had found the love of his life. Her name was Veronica Collins and she wasn't taking no for an answer. Lil Mike and I played on the same baseball team at the park. He was the pitcher of our team, while I played catcher and third base. Veronica and her Asian friend would come up there to see Lil Mike practice, standing behind the back stop to watch Lil Mike pitch. When I was catching, I could hear most of what they said about Mike. He would lose his concentration with Veronica watching him, throwing a fit and ready to leave saying, "Let's go, I'm cool, man that girl keeps looking at me." But when Veronica wasn't around he couldn't stop talking about her. He would tell me how he talked to her when he hadn't, trying to get me to believe he had found the courage to confront her. Without saying a word to Lil Mike, I would tell Veronica, "Don't trip. I'll get him to call you; he likes you but he's scared to talk to you."

I could tell you some stories of how long it took him to finally build up the nerve to approach her, yet I'll save you the laughs on his part. However Veronica was about her business when it came to Lil Mike. She got her man and they are happily married to this very day.

Veronica and I had some of the same classes and she didn't understand why I didn't do anything in class. I just didn't care. Many of us Crips looked at studying and learning the things they were teaching us in school as a form of brainwashing and blacks trying to be white. We didn't want to be anything like white people because we all viewed them as crazy and murderous monsters who thought they were better than everybody else. We went out of our way not to resemble them in any way, shape, fashion, or form. This was one of the reasons we created our own language, so we didn't sound like white people, and to prevent white people from understanding anything we communicated about with each other. As you may know, without hesitation they deemed this language stupid, unintelligent, or Ebonics, simply because they couldn't understand it. Then here came many of their black agents, riding up in shining armor to the rescue. They were sent to attack us for using this sort of language, in spite of our being comfortable with how we talked to each other and understanding what we were communicating. How is it that this wasn't considered genius on our part? It was because we didn't sound like white people. The powers that be in America needed to have complete control of what we learned, and white folks wanted to be the ones teaching it to us.

Edison had become known to most of us as the battle field where we had to fight with Mexicans just because we were Black. What was crazy about that experience was during school hours everybody went to their classes or ditched, whatever they did, but as soon as the last bell rang all hell broke loose; it never failed.

Most of my homeboys had been suspended from Edison for one reason or another, including me. One day we decided we would get back at the administration for kicking us out of school. We broke into the school and ransacked it, wrote our names and gang on the walls. Big La La Neighborhood 6-Deuce Crips. I was proud that I was able to destroy something white people owned. No matter how wrong it was, it seemed like the right thing to do for us, so we did it and didn't have any regret.

I immediately checked into Charles Drew Jr. High School, adjacent to Russell Elementary. I was already familiar with this area because I attended Russell a few years earlier. At Drew I ran into Danny and Willie Thomas, my childhood buddies. A lot had changed for all of us. I was now a gang member, and they had matured as well. This neighborhood was the 89th Street Neighborhood Crips. I started hanging out with Gangster John and Andrae Brown (aka) Dray from Eight Nine, 89th Street. Gangster John was a couple years older and my neighborhood was allies with theirs, so he was like the senior member there for most of us. I didn't stay there long. I was kicked out just as quickly as I had been at Edison.

School just didn't sit well with me. When we thought blacks were acting all proper like white people or pretended they were better than us, we gave them the blues. We harassed them and called them all kind of names. We couldn't stand to see black people acting white. When I was going to Edison, Veronica couldn't stand to see Mike and I failing our studies, so she talked us into a contest to see which one of us could get the best grade in math. I told Mike, I would get a better grade than he would if I tried. He accepted the challenge. We studied together and Veronica helped me in class, but my mind always drifted off to something opposite of what I was doing.

Before we started this challenge I believed I was getting F's or D's in math. When our grades came back I had received a C- and Mike had received a C+. I was happy about that and so was Lil Mike. He wanted to continue our challenge. However I was through with that experiment. I had some Cripping to do, and I had every intention of adhering to its calling.

One night Lil Quake and Vantray Gregory, who would years later become known as Trip Box, along with Big Vince, Alan, Lil Will, Big Erin, Mr. Low, Lil Kev, Lil Mike, and I were over at Alan's house smoking weed out of a bong. Vantray had gotten so high he couldn't say my name Larry. He tried to call me, but he kept saying La, La, La, La, La La, La, La, La, La La, La, La, La, repeatedly. Everyone there laughed at him until their sides were hurting. The next day when we all got together and reminisced about the night before, they started mimicking Vantray and it never stopped from that point forward. Whenever my homeboys saw me, without hesitation they would start clowning. They would say, "La, La, La, La, La, La, La, La and it stuck. That's how I became known as Big La La, all because one night of smoking marijuana with my loved ones.

I still had to go to school no matter how much I hated it. My mother checked me into Bethune Jr. High. It was like all of the schools I had attended wrapped up in one. Most of my homeboys attended Bethune - Big Sike and Biscuit were running the school for my neighborhood when I got there. Big Sike was from 6-Deuce and Biscuit was from 68th Street. We were allies. Bethune was fun because I met so many gang members there that were from several different sets/neighborhoods. There were the Hoovers, 5 Trays, 4 Trays, and many other gangs, but I ran with Tony Boguard from PJ Watts. He lived across the street from the school. He and I ditched every day, until I got kicked out. I was so opposed to school and to authority figures that it didn't make any sense for me to be in their company because I was certainly going to disrespect them.

I had to go before the Los Angeles School Board in downtown L.A. so that they could personally evaluate me. They concluded I should be expelled from the entire school district, so I couldn't go to school at all. That was like going to heaven, if one existed. My mother was devastated yet she continued to encourage me to do better.

Lil Quake, Lil Bubble and I began hanging out with this pimp named Chinese. He was a black man 6'2, 160 lbs who actually knew karate. He had a chestnut brown complexion, wore Rick James extensions in his hair, and didn't have one single tooth in his mouth. Chinese was electrifying. His personality was likeable and everyone that came in contact with him loved him, unless you were his enemy then he was as unpleasant as any human being that I had known. But he was never that way with us.

Chinese took us deeper into the night life. During the early morning hours, I saw the most desperate of hearts, who sought comfort at the expense of enslavement.

> **AMENDMENT XIII**
>
> Slavery
>
> *SECTION 1.* Neither slavery nor involuntary servitude, except as a punishment for crime whereof the party shall have been duly convicted, shall exist within The United States, or any place subject to their jurisdiction.
>
> *SECTION 2.* Congress shall have power to enforce this article by appropriate legislation.
>
> Proposed January 31, 1865: ratified December 6, 1865; certified December 18, 1865.

I witnessed all ethnic groups, from the ghettos to the suburbs, purposely ignoring the laws simply to be pleasured, at the risk of violating Amendment XIII. The amendment is clear that as a punishment for crime whereof the party shall have been duly convicted, slavery is acceptable in the United States, or any place subject to their jurisdiction. Slavery is still alive and growing in the United States as you shall see, but it didn't bother us blacks, because involuntary servitude was attached to our inner core. America will never voluntarily allow blacks to be free of its grip.

Chinese was fierce in the streets. He would talk women into selling their bodies for him and they loved pleasing him. He was gifted in the art of persuasion. I used to watch him at work and be just as mesmerized as the women he captivated. He was a true pimp, and I did everything in my power to protect him when we were in the streets. He was the definition of a jack of all trades. He made his money wherever money was being circulated; he had his hands somehow involved in the transactions. I watched him cheat people out of every last dime without any compassion; it was all business with him. My experiences with him taught me a lot about the darkness of the streets, and prepared me for the trials and tribulations I would encounter in the future. I grew a thick layer of skin, becoming desensitized to many things at a very young age. I came into contact with the meanness of hearts because of my association with him, and I learned all that anyone could ever learn about women because of him. I saw the sweetest and the most aggressive women be broken by him. I idolized Chinese, without question. I refused to allow America to tell me who I should accept as role models in my life. I loved all the characters around me.

One day Lil Quake and I were hanging out in front of my mother's house and I had a gun on me. Chinese pulled up in a Lincoln Continental he had just bought from my uncle. He asked me did I know anybody that was selling a gun because he needed one right now. I told him, "I have a 22 on me; you can have it if you need it." He told me that he did and gave me $100.00 for it. He fired it in the air to make sure it worked. After he ascertained that it did, he took off to wherever he had to be.

I saw him two weeks later and he had gotten shot several times in Hollywood. Mr. Low and I were walking down Compton Ave and Chinese pulled up and jumped out of his car and said, "La La, I need to talk to you. I got shot the fuck up that night using that bullshit gun you sold me." I asked him what happened. He said, "I tried to use your gun, but it didn't go off and the motherfucker that I got into it with shot me because the goddamn gun misfired. You owe me a hundred dollars." I said to him, "I don't owe you shit. When you left with it, it worked. What happened from the time you left me until the time you got shot is on you."

Before we could finish talking to one another Mr. Low interjected, "Cuzz, my homeboy don't owe you shit." Mr. Low didn't get his last words out of his mouth before Chinese hit him in it. Mr. Low took off running like we used to see him doing from the police when we all were younger. Only this time he had crazy-ass Chinese on his heels. Mr. Low ran inside Slauson Farm Grocery Market located on Slauson and Compton Ave. I yelled at Chinese "Leave cuzz alone. He don't know, cuzz." Mr. Low thought he was being a homeboy by standing up to Chinese for me, but it wasn't necessary because Chinese was only talking shit. He wasn't serious. He was letting me know that the gun misfired and he could've been killed. He was mad that he was caught in a situation like that and when he saw me walking down the street he got that shit off his chest, but he loved me too much to do anything to me. I was his project, to make me become like him, so he wasn't going to destroy me, and I wasn't going to allow him to either. He knew I wasn't going to give him shit. If I had made any attempt to act like it was because of me that he got shot, Chinese would've whooped my ass for being a punk. Chinese wanted me to be ruthless like him. So he would often become extreme with me to prepare me for the world he had invited me into. And for the most part he needed to know that I had his back when we traveled the city, which I did. I loved Chinese, just as I loved Big Quake, Big John, Baby Alton, and the others.

After trying to beat Mr. Low about the head with his pistol, Chinese said, "You better talk to this motherfucker then, before I kill this punk. This motherfucker bet not ever get in my business." Mr. Low was scared to death; he instantly knew he had made a grave error in challenging Chinese.

Chinese may have been a pimp but he wasn't a soft one. He was a ruthless one, who I respected immensely. Chinese granted Mr. Low his pardon and finished our conversation, saying, "I'll get that $100 dollars from you later, and be ready. Tonight we're going out on the stroll."

When I was much older I understood more of what he constantly would say to me, such as, "The game is not to be told, it's to be sold." Because I surely had to pay. He got his hundred dollars out of me plus a thousand years of interest for all my labor to help his game. I cherish every minute I spent with him.

I started to hang out with my homie Big Spike who lived inside the Pueblos Projects. Spike didn't know Jack (aka) Nu Nu, who was from Six Deuce. However one day we all were over to Big Vince's house shooting dice. Big Spike was on the dice and Jack walked up. Spike looked up and saw him standing there, and tried to rush him, saying that Jack was a Blood. The rest of us told Spike, "Cuzz, you're trippin. Cuzz is from the hood." Spike assured us he had seen Jack inside the Projects wearing a red rag on his head, and that Jack didn't know he was also from the hood. We couldn't believe it because we used to go inside the projects with our blue rags on to visit him and most of the youngsters in the projects all went to school together at Edison Jr. High.

Jack took off running across the tracks that separated our neighborhoods, screaming, "I'm going to kill you mother-fuckers." We sent word to Jack that whenever we saw him again he should know we intended to peel his ass back.

That day would come sooner than we expected - not on the street but in Juvenile Hall. Juvenile Hall is a detention center used for housing juvenile delinquents. Lil Will, Lil Caver, and I were in Juvenile Hall for grand theft auto. We heard that Jack was in the hall for murder. He had allegedly given a gun to one of the dudes inside the Projects that was a Blood. It was his mother's gun, the same one I had carried. Supposedly Jack didn't know what dude's intentions were when he gave him the gun. The dude shot and killed a Crip and ran back and gave Jack the gun, so he became an accessory to murder. When we heard this we thought he had lost his mind. How was it possible that he could turn on us when he hadn't lived inside the Projects a full year, and had lived with us most of his life?

He had betrayed us in a way that was unforgivable. We had become enemies, and vowed to seek the other's destruction on sight. We got our chance one morning when we were on our way to court and happened to run into him. But some dudes from another neighborhood gang were about to jump on him for a crime he allegedly committed on one of their homeboys. When we saw him in that situation, Lil Quake and the rest of my crimies still wanted to get him, but I talked them into supporting him and we came to his aid reluctantly. Eventually we allowed him to come back home and he worked his way back into good graces with the Crips. It wasn't that easy. Cripping ain't never been easy.

Avalanche

Things started to explode in every direction, to levels that weren't foreseeable for scores of us. Raymond Washington moved from 76th between McKinley and Wosworth to 64th and San Pedro - my neighborhood, the Sixty Second Street Neighborhood Crips.

Raymond had never given up on bringing all the Crips back together, at least on the Eastside. Big Tookie and other Crips on the Westside had become just as influential as Raymond, so his efforts with them would have probably been futile. So he called a meeting at Bethune Junior High School. He communicated with other gang leaders on the east side; Donald Kelly, Fast Black, Big Bubble, Big Doc, Pepe, J Box, Big Quake and others. He presented his idea for unifying the entire east side, expressing that he would drop the "side" out of East and replacing it with East Coast. However, every gang on the east side had their own leaders. Grape Street, Kitchen, Avalon Garden, Four Trey gangsters, Hat Gang, East Side Kids, Block Crips, Neighborhood, Front Street, Back Street, 118 Blocc, New Homes, Aliso Village, 190 Delmo Blocc, Five Trey, Shacc Boys and a few other east side gangs would all have to agree. Of course many of the other gang leaders didn't want to give up their leadership role, so they declined, not without a fight. Those of us that had agreed to the merge decided to press the others to join. So, not in this particular order, the following neighborhoods agreed to join the union: First Street, Sixty Second, Sixty Eighth, Sixty Ninth, Seventy Sixth, Eighty Ninth, Ninety Seventh, 102nd, 43rd, 190th Blocc, 118th Blocc, 66th street, 59th street and 1200 block located in Riverside.

We then became known as 6-Duece Neighborhood East Coast Crips. Instead of us writing 6-Duece we wrote 1Str., 59th ,62, 66, 68, 69, 76, 89, 97 102, 118, 190, 1200 as one gang. The 43rd street gangsters decided against joining our union and went back to their original roots, but remained allies with the 6-Dueces.

Other Eastside Crips sets refused to join, which is typical of blacks, isn't it? So we remained divided. Raymond had a great idea to make us stronger, but you had those that decided to stay on the plantation. Divide and conquer, a tactic that has been used against us from the beginning of time, still works.

We were by far the largest gang in Los Angeles County. The closest gang to us in numbers was the Hoover Crips, who had 43rd, 52nd, 59th, 74th, 83rd, 92nd, 94th, 107th, 112th street Hoover Crips, and they were just as fearless as we were.

I was blessed to meet gang members from everywhere. We roamed the city looking for difficult obstacles to overcome, whether other gangs or authority figures. The East Coast Crips had too many leaders from different streets, all qualified to be bosses. Some had talents the others lacked, and then there were those who possessed all the qualifications. From 62nd Street was Big Bubble, Dog, Big Sadd, Keyboss, Big Casper, Big D, Snow, Lime, Big Quake, Big Oscar, and others. Yet Big Quake was my favorite of all. From 68th Street were Ronnie Bam, 8-ball, Owl, Wolf, and Dog, from 69th Street, Big Doc, Smiley, Mitchell Glover, Poppa, Godfather, Vertise Swan, Lumberjack and others. From 76th Street were Baby Too Cool, Big Bob, Cry Baby Sal, Lil Bean, Cat Ceasure, Devil, Big Tweet, Spook, Skull, Bamps, Snake, Monk, X-Ray, Big C, Kool Aide, Terry Simmons, Kenny Carter, Eddie Hawthorne, Pit Bull, Number One, Batman and others. They all started out at about the same time as the Shacc Boys. From 89th Street was Big Duck, Trick, Gangster John, Crazy Dave, Wolf, Big Tuff, Rin Tin, 40 Ounce, Buzzy, Tom Tom (the mini bike bandit that dragged me down the street years earlier for sport), Big Dirt, Tee, Wayne Dray, J-Bone, Bat Man, Snake, Neck Bone, Spike and others. From 97th was Big J-Box, the night stalker. J-Box is one of many East Coast Crips that I can say taught me the meaning of play-no-games. He is the ultimate cap peeler. Big Murk, Charlie Mac, Lucious Bell, Bamp, Hound Dog, Gary Welch, Larry Welch, Big Poncho, Big Ant, Pie, J-Bam, Ron Ron, May May, Money, Hit Man, Big Soul and others. From Q102 there was Crazy Crip, Pee Pee, Twin 1&2, E-Man, Frog, J.R., Termite, Rick Rock, Mel P., Weasel, Sugarbear, Doc, Bucker T, UT, Big Carl, Monet and others. There are so many original Crips that came from Q102 set, it would take me too long to list all these men that made us proud. From 118th block was Lil James; he was the founder of the block heads. However G-Man, BK, Capone, Riff Raff, Lil Evil, Hot Dog, Lil Tiptoe, Buck, J-Bone, Evil, Gangster Rat, Old Man and many others are the tangible pieces that made the set run like a well-oiled machine. From 190th street (block), these young men were always accused of being too wealthy to be thugs, but they, for the strangest of reasons, proved to everyone that they were reckless and just as filthy as those considered vulgar. I'll say up front that there are too many 190th Street gang members to name, so don't take it personally. My favorite without question is Bruce Millsap (aka Loco). Other notables were Ken Dogg, Tom Slicc, Fly, Gangster, Sike, Black (aka Lil Loco), Frog, Meco, and others. From 59th Street there were reputable brothers like Big Slim and T-Tiger, and from 1200 block I only had the opportunity to meet Lazy Dee, who was turned all the way up. From 66th Street Brotherhood, there was Rocc, and too many others to name. From 1st Street, there was T-Bone, Ace, Bull Dogg and a host of others. Those would be my homies for the rest of my life. We were committed to one another, to death do us part, or at least until the hypnotic state of mind wore off, whichever came first.

Many of us continued the trend the first generation of Crips started. We would travel to downtown Los Angeles, to the State Movie Theater. Big Sike, who was the leader of my generation of Crips, was 6'3 and 200 lbs. at the youthful age of 15, and he was truly a great leader. He was intelligent and thought everything through. He wore a gigantic Afro and told jokes every chance he got.

AMERICA'S CONDUCT

For personal reasons, I haven't spoken much about the female gang members, but I do want very much for you women to know about the contributions you all made in our movement, and the joy, excitement and pleasures you all provided us. You know who you are, Crip Here!!!

I was dating a young lady named Christine Murphy, a track star at Edison Jr. High School. She ran like a Cheetah, smooth and effortless. She didn't lose many races, that's for certain. Because of her, I was able to meet Olympic legend Jesse Owens, at U.C.L.A. during one of her track meets. She lived directly across the street from where the 56th Street Blood Stone Villains hung out. I knew most of them because we all went to Edison Jr. High School and played sports together at Bethune Park, before many of them became gang members.

I went to a lot of their parties and they never said too much to me, other than what's up, how was such and such doing, etc. They never acted like they didn't want me coming over there, at least I never felt that way. But Christine started telling me they didn't like me coming over there with my blue rag on. Shit, in my heart I never thought for one minute that they would challenge me. Surely they all knew I was from 6-Duece, and to be honest, Big Quake pumped fear in many people's hearts on the eastside.

In summer of '79, a concert was held at the Coliseum, The Funk Festival. Parliament, Rick James, Bootsy Collins, Confunkshun, and other groups were there. I didn't know so many Crips existed until I saw what looked like a million of them. The Coliseum was full, from ground level up, with a sea of blue and red rags. I ran into Chinese, and I saw Big Took standing in front of the Coliseum with his shirt off, flexing his muscles as he always was doing. This was what made us happy - going to events, enjoying each other's company as best we could, until someone found a reason to explode, a reason that would surely be justified under ghetto laws. Hence modus operandi.

People were smoking sherm and taking off all their clothes, running around like they had lost their mind. It was funny to some, and disgraceful to others. Although we were all black people, we had different views on life. I thought it was funny until I took the time out to really reflect on what my journey has been all about. Then it became clear to me that some of the things I did were due to my immaturity and lack of experience in life. It appeared to me that whatever chance black people had to pull themselves up had been lost at this point, because the ride I was on was surely of a destructive nature.

After the concert, it was back to our part of town with no signs of letting up on the path of destruction. Bethune Park was giving a dance this particular night, and I had been hanging out with Big Sike, Spike, CL, Fish, and Big Fluxx. We would go some of everywhere, but tonight the dance was our destination. I wanted to get home early so I could iron my clothes and be Crippish for the Crip Walking Contest.

Everyone knew Lil Oscar was sure to win, as he did any time he was lucky enough to be around us. He, like Mr. Low, stayed in placements and was very seldom home with us, unless he was AWOL (absent without leave) which he would often be. I recall how the people would come out to get him and he would be ready to jump off the back of his second story porch. Big Quake used to tell him to go back, that he would be home with us next week. He didn't want to miss anything when he saw us about to go out. Everybody loved him - Lil Oscar was larger than life to us. He won every Crip Walking contest he entered, hands down. He was dazzling with his feet, excellent, a true professional. He could slide across the floor, light as a feather and his feet moved as he commanded them, with ease. It was as if he was sliding in oil, only he controlled his every move.

My homeboy Big Sike used to see how Boxco acted towards me and couldn't believe I hadn't whooped his ass, because I was kicking everybody else's ass that I had conflict with. He used to tell me, "Cuzz, you can whoop Boxco, I'm telling you. You're scared because he is your brother. Fight him like he's not your brother. I bet you whoop his ass."

I heard Big Sike, but I didn't really pay much attention because Boxco was a damn fool, and I knew that much for sure.

I went home to get dressed for the dance. I started ironing a pair of Boxco's pants, some blue khakis, and a black Monte Carlo shirt. I felt good and knew I was going to cut the dance floor up that night. Boxco walked in and saw me ironing his pants. Not only did he not want me to wear his pants, he wanted me to give him the ironing board immediately because he was also going to the dance. This is probably the first time I stood up to him. I didn't want to, but I knew the time had come. It was necessary. I was now 15 years old and it appeared he didn't respect me at all.

Finally the great show, Boxco vs. La La. He continued to insist that I give him the iron, but there was no way that was going to happen. I had made my mind up that I was going to fight him today. In my heart I always truly believed that I could beat him up if I really fought him, because I was really a good fighter. Boxco never let up, "Give me the iron, cuzz." "Nah wait until I'm finished cuzz." "You're finished now!" "No I ain't." "Yes you are." "Cuzz I ain't gone be but a minute." "Fuck that shit. Give me that motherfucking iron, cuzz." I just continued ironing as if I didn't hear him. My homeboys, Big Sike and Big CL, were standing outside waiting on me. Boxco grabbed at the iron and all I remember from that point on was me whooping his ass something fierce. I beat him mercilessly. We had an upstairs inside of our apartment complex, and I whooped him down the stairs into my mother's living room. She was in her room when she heard us coming down. When she opened her door, I saw her watching me as if to say, "There you go, you're growing up. You're there now, Larry. Be a man and stand up to Bobby. Don't be afraid to stand tall." Instead of my mother telling us to stop fighting, she said, "Larry, take him outside. Ya'll are breaking up all my crystals." Outside we went, never stopping for a break. Big Sike, and CL were cheering me on, "Beat his ass, La La." I felt God within me. I was determined to be victorious, and I was. I conquered Boxco with ease, and in his eyes I saw defeat. My sisters stood by, knowing there would be no more punches thrown unless I was the one throwing them in our defense. There would be no more smart remarks, no more unexpected wakeup calls. This house would be run fair, and everybody would get their equal share. If Boxco took too much of anything, I would have to take him on once again, and I was prepared to do so. Boxco had enough and he threatened to shoot me, but I knew he wouldn't because I never saw him with a gun. That was his last attempt to scare me. It didn't work. I told him to come off the porch, "Let's finish what we started." He wasn't having any part of it. I had represented myself and sisters properly. My mother was standing there, and she witnessed me overthrow the boss of the household. She told me, "Larry that's enough."

I was the new boss. Boxco and I would have only two more fights in our lives. Once, we fought over a card game in which he refused to pay me. We fought until he did. And the second time came in our adult life. He came by my mother's house while she was gone, and without going into any stark detail, I will simply say that he disrespected her house. Well, I won that battle as well.

On our way to the dance, Big Sike was happy for me. He kept on saying, "I told you, cuzz. I told you that you could whoop Boxco." I was elated and sad at the same time because I loved my brother and in some ways I felt like I had damaged his pride, something we all strived hard to maintain. I didn't want to hurt him, nor did I want to be his elder. I just wanted him to respect me and my sisters. But I saw in his eyes that he was crushed. I left no doubt during our fight that he could not whoop me.

When we arrived at Bethune Park, my homeboy Lil Oscar, Big Quake and the rest of my homies were already Crip walking. I couldn't enjoy myself as I had in the past because I kept thinking about my brother. He kept staring at me like he wanted to kill me. From that point on, there would be no turning back for me. There weren't going to be any more days of suffering like when I was much younger. If he wanted to try his luck again, he was more than welcome. In my mind I was not going to lose.

I stopped seeing Chinese as much as I once had. I had continued to run with him from time to time despite being a Crip. I loved being around women, plus I was able to experience many sexual encounters with women, as Lil Quake can attest to. One day I went to his mother's house and asked her where Chinese was. She told me he was in jail, but she didn't tell me why.

In the streets, rumors were that Chinese had murdered this dude in the street over some hustling debts. Chinese was so vicious, he burned the dude up, put him inside his trunk, took pictures of him and sent them to the alleged victim's family for a ransom in order to retrieve his body. Chinese wasn't anybody's joke, trust me.

One night a couple of my homeboys and I were standing out in front of my mother's house and saw the sheriff's car drive up. We didn't know why they pulled up, and people started running, because they had all done something wrong. They didn't know what wrong had caught up with them, but they definitely weren't going to be stuffed inside anybody's cages. However, they weren't there for any of us. They went to Chinese's mother's house. Mrs. Oliver's house was directly in front of my mother's house. They got out of their car and walked to her front door and knocked. Mrs. Oliver's answered and all we heard was a loud scream. She had been brought to her knees and was clearly in agony. They told her Chinese had been killed inside the L.A. County Jail. He was stabbed multiple times. I couldn't believe he would allow anybody to get that close to him to take his life. He was really one of the ghetto's thugs in South Central Los Angeles.

A lot of us went to view his body. I can remember thinking, "Chinese, you're free now. Those people don't have you locked up anymore." It was a shame that for many blacks, death is the only way they will ever experience freedom. I touched his hand, hoping he could pass his gift for being so deceptive with his hands on to me. He used to tell me all the time, "Never let your right hand know what your left hand is doing."

Soon after Chinese's death, many of us started going to jail. Mr. Low, Lil Oscar, Big Bubble, Big Sadd, were already embedded in the judicial system. Lil Quake was next in line; he went off to placement. We missed him a lot, and we sat around and talked about him, and how happy we would be when he came home. We missed his temper tantrums, and trust me he had plenty. He and I were always together, and I loved Lil Quake to death.

When he came home on his weekend passes we would violate every law known to man. When it was time for the van to pick him up to take him back to jail, he would always say to us, "Get everybody together and be in front of my house, so the other boys on the bus know that I am from East Coast." Whatever Mr. Caver wanted, he got. He wanted them to see us. I would always say, "Hell nah, we got something to do. We'll see you when you come home next week." He would go crazy on me, but we never let him down when the van came. We would always be there with him wearing our blue rags on our heads, carrying our walking canes. Mr. Low, no one could out dress him. He was the ultimate Crip dresser. He would be dipped in the very essence of what the Crips stood for. We truly believed in Raymond Washington's ideas, and we bled blue. Mr. Low without question represented that. We were Crips in that area. We would hoo-bang on everybody on the van as they took off. Lil Quake would throw up his two fingers representing 62nd St. 6-Duece and we all would miss him instantly.

Next it was me off to camp. My experience going through juvenile halls to camp was something to remember. It was as if the rules inside these places were set up to make you fail and lose perspective in life. Because one thing is for sure, by the time you went from one stage to the next as a gang member, there was no doubt you'd be much stronger physically and mentally, or broken both physically and mentally. There would be no slipping through the cracks there.

The way it was set up in juvenile hall, camps and youth authorities were by whatever set you were from. Whoever your enemies were, it was your duty to fight them the moment you saw them, no matter what. If we, as a unit, were walking to school and saw someone from a neighborhood we didn't get along with in another unit going in the opposite direction, we had an obligation to run out of line to attack that person. If we didn't, the other gang members would frown upon us and look at us as punks. The pressure was great to perform, and perform we did. Black people were taught early on how to destroy themselves, and we took pleasure in doing it.

When I arrived in camp, I was sent to Camp Scott and Scutter. By this time I was far beyond the kids my age in maturity and street experience. I had seen and done it all. I had the experience of Raymond, Big John, Big Quake, Baby, Alton, Big Bubble, and Chinese in my life, so this was like being around little kids to me.

However, I was blessed to run into some other youngsters that had shared many of my experiences. Old Pappy from Atlantic Drive was 15, but he easily looked forty. Roderick Scott (aka Big Rod) was from Atlantic Drive, but he also claimed Santana Block Compton Crip. I asked him, "How could you be from both sets?" He told me, "I'm from the Drive but Santana Block is like my hood too." He told me, "I'm from the Big Black Banana." He was my closest partner there. He was 15 and the biggest youngster there, 19" arms, massive chest and one of his legs was shorter than the other, so he walked with a limp. Ricc Rocc from my hood was there. He was a bully; he was just as big as Rod. He left shortly after I got there, and to my surprise he got at my sister and started dating her. I never in a million years thought my sister Debra would date someone like him, but hey, Debra showed all of us she did as she pleased.

Mad Dog and Lil C from 60's were solid and Curtis Bittles from 83rd Street Hoover Crips was pure evil. We shared some fun times together. I wasn't there a month before I received a letter from Lil Kev telling me Raymond Washington had been killed in front of his house on 64th and San Pedro. Somebody allegedly drove up to his house and called him to the car. When he walked up to the door of the car, someone stuck a shot gun into his belly and blew him off the face of the earth. That was one of the saddest days in so many people's life, and the happiest in others.

Raymond was loved and hated equally. I loved all that he stood for. I was sad after hearing he had lost his life to the meanness of the streets.

My time in camp was spent perfecting the art of masking and disguising, because now I was directly encountering white people who were responsible for determining whether or not I would be allowed to go home, based on my conduct there. I found that to be ironic. Here again, black people's conduct was being evaluated by a race of people whose conduct was never evaluated or rated as to their moral aptitude and station in anyone's society. I hid all of my mischief there by going inside the laundry room to do all of my fighting. The counselors there thought that I was a programmer, mainly because of my learned abilities to deceive them just as they have done to African Americans for centuries. I managed to get out that place after being there for four months.

Devastation

When I arrived home my mind had sunk deeper into an abyss. The experience I shared with other gang members had influenced how I acted at the detention facility, and how I would act in the future, in a negative way. I wanted to be looked upon as one of the most infamous gang members in Los Angeles, and I wasn't going to be satisfied until I accomplished that goal.

My mother checked me right into Fremont High School. All of my homeboys where going to school there, and most of the Crips from the surrounding areas. I ran into Danny Thomas in the school office while I was checking in; he had gotten into trouble in one of his classes. He asked me where I had been; I told him I had just gotten out of camp.

Fremont High was a well-known sports school. My cousins Robert and Lonzo McDaniel, as well as Terry Laffitte were all football stars on the varsity team. Robert played safety, Lonzo and Terry played on the offensive line. Then there was Boxco, who ran track. Can you believe that - Boxco taking the time out to participate in sports? I'll never forget Boxco had my family come up to the school to see him run. He looked the part of a track star, mainly because he was built like a body builder. In fact when he was attending Edison Jr. High School, his body was so defined the yearbook committee created a category just for him in the yearbook. The category was "Biggest Chest", and they had Boxco take off his shirt to pose for the picture. The caption read, "Mr. Boxco, the Shirtless One." So when you saw him on the track, you just knew he could run anyone down. But on this particular day, he was lapped and waved off the track. He thought he was about to win the race when one of the officials ran onto the track, waving him off to the side. We laughed so hard, we were all crying tears. The race was the metric mile which consisted of four times around the track, so for him to get lapped in such a short distance was hilarious to us.

I did attend classes at Fremont, but only for the purpose of messing around with the young ladies there. I was a full-fledged gang member; succeeding in life or chasing the American dream had escaped most of us. It just was no longer in our immediate thought process. We had declared our death to the streets, so to speak, because all we did, every single day, was wake up and plan our day exactly as we had the day before, with only one exception. The victim we would choose to victimize always depended on the occurrence of the day.

Most of my homeboys that were my age attended Fremont, e.g. Big Ed, Big Sike, Lil Man, Lil Sike, Big Snake, C-Bone, Lil Quake, Big Moe, Big Mark, Mr. Low, Too Tall, Bam, Crazy Lar, Greedy, Bulla Cow, Ricc Rocc, Rat, Chumly, Big Vince,

Insane Wayne, Drake, Biscuit, 68th St., and many others. Most of what we did was roam the hallways harassing people.

Fremont was the school where Raymond Washington had started the Crips nine years earlier, and it still was a Crip school during this time: the Hoover Crips, Kitchen Crips, Avalon Garden Crips, Eight Seven Gangster Crips, and a heavy dose of East Coast Crips 1, 62, 68, 69, 76, 89, 97's. Our meeting place every day was on 74th and San Pedro, at the arcade, where we played video games and listened to music, all during school hours.

Trouble, for me, was inevitable; it was the manifestation of what I had become. My mother never gave up on me, when she probably had every excuse to do so. I believe that she basically just refused to acknowledge that I had become this infamous being.

Lil Bubble and Lil Kev were going to a probation school on the west side, near the Jungles, an infamous Blood area. Lil Bubble told me about a young lady named Vivian Dozier, (aka Yogi). I had a reputation for macking at the ladies, and Vivian was a young lady that was fast and slick. So Lil Bubble told her he wanted her to meet me. I told him whenever he wanted me to go to his school, I would. He had gotten into it with this Blood dude that Vivian was dating. So one day we went up to the school to get at the dude, but the guy didn't come to school. That was not necessarily because of us - he had no idea we were coming. Lucky for him. Vivian didn't come either, but she had heard about some East Coast Crips coming up there looking for her man, and that I was one of them. She asked Lil Bubble for my phone number and called me. I was a hard core gang member and I lived and breathed East Coast 6-Duece Neighborhood Crips. So when she called me, that's what she got. She called and asked to speak to La La.

La La: "This is he, what's up?"

Vivian: "I heard a lot about you."

La La: "Who is this?"

Vivian: "Vivian."

La La: "Vivian?"

Vivian: "Yeah, I go to school with Lil Will. He told you about me."

La La: Oooh, Yogi."

Vivian: "Yeah, what's up?"

La La: "Nothing."

Vivian: "I just wanted to meet you. Lil Will made it sound like you were a killer or something."

La La: "Nah, baby, I ain't no killer. I'm from East Coast Crip though."

Vivian: "I'm from 107um (one O sevum) Underground.

La La: "Is that right? I heard you were talking to a Blood dude from the jungles. Poppa T or something."

Vivian: "Yeah, he's cool."

La La: "Well I want to meet you. When can we meet?"

Vivian: "I don't know. I want to meet you too."

We talked for weeks, and often we would fall asleep on the phone. Then one day, out of nowhere, I was at home looking out of the window and saw Lil Bubble and a young lady about 5'3", 120 lbs, with a yellow complexion and brown hair in a mushroom style. She was bow legged, with a gap between her legs that stood out a hundred blocks away, big breasted, little freckles in her face, and pretty brown eyes. I had no idea this was Vivian. She told him at school to take her over to my house. They walked to the door and I still didn't know who she was, because Lil Bubble was truly retarded. There was no telling what he was up to. When he knocked on the door, I opened it and she stood there, looking shy. I asked him, "Cuzz, who is this?" He said, "This is Vivian." I replied, "So you're Vivian? Come in, but not you, cuzz. I'll catch up with you later cuzz."

Vivian walked inside just staring at me. I was 15 years old at the time, approximately 5'9, 160 lbs, brown skin, a little Afro, with brown eyes and a silver cap in my mouth, and dressed for danger, with a blue rag hanging out of my pocket. We went upstairs to my bedroom and talked. I asked her what made her just come by without telling me. She said, "I just wanted to meet you." I asked her, "What's Poppa going to say about you just wanting to meet me?" She said, "We're not really together."

La La: "Is that right?"

Vivian: "Yeah."

La La: "You're pretty, I didn't think you would be so beautiful. You look nice."

Vivian: "Thank you, you look nice too."

La La: "So what am I going to do with you?"

Vivian: "If I have to tell you that, then I should not have come. Do you have a girlfriend?

La La: "Something like that."

Vivian: "What do you mean by that?"

La La: "I mess with a few girls, but I wouldn't say that they're my girlfriends."

Vivian: "Well we are going to have to do something about that. I want to be your girlfriend."

La La: "You know that I'm a Crip?"

Vivian: "So what."

La La: "All you women say so what, then always sweating us when we're with our homeboys."

Vivian: "I ain't worried about that, I know you're going to wanna be with me."

La La: "You do huh?"

Vivian: "Yeah I do."

We kissed and I was lost in the depths of her passion. I wanted more, but she couldn't stay because she took a detoured route home just to meet me. Her father and step mother stayed on her about being responsible, so she had to stay in congruence with her time restraints. I offered to ride the bus with her all the way from Slauson and Compton Ave to 108th and Western, which she accepted. I walked her near her home, but made sure to keep my distance. She didn't want her father to know that she was with a young man. So we kissed and then she told me to be at home and she would call me in an hour. As I walked back to the bus stop, I encountered several 107um (one O sevum) Underground Crip members. Choo, Lil Man, Red and several more young men approached me and asked where I was from. I told them 6-Duece Neighborhood East Coast Crips. After they all introduced themselves they told me they thought I was from Hoover. They were at war with the Hoover Crips during that time, so they stayed vigilant in their area. I was only there for one reason, Vivian, and I was willing to cross any hot zone for her, as I would do repeatedly in the future.

I went right home to wait for her call, and as soon as I stepped inside the house my mother told me some girl was on the phone.

La La: "Hello."

Vivian: "What are you doing?"

La La: "Thinking about you."

Vivian: "Me too. Did some boys confront you?"

La La: "Yeah, why?"

Vivian: "Because they were talking about it. They said they thought you were Devil (Andre Randsom) from 107 Hoover"

La La: "Is that right?"

Vivian: "Yeah, he is coming over here doing all kinds of crazy shit, so they're looking for him. They were about to shoot you."

La La: "Well baby I'm glad they didn't because if they had you would've had to avenge my death. Would you?"

Vivian: "I don't even know you like that."

La La: "Aren't you my woman?"

Vivian: "Yeah."

La La: "So you mean to tell me if they had shot me, you wouldn't avenge me?"

Vivian: "Yeah I would've."

La La: "Yeah right. What would you have done, look at them with your pretty eyes until you killed them like you did me?"

Vivian: "What do you mean by that?"

La La: "I like you a lot."

Vivian: "If you like me like you say then you should want to be with me instead of your homeboys."

La La: "I knew you would start that shit."

Vivian: "Nah, La La, I dated this boy that was a gang member before, and he got killed. I don't want that to happen to you."

La La: "Ain't shit going to happen to me."

Vivian: "How do you know that?"

La La: "Look, I got to go. I'll call you back."

There was no way that I was going to trade in my blue rag for anybody. I had been a Crip since I was 10 years old. I was now 15, so a 1/3 of my life was dedicated to this lifestyle. Five years of my life had been formed around all of these men that I admired. Here comes Vivian, asking me to choose between her and my homeboys. That was an easy choice. I chose this Cripping, hands down. She called me and asked how I was doing. I told her "I'm straight and I don't like the fact that you tried to come between me and my homeboys. If I decide that I want to be with you like that, it would be up to me to make that decision." I wasn't going to allow her to give me an ultimatum, because she would not have liked my choice. She said she understood, and that I thought that I was hard, meaning a tough guy. We got back on track, and I spent most of my time with her, until it became so noticeable that my homeboys started to comment on it, first playfully, e.g. "La La, where you been? With Vivian?" "Yeah, cuzz. Why?" "Oh cuzz, don't get all serious." "Cuzz, ya'll act like ya'll mad that I'm kicking it with my woman." "Ooh, your woman huh?" "Yeah, my woman." "What about us?" "What about ya'll."

This, of course, was Lil Quake, Lil Bubble, Big Vince, and Lil Kev. All of them didn't feel this way. Lil Quake was for me but he noticed that I had stopped hanging out as much. My mother loved Vivian because I wasn't getting into trouble as much. She noticed that I was in the house at night, talking on the phone to Vivian, so she supported my newfound love.

I met her father, sisters and stepmother. For some reason, Vivian always thought her stepmother didn't like her, so she wanted to live with us. I told her she was trippin because when I was around her family, I didn't notice the things Vivian spoke of. She was adamant about it, so she spent several nights a week with us, which I loved. I had become a young lover boy. We walked down the street holding hands; I held her hand with one hand and with the other I held a gigantic boom box, blue rag hanging out of my back pocket, even though I had stopped hanging out with my homeboys altogether. I hadn't even noticed it because I still wore my same Crip attire every day. But my days and nights were spent solely with Vivian. Lil Bubble became incensed by my actions. One day he saw Vivian and I walking down the streets together. He crossed the street, talking shit to me about me not hanging out with them anymore. He asked me why I had the blue rag tied on my head if I wasn't Cripping no more. Now Lil Bubble couldn't whoop me if I was blind and had no arms. That was the closest he would come to being victorious over me, so this matter I was about to handle quickly. I put my radio down and he ran across the street. I told him, "Cuzz, you don't tell me how to Crip motherfucker. I'm kicking it with my woman. If you don't like it, let's get down punk." He said, "I ain't trippin like that; I just missed you." "Cuzz," I said, "I don't give a fuck. Fuck you, punk." Lil Quake was there and sided with me. He said "Cuzz, don't trip off Lil Will's retarded ass." I wasn't and didn't. Vivian just stood there, trippin off the whole thing.

When we got home, she told me that she didn't want to come between me and my homeboys. I told her that she wasn't, that I will always be a Crip. I told her that I want to kick it with her, and that it was my decision. I also told her not to trip on Lil Bubble. He's just mad because I don't fuck with him no more. One day, like a little bitch, he yelled across the street while Vivian and I were walking, "I shouldn't have introduced her to you." I shouted back, "I'm glad you did."

I still loved my homeboys and would do anything for them, but I loved Vivian as well. She was a woman, so I preferred to be in her comforts, and she made me feel good. One night, Vivian was back home with her parents and I was on the phone with her. Lil Bubble came to my window screaming my name. "La La, La

La, La La." I looked out the window and asked him what's up. He shouted, "Lil Oscar just got shot." I thought that he was bullshitting, and that this was his way to get me to come out and kick it with him. I asked him to repeat what he just said; he said "Lil Oscar just got shot on 59th and San Pedro." Vivian heard him through the phone. I told her I had to go and she responded, "Be careful." If this was true, my love fest with Vivian was surely over, without question.

When we all arrived on the corner of 59th and San Pedro, directly in front of my home girl Cookie's house, there Lil Oscar lay dying, if not already dead. It was the latter, nobody wanted to believe it. From that day forth, none of our lives was ever, ever the same again.

Big Quake rounded up everyone. We set our sights on one particular neighborhood, and we didn't let up. That seed of black hatred had been sown, and we would see to it that we nourished it forever. A lot of people lost their lives because of this ideology. Vivian lost me to the streets. We still kicked it, but it was different. She acted as if she understood.

Lil Oscar, the dazzling Crip Walker, was no longer with us; he was our second casualty of war, but my first. Big Snow had been killed before Lil Oscar, but I hadn't known him, so Lil Oscar was the first death that I had experienced as a gang member. That tragedy set me off, and my life never recovered. I surrendered my soul to the streets and became engulfed, totally committed to insanity. Lil Bubble delivered the message that pulled me back into the streets. He had been successful in his endeavors.

AMENDMENT II

Right to Bear Arms

SECTION 1. A well regulated militia, being necessary to the security of a free state, the right of the people to keep and bear arms, shall not be infringed.

Proposed September 25, 1789; ratified December 15, 1791.

We all felt like this Amendment applied to us, even if it wasn't written for us by the forefathers of America, and we intended to exercise that right to the fullest extent. I kept all the guns, so I still had dealings with all of my homies.

One day, Lil Bubble was determined to come between Vivian and me. I was at home with Vivian when he came and knocked on the door. I let him in and he asked me for a shotgun. I asked him why; he told me some Florence 13 gang members had tried to jump on him. I didn't believe a word he said and I definitely wasn't going to give him a gun. That was for sure. I told him I would go around the corner with him to address the issue. We knew all of the F-13 members, and they knew we weren't to be played with. I took the shotgun myself. Vivian pleaded with me not to go. I told her I'd be right back, thinking Lil Bubble was playing. When I walked outside Big Ed, Snake, Lil Kev, and I believe Art were outside waiting. So we walked around the corner and sure enough, there they were, the Florence 13 standing around acting like they were us. I approached Cowboy from F-13, who thought that he was some major motherfucker. I asked him, was there a problem with Lil Bubble. He told me some bullshit, and I shot him. They started running, and we went on a tear. The police were looking for me. I went home and told Vivian I thought that I was going to jail, so I left. The police came to my house, telling my mother if I didn't turn myself in that they were going to kill me when they saw me in the streets. My mother told me to come home so she could take me down to the police station for questioning. I turned myself in and received a 5 year sentence in the California Youth Authority. That was the second time Lil Bubble pulled me into the streets.

Vivian was devastated. I had broken her heart, and I missed her greatly. She moved in with my mother permanently. My sisters and she got along well. I was happy that she was comfortable there. I didn't worry that much about her, because I knew she had a place to stay.

Voyage

The system called me a menace to society, and there I was thinking, "What does that make the system?" Really, stop kidding yourself and find the courage to be truthful. What does that make America's behavior towards African Americans? Scores of black people are so afraid to upset white people they are often heard shouting, "The past is the past; all that stuff is over."

Many blacks believe America has been more than just and fair to black people. Well, the Sixty Second Street Neighborhood East Coast Crips didn't believe any such thing. I, for one, knew that was bullshit, and I wasn't going to allow any black face dressed in a suit to tell me anything different. I would find out how unjust America could be in the most profound way imaginable a couple of years later.

I was sent to Fred C. Nelles Youth Correctional Facility in the early part of 1980. Before I arrived there I had the pleasure of meeting so many Crips and Bloods whose Do or Die attitudes were identical to mine. That set the stage for many confrontations.

My mother was lost for answers when it came to me. Just a year earlier she had lost another baby, my little brother Demitriaus Warren, by this man named Terry Warren. The baby was stillborn in February of 1979, so she was going through some rough times.

When I arrived at Nelles, I was sent to Adams Cottage, the orientation unit for all new arrivals. Fred C. Nelles had approximately ten or eleven cottages, all named after former presidents: Adams, Monroe, Roosevelt, Kennedy, Hayes, Washington, Cleveland, Tyler, Madison, Taft, and Jackson. How ironic that these buildings named after presidents were used to enslave young Africans.

AMENDMENT XIII

Slavery

SECTION 1: Neither slavery nor involuntary servitude, except as a punishment for crime whereof the party shall have been duly convicted, shall exist within the United States, or any place subject to their jurisdiction.

SECTION 2: Congress shall have power to enforce this article by appropriate legislation.

Proposed January 31, 1865; ratified December 6, 1865; certified December 18, 1865.

LARRY DAVIS

I would have preferred to be locked up in Malcolm X, Martin Luther King, Marcus Garvey, Frederick Douglas, Nelson Mandela, Harriet Tubman, Mary McCloud-Bethune, Raymond Washington, Louis Farrakhan, Muhammad Ali, Stan "Tookie" Williams, or George Jackson cottages, but you know, like I know, that the anti-black establishment would never name these particular buildings after prominent people in the black experience. One reason is that doing so would contradict the disenfranchisement movement that is geared to maintain class and status, or lack thereof, within the black community. These African Heroes were not spotlighted, mainly due to their infectious ability to inspire change in the people, the kind of change that the governing establishment does not want to transpire amongst the people, especially black people. Now if those Africans had been slave owners, their names would have been plastered all across America in shining lights.

Each cottage was designed to house certain prisoners, e.g. Cleveland and Roosevelt were the working cottages for the institution. Cleveland occupants did all the cooking, so it housed the kitchen workers. I had two partnas over there from Harlem Crips Rolling 30's, Killowatt and Maxwell. Roosevelt was the cottage that housed all the institution's maintenance workers. In that cottage I had a couple dudes that I associated with. Lil Country, who I had known from the streets, was a bully most of his life and it hadn't stopped in the Roosevelt Cottage. Jack (Nu Nu) was there as well. He had been convicted for that aforementioned murder, so he stuck by me to the bitter end and made it out unharmed. Taft was known as protective custody, for the weak and vulnerable prisoners, who were in need of close supervision. These inmates were predominantly white boys, who were often beaten half silly. Everybody knew the administration had to protect white boys. Their parents had the means to hold the institution accountable for their children's safety, so they were guarded with great care. Jackson Cottage was for the little kids, ten, eleven and twelve year olds. One of my partnas in Jackson Cottage was Trey Dee from the Estsidaz, Insane 21st. He was something else. Many of the Crips there couldn't believe how little and short he was. He reminded me of myself when I was ten years old. He was just as active as the older Crips there, and he was as disruptive as anybody there. Every time we looked up they were sending him to the hole. The hole is a room not much bigger than most people's closet, where they send you when you misbehave. An individual could be in there for 24, 48 or 72 hours depending on the severity of the rules violation. Tray Dee lived in there. Also over in Jackson Cottage with Tray Dee was Lil Tee and Lil Killer from 83rd Street, Hoover Crips, who gave Tray Dee a run for his money. They were all identical in their conduct. They walked around with their pants hanging off their asses, khaki suits, blue rags tied everywhere, and they were shorter than Tray Dee. It was clear to everyone there that those three youngsters were serious about what they believed in, and we had to make sure we protected them from our enemies. Washington Cottage was for immigration prisoners. Kennedy Cottage was for prisoners who had used too many drugs and had become so addicted they needed treatment. My next door neighbor Dee, from the Grandee's 165th Street was on this unit. I couldn't believe it when I saw him "What the fuck are you doing over there?" He told me that he had started smoking this chemical called "Sherm." This chemical in part was used as an elephant tranquilizer. What would make a person want some shit like that? Black folks were trying to escape all of the opportunities afforded them here in America. Why would they be doing this, except to run from the possibility of being successful?

Tyler Cottage was for prisoners that were thirty days or shorter to going home. Monroe Cottage was for the 14, 15 year old prisoners who had no intentions whatsoever to follow the rules there. Del Dog ran that unit; he was from 89th Street Neighborhood East Coast Crips at the time, but he would later be known as Del Dog from Main Street.

Madison Cottage, known as the Mad House, was primarily a Blood unit for red rags. Most of the other units there were full of Crips, and we fought Bloods every chance we got. Most of the time, we took our aggression out on each other in sports, mainly football. Each unit had its own tackle football team that played each other unit, so there was no way you weren't going to run into whoever your enemies were. Border Rat, a notorious gang member from Inglewood Family Bloods, thought he was unstoppable on the football field. I looked forward to engaging him.

Hayes Cottage was known as the Hell House. It was for the most aggressive prisoners, whose next stop was Youth Training School (Y.T.S). I was sent to Hayes, where I ran into my partna Roderick Scott (Big Rod), from Atlantic Drive Compton Crips, and Curtis Bittles from Hoover Crips 83rd Street. Curtis was in for murder which didn't surprise me. He was sadistic, but no one could tell by looking at him because he looked so normal.

I ran into my homeboy Phillip Anderson, aka Pee Wee; he told me about all the dos and don'ts of Nelles. This was a children's prison, but the people that had come before us had left rules behind that every generation of prisoners followed. Those were the rules Pee Wee was instructing me to adhere to.

For instance, Fred C. Nelles provided combination locks to every prisoner, but the prisoners themselves prohibited the use of locks, especially in Hayes cottage, the Hell House. If someone stole another prisoner's property, the person whose property was stolen had to go around and tell every person in the dorm that if he was the person who had taken your stuff, fuck their mother, father, homeboys, their neighborhood, and every single person who had died in their family and them as well and whatever else you wish to add to the list.

Then the person who was responsible for taking your things had to step forward and claim his responsibility. Then you had to fight whoever the culprits were. All of these things were surely things that would prepare us for the realm of society we lived in. This would **surely** teach us how to be productive citizens right? How were these things supposed to prepare us for society? They were assurances that we would be worse off than we were before we got there, certainly by the time many of us went up for parole.

I didn't care what the rules were; I was now a well-known gang member so I didn't believe any of those things would happen to me. I had proven myself on the streets, in all the Juvenile Halls, and at the Youth Authority Reception Center, S.R.C.C. I had fought my way through them all, not coming close to losing a single fight. I had a reputation for kicking asses just as Big Quake had, so I felt confident I wouldn't be tested.

One day I came inside to go to my locker for some cigarettes. I always wondered how was it possible for us to be allowed to smoke at such a young age. When my family lived in Watts, I had to take a hand written note to the store with my mother's signature on it. But there in Y.A. we could buy them out of the commissary at the age of 15. How about that hypocrisy? Without question it would be justified, right? Sure it would, by some black people running to the rescue of white people expressing why it was okay for us to carry on in this manner.

When I got to my locker and saw that my cigarettes were missing, I thought at first that I was at the wrong locker. But it was my locker. I went and found my homeboy Pee Wee and told him, "Cuzz, somebody stole my shit out of my locker, what am I supposed to do?" He told me to go around and tell everybody fuck their mother and father and all the other things I mentioned earlier. I told Pee Wee, "Cuzz, why didn't you tell me they were going to take my shit?" He said everybody had to be tested and he knew that I would kick their asses. I didn't understand his reasoning, because we were from the same neighborhood. We had an obligation to one another in spite of being in prison. If I had been in the position he was in, I would have told him, so we could kick their asses together when they stuck their hands inside of his locker. Nevertheless, a dude named Capone from W.V.G. (Watts, Vecindario Grape Street Crips), and his accomplice, Blue from Oxnard, stole two cartons of Kool cigarettes out of my locker. I went around screaming at the top of my lungs, "Whoever took my shit out of my locker, fuck everything you love and all that you don't love. This is East Coast Crips."

They both approached me and told me that they wanted to fight me for my shit. I thought this had to be a joke. There I was standing in front of two human beings that had taken my shit, telling me to my face they wanted to fight me to keep it. I had two choices, I could have said, okay, I'm trying to reform myself, and allowed them to keep it. Or I could choose to kick their asses to prevent the rest of the prisoners in the cottage from taking my things the entire time I had to be there. That wasn't a difficult choice for me to make. I chose to kick off on their asses.

AMERICA'S CONDUCT

First I took Capone, in a fighting room designated just for these occasions. I beat him so bad he hid under the bunk and refused to come out from under the bed. Next was Blue, I fought him in the same room, while Capone was still hiding under the bed. I hit Blue in his jaw so hard he ran out the room screaming like he was about to die. I wanted my shit and I wanted to beat their asses for trying me. I told them they better go get my shit and they did. Finally Capone came out from under the bed after he was certain I was through with his ass.

My homeboy Pee Wee came over and told me, "Cuzz, don't take it so personal. It's only a test to see if you will fight. I knew you were going to beat their asses, so stop trippin, cuzz." I didn't like that; I wasn't going to steal nobody's shit just to see if they would fight. All anyone had to do to accomplish that task was to go up to the person they suspected of being fearful and ask them or disrespect them. Stealing wasn't necessary I thought.

My mother, sisters and Vivian came to see me as soon as I got there. I was so happy to see them. I missed my mother a great deal. Although I continued to disrespect my mother's wishes for me, I loved her with all my heart, and I can honestly say I believed that I was doing the right thing by disobeying America's Laws.

The counselors saw Vivian in the visiting room and couldn't keep their eyes off her, literally telling me how beautiful she was. "La La, you have a fox on your hands," they said. I felt the same way and wished there was some way I could have laid that fox down and loved her with great passion.

It was going to be hard to keep Vivian by my side because she was a young lady that was too beautiful to be held down, but, hey, I was inclined to try. She swore she would be by my side, but she was too young to endure the hard aches of loneliness; she was sure to fly away. One thing I hadn't planned on was my cousin, Big John, taking her away from me. My mother kept telling me she thought they were messing around with each other, but I didn't believe it. I asked him when he came up to visit me, was he seeing her. He told me that he wasn't, that they were only getting high together and that my mother was trippin. I didn't think she was trippin, but I had so much love and respect for Big John that it really didn't bother me that much if he had been messing around with her. But I can assure you that Jannie Mae Davis was going to say what she thought and what she knows.

I didn't actually find out that it was true until years later, after I asked him again. He told me, "Cuzz, don't ever ask me about any women, because you will find out about women as you get older." I took that to mean yeah, he was messing with her and that was a lesson for me early on in my life.

After I settled in as best I could, I learned the goings on around there. I noticed Nelles was actually like a high school program for those who could play sports. Nelles had two varsity programs there that traveled outside the institution to play high school programs on the streets, i.e. football and basketball.

I played quarterback and linebacker on the football team, and I played point guard on the basketball team. Both teams were gang infested with hard core gang members, Crips and Bloods who had football and basketball backgrounds.

One of my buddies, Killowatt, played wide receiver. He caught anything thrown near him a high percentage of the time. On the basketball court, he played point guard and shooting guard. He was an outstanding ball player. He and I were so competitive it sometimes hurt the team. I thought for sure that I had the best passes on the team, and he believed he had the best passes. So that was a recipe for disaster whenever the coach put us out there together. We would overpass to one another trying to show off each other's passes. The coach would scream at me more often than he would Killowatt, "Jesus Christ Davis! Shoot the damn ball!"

As I got to know the people there, I discovered that a lot of the youngsters were there for murder, and some for multiple murders. How could this insanity be explained?

My homeboys had started to get locked up, one after the other. First Big Fos, Big Spike, Big Sike, Big CL, Chummly, and Big Drake all came in for murders. It seemed like just a few years earlier we all were running around drinking beer, smoking weed and worrying about what we were going to wear at the park dances, but the stakes had gotten higher for everyone involved in gang activities and the institutions were reflecting this fact. The gambles were our lives, and many of us stayed in the game and refused to fold our hands of commitment to our neighborhood. It was clear for everyone to see it was Do or Die.

CL, Biscuit, Gangster Rat, Spike, and Stacks from East Coast all made their way to Nelles. We were happy to see each other. I was able to change the stealing policy so they didn't have to go through that ritual. I knew them from the streets and I knew they all were warriors from my neighborhood. If there was going to be any fighting we were going to be doing it together.

CL and Biscuit immediately joined the football team and we traveled outside the institution every weekend, and a few week days. As much as we left the institution, it started to feel like I wasn't even in jail.

One night I was in the dorm, lying down on my assigned bunk, and the counselor called me into the office and told me I had a phone call. It was my sister Debra, calling to tell me that my mother had her baby. It was a boy; I now had a little brother, Terrance Warren, born 9/11/80. I was happy about the news because her last child didn't make it. I went back to my assigned area and told CL about the news; he was happy for me. He had a baby boy himself and was only 13 years old.

AMERICA'S CONDUCT

As soon as it was possible my mother brought my little brother to meet me. I held him like he was a fragile piece of glass that I didn't want to break or drop. My mother was a nurturing mother all over again and I couldn't help but think about Shenette; she was no longer the baby of the family. That spot now belonged to Terrance, and I would have to protect him as I had her.

Basketball season had come around again. They only had one position open for a point guard. The coach allowed Tank McGruder and me to try out for that position, and I won the job. Tank McGruder was the best running back I have ever seen in my days of playing football. He was our tailback on the varsity football team, but when it came to Basketball he didn't stand a chance to get that spot. Tank was from W.V.G. I played football against him when we were youngsters. He played for Mona Park Sheriff's League, and I played for Bethune Park and Roosevelt Rangers Sheriff's League.

Our team members included Christmas, a Piru Blood gang member. He was 6'1" and 235 lbs. Pierre was 6'0" and 185 lbs. He was from Insane 21st Long Beach. For the life of me I can't recall this brother's name, but he was from Inglewood Family Bloods gang and myself. Others were: Killowatt, a Rollin 30's Harlem Crip who was 6'2 and 185 lbs, Fatso from 120th Raymond Ave Crips, 6'3" and 180 lbs, Monroe from Nickerson Garden Bounty Hunter's Blood, 6'4" and 190 lbs, Vincent from Venice Shoreline Crips, 5'11" and 175 lbs, Russell, who was non-affiliated, 6"3" and 200 lbs, and Ransom who happened to be a pimp in for murder.

On one of our night games Ransom decided he was going to escape after the game. I believe we played North Hollywood High. After the game, he took off in an all-white sweat suit. Ransom was 6'3", 180 lbs, high yellow complexion, and wore one of the largest afros in the world. Once the coach realized Ransom had taken off, he called the police and they found him standing on the side of somebody's house. There's no way he should have been caught that night. We didn't have any supervision; any one of us could have taken off anytime on trips outside the institution. The administration trusted that we wouldn't go awol because everyone there was going to get out at some point, even those in for murder. Under juvenile convictions, the longest they could hold us was until we turned 21 years old. The police stated in their report they spotted Ransom's white sweat suit. They brought him back to the institution after taking him to the hole for several days. When he got out of the hole we all asked him why he wore a white sweat suit if he was going to leave at night. He said he didn't have any intentions on leaving until he thought about it at that moment. Still he should not have been caught that night. We literally could be in the company of society without separation from them. It was the easiest time I have ever done.

Killowatt and I had developed a close friendship. He always talked about one of his homeboys named Big Bob, who had been in Y.T.S., and had a reputation as a hard core gang member from the Harlem 30's Crips. Killowatt had a great deal of admiration for Big Bob, until he started to admire himself more. He loved himself more than Christians admired Jesus Christ. Killowatt was good for some side-aching laughs.

One night we had a playoff game on Catalina Island. Our team traveled over there by boat. It was a fun experience for many of us. Once we arrived over there they allowed us to call our loved ones to let them know we hadn't drowned in the ocean on our way there. I noticed that Kilowatt was laughing like his usual self. I asked him who he was talking to, he told me his home girl, Big Bob's sister. I asked him to let me speak to her and he handed me the phone. I took the phone, and asked her name. She said, "Lil Bit." I asked her what her real name was, and she said Jackie. She then asked my name, I told her, La La. From the time I accepted the name La La, I never ever told anybody I met that my name was Larry. La La would be who I became the rest of my life.

She asked me where was I from. That was the kind of conversations I love having because I knew that I belonged to something meaningful and I loved telling people that I belonged to the East Coast Crips. I told her I was from 6-Duece East Coast Neighborhood Crips. She told me she knew some of my older homies Big Fox and Big Casper, through her brother's association with them.

We exchanged our information to write to one another. It wasn't anything serious, in fact, I didn't have any intention to really meet her once I got out of that place. I told her that I would write to her and she communicated likewise. I wasn't trying to pursue her nor she me at the time. I had no idea who she was with and I still had a heavy case of Vivian in my heart.

Anyway, in the playoffs we dominated all of the teams in our division. Christmas was one of the most outstanding players in the league on our team. He was a scoring machine and one of three Bloods on Hayes Cottage. On Hayes Cottage, the Crips didn't allow Bloods to live in the dorm. Each time the institution sent one of them over we sent them back out in record speed. Christmas was the first Blood sent over there who refused to leave. He was a young man who had heart and was determined to show us he was the real deal. I don't know if the administration wanted to get him punished or if they thought he could make it over there. Thus far none had.

I believe Dirty Red, from Long Beach Insane 21st Crips was his first battle of many. I had never been into jumping on no one and to this very day I have never partaken in such an act. I have always believed in men squaring off and let the best fighter win no matter his affiliations. Christmas took on all comers, big, small or fat. I loved that about him. I was impressed by his heart.

The Crips over there could have removed him, as they had all the Bloods that came through there, but they respected Christmas' heart and allowed him to stay. He wore his red rag on the unit in the midst of all the Crips. That didn't stop the rest of the Bloods in Nelles from being attacked; they still got it every chance that was available.

Now that Christmas had survived what nobody thought was possible, the administration thought the door was open for Bloods to be sent to Hayes Cottage. So they sent a notorious Blood gang member from the Nickerson Garden named Bill Bill over there. His enemies there were the Grape Street Watts Crips, Tank McGruder, Lil Billy, Taco, Capone, Solo, Sleepy, Boo, and so many more until it would take forever to mention. He surely was in for the battle of his life. He and Tank knew each other from the street and they really didn't dislike each other like most of the Crips thought.

The Crips approached him and told him that he had to leave the unit and go to another unit where the Bloods were. He told them that he wouldn't, and unlike Christmas, they beat Bill Bill senseless. I didn't like what I saw but I knew they were doing Crips the same way on the other units so I never attempted to stop it. I just wasn't going to get involved in it.

Bill Bill was approximately 5'6 190 lbs. He looked like a firm built Pit Bull, and just as strong as one. He placed his back up against the wall while six or seven Crips were mangling him beyond recognition. He displayed toughness I've rarely witnessed in men. He refused to hit the ground and repeatedly kept expressing, "I'm not going anywhere." I remember asking Christmas, "Why aren't you trying to help him?" His exact words to me were, "Didn't nobody come over here to help me when I was fighting all the Crips over here, so they have to experience what I had to." Bill Bill became enraged. He started telling the Crips, "Come on motherfuckers, let's get down," pressing his back firmly on the wall throwing punches at any and everything standing in front of him. Then he started telling the Crips, "What's up, you motherfuckers? Don't want to go heads up?"

Reese Cup from Long Beach Rolling 20's stepped up to the plate. Bill Bill focused in on Cup, and let off a thunderous blow separating Cup from his front tooth, which fell out of his mouth. They immediately began crushing Bill Bill, but he still never hit the ground. I think Biscuit told them that was enough. They gave him a pass to stay on Hayes Cottage. I was impressed with Bill Bill as well. He and Christmas became good buddies after that. One more Blood came over there after that, Too Cool, from Bounty Hunters. He had a fight with somebody from Grape Street. It wasn't anything spectacular. They let him stay because of Bill Bill. He didn't have to endure what Christmas and Bill Bill had to. They were the last of the Bloods allowed on Hayes Cottage.

LARRY DAVIS

We went on to the Championship in basketball, to play Montclair High School, at the Los Angeles Sports Arena, and lost 62-61. This also happened to be my last year there. I was six or seven months away from going to the parole board for release. I didn't see why they wouldn't let me go unless I went in there and became tongue tied like many people did when asked, "Why should we let you go?" The wrong answer always got each of them another year to think about the reason. How much power is that for someone to have? A great deal I would imagine.

My sister Debra had given birth to a baby girl Myesha Johnson (4/19/81), by Ricc Rocc the spray painting king from Sixty Second Street. I thought to myself she must be serious about him she's bringing children into the world for him. Debra brought the baby up to see me and she was just as pretty as Shenette was when she was a baby. I kept thinking this can't be Ricc Rocc's baby, because she looked more like Alan Gibson, but she swore it was Ricc Rocc.

Football season had begun and this was my last year there. I met another cat by the name of Don Juan, from 83rd Street Hoover Crips. He played on the football team with me, both varsity and Hayes Cottage. I met his family, sisters in particular, Sue, Gail, and Nita Jean. Sue was crazy over me but she had too much going on in her life for me, so I never pursued her like she wished I had. I say this because at that time I truly was in love with Vivian, and no woman stood a chance of capturing me.

The counselors on Hayes Cottage, without me knowing it, decided it would be best to send me to Roosevelt Cottage my last six months so I could get a trade before I went up for parole. My mind was so destroyed I felt like they were disrespecting me by kicking me off the cottage. I swore to them that when Roosevelt played them in football that I personally was going to crush their spirit. Hayes had the best team in the institution for years. I didn't want to leave CL, or Biscuit, but I was going over there with Nu Nu from 6-Deuce, Spike from 76th Street, and Gangster Rat from 118th Street East Coast Block Crips. Gangster Rat was a trip to me because although he was from 118th Street, he was like Big Rod from Atlantic Drive, and because of his love for Santana Block Crips. Gangster Rat was in there for murder as well. He allegedly killed a well-known Piru out of Compton and the Santanas knew him well. This would be the first time I got the chance to see my partna Big Rod interact with the Santanas when they came up to visit Big Hub and Tee Wee from Santana. They also were in for murder.

When they came up they called out Rod, Rat, Tee Wee, and Hub. I hadn't seen so many gang members be let inside an institution as I had the Compton Crips. When they came in, there were no questions about who they were.

T-Bone and Sag are two names I do remember. I can't remember the other members. I was impressed with their union and how they appeared to love each other. For the first time I saw how Big Rod could love his neighborhood and Santana Block Crips. I never gave him no more lip on that conflict of interest.

Sure enough, after I went to Roosevelt Cottage we won our division and had to play Hayes in a playoff game to go to the championship to face Monroe Cottage, Border Rat's unit. Out of the gate I ran a 99 yard touchdown on a quarterback sneak from the 1 yard line. Spike played wide receiver. I fired the ball at him after moving the ball up and down the field on them, while Lil Country, the Cottage bully ran all over them. They couldn't believe it. They wanted me to throw the game because I had always been a Hayes resident. CL and Biscuit were telling me "Cuzz, fuck them busters over there. This is the Hell House." "Stop us if ya'll can." We won and moved on to the title game.

Finally the showdown came with Border Rat and me, The Mad House versus the Rough House. All during that week before the game I use to see Border Rat walking around with his cottage. I told him when I caught him that I was going to not only whoop his ass, I was going to break his ass up on the football field, and I meant every word of that.

The only reason I wanted to kick his ass was because he had been walking around there like he was some bad ass, and the people that were at war with his neighborhood acted like they didn't want to beat his ass. One of my childhood buddies, Donald Miles, aka Devil, from Shot Gun would have destroyed him without question, so I wanted to get him for Devil. My neighborhood focused on Swans, Villains, Outlaws, and Pueblo Bishops.

In Nelles we had a policy that the immediate neighborhoods of their known adversaries handled their own enemies so for me that would have been far reaching had I kicked off into Border Rat's ass. Acceptable but not really my duty. Inglewood Family enemies were Rollin' 60's, Shot Gun, Hoovers, 8 Tray Gangsters, Raymond Crips, Underground Crips, etc.

Coach Carter was one of our counselors on Roosevelt Cottage, a black man 6'0" and 140 lbs maybe, shit-talking, crazy motherfucker, who should have been in there with the rest of us. Most of the prisoners there respected him, and the scary prisoners feared him because Carter would make them stand up for themselves when he saw others trying to take advantage of them, and that was the scariest thing in the world to them. He encouraged them not to take anybody's shit. If you thought you were hard, Carter would call you on it. He made Lil Monster, from 8 Tray Gangster, fight Lil Country, the bully, because Carter felt like Lil Monster was scared of Lil Country. Lil Monster lost the fight but he stood up for himself, and that was all that mattered to Carter. I had to sneak around when it came to my fighting. Carter used to tell me, "Shit motherfucker, you ain't gone get me fired for killing somebody in here." He knew I was out for blood.

Before the game, I told Carter to let me play inside linebacker so that I could fuck Border Rat up. He played running back, but O.J. Simpson he wasn't. They had the ball first, and ran a 32 blast. It would be the last time he would touch the ball. I shot through the gap stopping Border Rat in his tracks, wrapping his legs together like they were shut tight between the grips of a vise, twisting them until I heard the sound of his bones pop. He didn't scream, in fact he attempted to get up and walk but came crashing back down, looking at me standing over him screaming, "East Coast Crips." His leg was broken. Instead of us becoming reformed inside there, most of our minds had sunk so low, to levels of savagery.

I only had a couple of months remaining, so they approved eight hour passes for me to go home on the weekends. I went home to spend a few hours with Vivian and a few of my homeboys that I was happy to see.

Vivian no longer lived with my mother. She had moved in with an older man, but still came to kick it with me. I understood that I wasn't ready for a relationship; in fact I hadn't the slightest clue of what a relationship consisted of. If it didn't have anything to do with gang activities I was clueless.

Vivian's life consisted of paying bills, managing a household, driving her own car, doing grown up things, the opposite of what I had been doing. Thus far, I hadn't accomplished anything in my life, yet I thought that I was grown. I was still being cared for by my mother. I hadn't owned anything in my life. I had yet to pay any bill, ever, and didn't know what a utility bill looked like. I never looked at her situation as being disloyal. I put her in that situation because of my lack of understanding of who I was. She now had a man and she was now a woman, whereas I was looking for my girlfriend, still ready to pursue a destructive path of madness. I definitely wasn't ready for her, or she for me.

Before I went to the board, my partna Andre Brown, aka Dray, from 89th Street East Coast, had become real close. He was a few weeks behind me to go home; he was on Roosevelt Cottage as well. We exchanged addresses and promised to continue our friendship.

When I went before the board they asked me how did I know that I was ready to be sent back out into society and why should they let me go? Until I had to face it, I hadn't understood what kind of pressure those who went before the board were under. Now there I was, thinking it really didn't have anything to do with whether I was fit to be sent back out into society. What mattered was whether I had the gift of gab, to impress upon the board members why they should free me. I was lost for the words to organize that argument, so I just sat there thinking of what to say. It had become clear to me that my sentence meant absolutely nothing. Though I served every day of my sentence, these petulant pawns posing as administrators had the power to make me serve another full year before being given another opportunity to go free. If I said something wrong or something that could be construed as negative, that would have been enough for these people to exercise those powers.

Then, without warning, the Program Administrator stepped in and worded my argument for me, without me saying a word. I was paroled on 11/18/81. Before I left, the Counselors allowed many of my homeboys to come by to see me off. I was sad to leave behind CL, Biscuit, Dray, and Nu Nu, but, hey, the show must go on right?

My mother and Aunt Jean came to pick me up. I had $3,500.00 on my account from my father's social security, so they gave me a check for that amount. I gave the entire check to my mother as we drove off into <u>THE LAND OF THE FREE AND THE HOME OF THE BRAVE.</u>

ZONKED

It felt really good to be back on the black top. I was much stronger physically, because I played football, basketball and lifted weights the entire time I was in Fred C. Nelles. But mentally I had sunk deeper into darkness, because I continued on with my contribution to black people's destruction by confrontation, i.e. any and all enemies to The East Coast Crips, which were predominantly African Americans. I wore a fairly large Afro that was usually braided; French braids most of the time. My sister, Debra, had a gift for braiding hair. She was able to do the Allen Iverson style braids long before most of White America had taken offense to him introducing them to The National Basketball Association.

I decided I wanted to put a perm in my hair for two reasons. One reason was when I was younger my partna Lil Mike wore one. He was a young player and it symbolized that those who wore perms were players in the game of life. I don't know why or how we thought of something so stupid, yet we had. I was openly rebellious, so I saw it as my way of showing that I had no intentions of conforming. Two, I liked the blue rollers that were used to roll my hair, so in my mind it added to the blue that I already wore, and left no doubts that I was a Crip. I went everywhere with blue rollers in my head and a blue rag tied around them.

Without hesitation, I began building on my reputation in the inner city gang life by roaming the streets of Los Angeles, chasing behind all the crazy shit the Crips had done before me. It was as if I had not learned anything constructive while in Y.A., which I had not, to be honest. Jail had made me worse off, and some of what was going on inside it I brought to the street with me. There I was, much older, yet the same experiences were hunting me as when I was at Russell Elementary. If the system was ideal, once I had been convicted and sentenced to 5 years to the California Youth Authority I should've been placed in an environment conducive to growth and prosperity, but it was the complete opposite of that. I really hadn't been conscious enough to understand that the environment I had been placed in was a direct reflection of the society I had come from. Everyone there was being tested for their strengths and weaknesses, exactly the way we were in society. We were there to be exploited, and proving ourselves to be strong only contributed to our mental weakness, because we had to become savage to survive. We had to use our animal instincts as opposed to our ability to be rational. Rationality there would've without question got our asses beat.

While I was in jail, most of my homeboys from my generation had taken my older homeboys' names. When we were younger everyone had their own names for instance Lil Caver was how we referred to him but he had taken his brother Big Quake's name becoming Lil Quake. Crip roll call: Big Ed had begotten Lil Ed, Big

Lime, Lil Lime, Big Bubble, Lil Bubble aka Lil Will. Big Snake, Lil Snake, Big Sike, Lil Sike, Big Wooda, Lil Wooda, Big Sadd, Lil Sadd, Lil T-Dog, Big TC, Lil TC, Big Moe, Lil Moe, Big Dee, Lil Dee, Big Spike, Lil Spike, Big Duece, Lil Duece aka Lil La La, Big Crump, Lil Crump, Big Fish, Lil Fish, Big Greedy, Lil Greedy, Big Mont, Lil Mont, Big Boxer, Lil Boxer, Big Willie Blue, Big Spark, Big C-Bone, Lil C-Bone, Big Casper, Lil Casper, aka Big C-Bone, Big Ghost, Lil Ghost, Big Fox, Lil Fox, Big Choo, Big Bam, Lil Bam, Crazy Lar, Crip Cal, Bulla Cow, Big Scotty, Lil Man, Baby Man, Big Stoney, Lil Stoney, Big Fos, Lil Fos, Big Oscar, Lil Oscar, Big Kay Kay, Big Greg, Big Mark, Big Too Tall, Big Snow, Big Ray Dog, Lil Ray Dog, Big Rat, Lil Rat, Big Mouse, Lil Mouse Big Tav, Big G-Bone, Lil G-Bone, Big Sugar Bear, Big Goody, Big Erin, Big Vince, Mr. Low, Big Ricc Rocc, Lil Kev, Blacc Jesus, Lil C, Big Pound, Big Ray, Big Drake, Lil Drake, Chumly, Art, Big Nutty, Lil Nutty, Big Gangster, Lil Gangster, Big Black, Cricket, Big Andrew, Big Walt, Big Insane Wayne, Big Fluxx, Lil Fluxx, Big Rocc, Big CL, Lil CL, Big Brown Eyes, Big Lou, Dirt, KT, Soul, Big Melvin, Big JC, Lil JC, Big Tim, Big Hyme, Big Maniac, Ben, Karte Mike, Big Crook, Devil, Big Dino, Nu Nu, Big Worm, Young Rob aka Baby Fluxx, Bob Cat, Big Country, Big C. Rag, Lil C. Rag, Big Hamburger, and many more. Now all these names I've mentioned have "Baby's", Young's", "Tiny's", "Infant's", and "Newborn's" named after them, so multiply times baby, young, tiny, infant, and newborns scattered throughout the inner city of all gang areas with the mentality I've described.

Lil Sadd, Baby Bubble, Termite, and the Lil's had taken off on their plight of madness and hadn't disappointed those that had an appetite for blood and chaos.

Lil Sadd came by my house the day after I got out. I didn't know him before I went in because he hadn't yet started gang banging, but he certainly learned, and he was my type of street guy. Lil Sadd was a small dude, 5'8", 140 lbs maybe, light skinned, short hair and light brown eyes. You would be sadly mistaken to take him to be the friendly kid. The ice cream truck was coming down the street and I told him to stop the truck, I wanted to get me a banana split. As I stood there buying the ice cream, Lil Sadd was writing all over the man's ice cream truck while the man stood there looking. The man asked him not to do it but Lil Sadd ignored him and kept on writing words, e.g. Lil Sadd, Baby Bubble, Big La La, and a thousand more names. I remember thinking Ricc Rocc all over again. Raymond started something that would last forever.

It was time for me to hang out with some women I used to date, one of my home girls named Lil Cee in particular. But I needed to quench my thirst for some new women. My sister Shenette's friend, Kathy, who has always been crazy over me, reluctantly introduced me to one of her friends named Sidney Robinson. She was 5'7", light brown skinned, 135 lbs, long black hair, soft and sexy as ever. She lived in Duarte; we hit it off instantly I can tell you I was completely satisfied every time we got together. She was a beautiful young lady.

Sidney lived too far for me, plus I continued to run the street aimlessly, without a purpose other than to be seen and to destroy as many people's lives as humanly possible. When I was much younger I used to wonder why so many older men always stood around on corners every night and drank themselves into oblivion, and there I was a few years later, doing the exact same thing and loving every single minute of it.

One night I was at home watching a sporting event on TV and there was a knock at the door. I answered it and to my surprise there was Killowatt from Harlem 30's standing at the door. We greeted each other; I was happy to see him. I told him to come in he said "Somebody wants to see you." I asked who? He said, "Jackie." I was surprised because I hadn't called her since I had been out. We walked out to the car. I was dressed as I always was, Crip down from head to toe, a gray khaki suit, blue rag in my pocket, and my blue rollers in my hair.

When I approached the car there were three females inside it. I asked openly, "Which one of ya'll are Jackie?" Every one of them answered they were Jackie. The entire time I was in Nelles, I hadn't seen any pictures of Jackie, so I didn't know what she looked like. Plus at that time I hadn't learned to understand how my senses worked. Had I at that time appreciated the gift God gave us, I would've easily been able to pick Jackie out from the other two ladies by listening to the sound of her voice from when I used to talk with her when I was in Nelles. But foolish me, I was still a baby, growing up thinking I was grown.

Out of the three that were inside the car I was hoping the little black chocolate petite pretty young lady was her. I asked again which one of ya'll is really Jackie. All three again answered they were Jackie. I told them I don't have time to play any games with them and told Killowatt "Come on, Cuzz, let's go inside and talk." As we were walking away Jackie got out of the car and said "I'm Jackie." She was the one I was most attracted to; the little petite black fine thang.

I asked Killowatt was that Jackie, he said "Yeah, cuzz, that's Jackie." Later I learned the other two young ladies were Tan and Angie two of Jackie's best friends. Jackie and I talked; I asked her how was she doing and what has she been up to. She said not much, going to school. I also asked her did she know that I was out before Killowatt got out, and she told me no.

They asked me to ride back with them to their neighborhood which was on 37th and Western. I didn't mind and jumped right in with them. Killowatt and I continued our conversation, while the ladies had fun with themselves over Jackie's driving skills, or lack thereof. I asked Killowatt when he got out, he told me couple of days earlier. I was surprised to see him and to be truthful I didn't know if we would ever see each other again once I left that place. I was strictly an East Side type of fellow; Killowatt was the first West Side dude I had kicked it with other than my homeboys from East Coast Crips on the streets.

AMERICA'S CONDUCT

Once we made it to their neighborhood we ended up at Jackie's house where she and I talked for some time. We agreed that we would keep in touch with each other. Jackie was 5'3", 110 lbs maybe, dark skinned, had short black hair, full size lips and some beautiful brown eyes and a nice smile. I always told her she was beautiful enough to be a model, but I don't think she ever thought of herself as being beautiful, as I knew she was. To me, she was descended straight from African Queens and black has always been my favorite.

Jackie and I stayed in touch and often talked on the phone. We dated, but for whatever reasons we never became sexual with each other. We kissed but never attempted to sleep with each other. I would however go over her house so she could roll my hair and occasionally we ran into each other at parties and dances without knowing the other would be there.

Although I was out of Nelles, I never forgot how impressed I was with how the Santana Block Compton Crips came to Nelles to visit with Big Hub, Tee Wee, and Gangster Rat. To me, it showed they hadn't forgotten their loved ones, and when times got hard for their homies they were there for them. I always said that I would never forget about CL and Biscuit once I got out, and that I too would bring my homeboys up there to see them, even though I knew they weren't going to let us in to visit.

One weekend I rounded up approximately ten of my homeboys and told them we were going to Nelles to visit CL and Biscuit. Big Erin, Big Vince, Lil Kev, Lil Quake and several others rode up to the jail in stolen cars. Because we knew we weren't going to get in, we waited for CL's girlfriend Von to get in, and then we waited on him to come walking up to the visiting room. When we saw him walking up he had no idea that we were there waiting on him. When we saw him, we all started throwing up our signs, 6-Duece East Coast Crips. CL had a smile so large it made all of us feel like we had done a good deed. It made me happy that I was able to let my homeboy know that I loved him and I would never forget him, no matter what.

While I was out, my homeboy Andre Brown, aka Dray, was out so I started hanging out with him, Gangster John and Crazy Dave from 89th Street Neighborhood East Coast Crips. Dray was a ladies magnet. He was 5'8", light brown skin, and 140 lbs. He wore a large Afro and often dressed in Crip attire - overalls, Romeos, blue rags - and drank like a fish. Dray was dating this older woman named Lady. He was 17 years old and Lady was 30 years old, without question. They were made perfectly for each other. Dray was no joke; he didn't play any games. He could handle Lady without doubt. I witnessed him being the man all the time. Gangster John was dating her sister; I believe her name was Vivian.

One evening I got my mother's friend Jerry's car to pick up my home girls, Lil Cee and Co Co. We drove to 89th Street to hang out with Big T, Dirt, Dray,

Winbone, and many other 89th Street Crips. Everybody had been drinking. While Lil Cee and I were in the back seat making out, we heard gunshots. It didn't bother us, because it was not unusual to hear gunshots at any given time. Before we knew it, the policemen were there, tapping on the car window telling us to get dressed and get out of the car. When we got out of the car, they had us stand in front of their car with the lights blazing; apparently we had been positively identified as the shooters. Allegedly some Mexicans had been shot or shot at. I knew this was bullshit, yet the police took us down to the station for questioning. I didn't dispute that someone had been shot, or shot at, but I didn't see shit. I knew we didn't do it, and for them to say that we had was bullshit. Now, for those that don't know how the police department operates within the inner city, let me tell you. The Mexicans that were supposedly shot or shot at may have been real. In most cases the police department tries to get it right, at least that's what we'd all like to believe. However, in a lot of cases they really don't care if the person they're arresting is guilty or not, and that goes for the District Attorney as well. The truth of the matter is that in the urban city it is common for Black on Black, Black on Mexican, Mexican on Black, and Mexican on Mexican crime to take place, especially murders or attempted murders. In the eyes of law enforcement and the District Attorney, as long as these demographics are the predominant players, it doesn't matter much if the right suspect is arrested, tried and convicted or not. To them it has always been looked at as win win. If you come close to fitting the profile of the suspect of a crime, more likely than not that case is yours and you're going to have to prove that you didn't commit the crime. Try that with inadequate legal representation. Now my history made me a prime suspect in any shooting that may have occurred in that area.

They eventually released us to our parents. My mother and her friend Jerry came to pick me up and we went and got his car then drove back home. My mother asked me if I had done what they were alleging we had done. I told her no, and that if I had I would have told her, as I always did when I got caught doing something by the police.

Things for me weren't getting any better. I started to branch further out into the street. Gail, Don Juan's sister called me one day telling me that he was getting out of Nelles, and would I ride up there with her to pick him up. I told her that I would, and went with her to pick him up. I had been out only about two months now, so my face in Nelles was still relatively fresh to the staff that worked there. I didn't think they would make a big deal about seeing me back up there, because I continued coming most of the weekends to see CL and Biscuit, as they walked up to their visitors.

I waited inside the car, while Gail waited inside the building. Don Juan walked up with no idea I had accompanied his sister. When he got to the car he was surprised to see me. I greeted him and told him about all that was going on in the streets. My neighborhood and his neighborhood were at war with each other. Don Juan was from 83rd Street Hoover Crips.

AIDS was just being spoken of; it was something many of us had no clue even existed. I was telling him he had to be careful and to always put a condom on when he was with somebody he really didn't know.

I met Tray, Spoon, Clay and many others around his neighborhood through hanging with Don Juan. Tray and Spoon were brothers and from 83rd Street Hoover Crips. Tray was Gail's man, and Spoon was Sue's man. Clay was from 83rd Main Street Crips.

We hung out often, and had so much fun it was ridiculous. I remember one evening it was a close call for me and my association with them. Don Juan, Tray, Spoon and I were on 37th and Normandie at Gail's house. We left, going to 83rd and Main. As we were riding down Slauson, at Main, the car battery went dead, so we had to walk to Don Juan's house. We couldn't walk down Main, because being from Hoover made it impossible for them to get past my homeboys on 62nd, 68th, or 69th Streets. Bringing them through our hood was a complete violation on my part, which I couldn't justify. We definitely weren't going to get past 77th or 84th Streets. That was Swan gang territory, who were Bloods. It was around 11 p.m., so I decided we should try San Pedro, thinking my homeboys were probably hanging out in one of the many shacks that we frequently hung out in.

One of the things I hoped didn't happen was Lil Sadd being out and about. If he was it would be curtains for them; God himself wouldn't be able to save them. I told them, "Look my homeboys may not be out on San Pedro right now, so we might be able to make it past Gage. If we get past Gage, we're home free." Spoon and Tray were confident that my homeboys wouldn't trip if they caught them passing through. I, on the other hand, knew better and proceeded with caution. We began our journey and it wasn't long before we were at Gage. I remember thinking, "We made it." Right when I thought those thoughts, Big Quake and several more of my homeboys came out from everywhere. Quake called my name and said, "La La, what's up cuzz? Where are you going, and who are cuzz and them?" In my mind, I knew it was all going to end bad, but I really had genuine love for all of them and it was my duty to protect them. I thought they would do the same thing for me if the shoe was on the other foot. Now, in the gang world you can't pretend to be something or somebody you're not, and what I wasn't was a gang leader from 62nd Street East Coast Crips. Big Quake was still the boss, and I respected him fully. So I was completely honest with him. I told him that we were driving down Slauson and the car battery went dead so I thought the safest route was down San Pedro. Quake asked me, "Who is cuzz and them?" I told them they were from Hoover. Quake said to me, "Cuzz, you know better than to bring cuzz and them through the hood." The reasoning was that it's a violation to let the enemies know where we hang out, so we could safeguard our lives. By bringing them into the hood, I violated that law. I told Quake it wasn't my intention to bring cuzz and them into the hood, but the car broke down, leaving little choice as to which route we chose. He understood, and told me don't do it again. I was happy not to see Lil Sadd, because Quake had known the original Hoovers, and had some respect for their leadership. Lil Sadd on the other hand didn't respect any of them. He grew up hating them, and it would've been all bad for them had he been there. Quake and the other homies didn't let them get off easy. They approached them, letting them know that they were East Coast Crips, and telling them "Don't ever come back through our hood." Before we were confronted by Big Quake, I remember asking Spoon, Tray, and Don Juan if they knew him, and one of them told me he did. But apparently he didn't, because that experience would have gone a little bit smoother had they really known him.

One of my homeboys from 69th Street East Coast Crips, Lil Doc, had just been shot. He was 16 years old. He was at a party and was shot badly, paralyzing one of his legs. Lil Doc was to 69th what Lil Oscar was to 62nd Street Crips. Things for most of us became one big gun exchange after another.

Vivian and I had drifted apart and I heard she was using cocaine. I didn't know to what degree she was using, but this new drug called crack cocaine was being used by many black people in the inner city. Most of them saw it as a high society drug that upper-class white people used. If white people used it then it must be good. That was the way many blacks thought. I remember hearing people say "This is the white man's drug," making it appear privileged, so scores of black people flocked to it thinking they were high class drug addicts. Before many of them started actually smoking crack, they began crushing it up and lacing Marijuana cigarettes with it, calling it premos. Many people were doing it.

Big Vince and I used to get high on weed and Silver Satin, but I noticed he didn't like to get high on weed much anymore. He was the first of my homeboys I saw smoking crack, and he wanted me to try it. I swear to you, I didn't like how it made him act, so I refused to try it. When I was much younger, Jeff, my cousin Cal's man, used to snort cocaine with us and I thought it was a waste of time. I never felt shit, and didn't see how someone could spend the money they spent on it. I was content with my weed, and didn't trade it in for the white man's drug.

Many of my homeboys became hooked on crack, and haven't recovered to this very day. Big Quake, Bruce, Crump, Lil Sike, Big Bub, Big Lime, Big T-Dog, Goody, Asmoe, Big Greedy, Juice, Bay Bay, Brown Eyes, June Bug, Big Dee, and so many more of my homeboys were taken down by this drug. Because of the crack cocaine, my homeboys started to have money, money they never dreamed possible. Many of them stopped hanging out and doing all the things we had grown up doing.

AMERICA'S CONDUCT

Fremont High School was our hangout, but the drugs and flamboyancy of having money softened Raymond's image among the Crips.

After crack cocaine appeared on the scene, my Big Homies were weakened, and the Bloods became stronger and bolder, taking territory that had belonged to the Crips since 1971. Fremont High, the greatest prize of them all, the birth place of the East Side Crips, was lost to the Swan Blood Gang.

Before I went to Y.A., there were seven or eight dudes that had started their own gang called the 59th Street East Side Gang. They hadn't tagged themselves with the title Crips yet, but they hung out with us and we partied together a lot. Their leader was a dude named Big Whitey he was 6'1", 280-300 lbs, black as night, and had a million women. Whitey was a drug dealer and had plenty of money. With money came women in bunches. One of their members who I liked a lot was named Thag. He was originally from Compton Crips, but was related to Whitey's family in some way. Thag was a complete fool and was down for anything. I liked that about him; he and I were close, and often hung out.

Things for me were moving a thousand miles a minute. My little brother and niece were growing up fast, especially my little brother. He was a joy to be around. I think it was because he was the closest person to me that represented pure innocence. Whenever he climbed up the stairs and knocked at my door with his little hands, demanding entrance, I smiled widely at the very sight of him. He was 15 months old during that time. If I was playing music when he walked in the room, without hesitation he would begin to jump up and down saying "Get it, get it." That's what we used to say to him when he tried to dance, so he thought whenever he was dancing the words "Get it" went with it. Every time he heard music, he'd start dancing, hollering "Get it, Get it." I thought that was the cutest thing in the world. I loved my little brother and couldn't imagine life without him. My mother made sure we all spent time with him. I rode the bus places with him and my little niece, for the pure joy of innocence. Plus my niece was so beautiful I often used her to catch women.

I continued to visit with Jackie. I met her mother and she reminded me of my grandmother. She was quiet, but very motherly, and Jackie loved her to death. Most of the time it looked like she was off to work. Jackie acted quite respectful around her, like a little girl, so I knew she was a loving mother.

Without question I had not become rehabilitated, and I was engaging in unlawful activities as often as I possibly could. I always accepted the consequences for my actions, whatever they were. I understood the trick was not to get caught. Once you got caught, whatever your game was, it had failed, and the next phase of the game was to escape capture, using the code of the streets, and stay honorable in doing it, without fears or tears.

LARRY DAVIS

Early one morning, out of nowhere, the police came to my house looking for me for five counts of attempted murder. My mother came to my room, knocked on the door and told me the police were downstairs and wanted to talk to me about some people being shot on 56th and Ascot, between Hooper and Compton Ave. This was the Blood Stone Villains Neighborhood. I was familiar with the neighborhood, because my ex-girlfriend lived on the corner of 56th and Ascot. Allegedly, all of the victims were shot directly across the street from her house. According to the police, a baby was shot in the stomach with a 38 caliber, and four other people were hit by shotgun bullets. One person was shot in the nose, another in the back, and two other people had minor wounds. To top it all off, none of the victims were gang members. There were three females, one baby, and one male, or something like that. After hearing the police describe what had taken place, one thing I was certain of was that I wasn't the person who had done it.

I told the police I didn't know anything about the shooting, and I was certain if they showed the people over there my picture that they would verify the shooter wasn't me. They asked my mother if I would come down to the L.A.P.D. Newton Division.

When the interview began, I was sure they had made a mistake and I would be going home in a matter of minutes. For the most part, every single time the police had arrested me for something, I was 100% guilty of the charges. The exception was the incident where Lil Cee, Co Co and I were arrested for the shooting of the Mexicans on 89th Street. The difference between the 89th Street incident and this one was that I was there, on 89th Street, when that incident occurred. But the incident they were describing to me here, not only was I not there, I didn't know anything about it.

They told me this happened April 12, 1981, at approximately 8:30 p.m. That night, Big Vince, Big Erin and I went to Big Vince's little brother Dray's birthday party. He had just turned 12 years old and his mother, Ms. McGowen, wanted us to come, so we did. I had been smoking weed earlier that night, so I wasn't up for all that festive stuff. I didn't stay long and went straight home. Once I made it home, I remembered turning on the T.V., to a cable station to watch a movie, but an unscheduled hockey playoff game was being televised in its place, so I watched that.

According to the police, the suspects were allegedly in a blue station wagon with approximately four or five occupants. They drove around the block while the victims stood outside together talking. The suspects circled the block the second time, opening fire on the victims. I was allegedly identified as the shooter with the shotgun. I allegedly had hung out of the front passenger's side window and fired one shot. The blast from the shotgun gave off enough light for me to have been identified. This is so unbelievable it would never be attempted on the wealthy. This theory would only be practiced on the poor, and it is what we put up with in America's judicial system with regularity.

Could you imagine someone walking into a court room to testify against some rich person and beginning their testimony by stating "When the assailant shot me, I was able to identify him because when he shot me in the face, the light from the shotgun illuminated the inside of the car, making it clear for me to see him." Now, this is allegedly the person being shot giving this testimony. Not only would there have been a million different expert witnesses brought in to destroy that person's testimony, the District Attorney's Office would never have filed charges.

Now here is what was so stupid about that theory - I had known every gang member on that street since we were kids, and I knew where each one of them lived, house by house. I had never in my life engaged in a drive by. At that time, any person that I had ever shot got it the way Cowboy from Florence 13 had when I was sent off to Y.A. I have never been afraid to get out and shoot anyone, so for starters that was the wrong M.O. for me.

I thought because I had gone to Y.A. for the use of a shotgun, and these people were shot with one, that made the crime mine. I told the detectives, "Man I know them dudes over there. Ask them are they sure they saw me." One of the girls who had been shot allegedly identified me; she told the police she remembered me because I once dated her sister. I had no idea who this woman was or who her sister was. Then she claimed she used to see me at Fremont High School all the time.

No matter what evidence the police had collected, I knew it didn't affect me because I knew that I hadn't shot those people. As rebellious as I was and as corrupt as I knew the police department to be, I still didn't believe they would take an innocent person to jail. I played the game of "Don't get caught, but once you do, don't cry over spilled milk." I was okay with that game. But here, I hadn't been caught because this crime wasn't mine. So I waited for them to tell me my mother would be there to pick me up, but no such thing happened. They told me I was being charged with five counts of attempted murder. I still thought I would get out once the judge saw they had made a mistake.

I was sent to Juvenile Hall to stand trial. I remember on the ride over there thinking about my little brother. I thought about how he would climb up the stairs, knocking at the door to come in. But I wouldn't be there to answer this time. I didn't know how long it would take for me to get home to answer his little taps at the door, but I was sure I would be home soon.

Insanity

I arrived at Central Juvenile Hall distraught. I hadn't been aware I was suffering from a mental illness because of the past mistreatment of black people for so many years here in America. I thought that I was mentally healthy. That wasn't a good mixture, being in a state of delusion, but believing I was sound minded.

I was sent to G and H unit, where they housed inmates waiting to stand trial. In the past when I went to juvenile hall it didn't bother me, because I was guilty and looked forward to seeing my homeboys that had been picked up months earlier, or running into some of my partnas from other neighborhoods who I had done time with in the past. However this time was different. I didn't want to be around any of these dudes, my homeboys included.

I was a thousand times more street savvy than many of the youngsters there, and I was set on getting out of there one way or another. I remembered when I was much younger, how my homeboys would stand around and talk about their experiences in the Los Angeles County Jail. The way they told the stories, being in there was gratification, and they wore it like a badge of honor. If you didn't have that allegorical badge, it made you appear less of a reputable gang member. So I figured while I was waiting to get out I might as well do it in the Los Angeles County Jail. I told the counselors I didn't want to be in Juvenile Hall, asking them to send me to the L.A. County Jail. They told me they couldn't do it, that I had to have my lawyer pursue the legal avenues to sanction such action.

I didn't know they were considering trying me as an adult because of my age (17, five days away from my 18th birthday). This circumstance made for a perfect storm – my stupidity made it much easier for them to butcher me up, without all the games and tricks they would have to play in order to prosecute an innocent person.

The next time I was sent to court I had the usual ineffective assistance of counsel. He advised me that this was a fitness hearing, to determine if I was fit to be tried as an adult. I told him that I didn't want to be tried as a juvenile, and that I preferred to be tried as an adult. Instead of telling me "Man, you are crazy!" he just asked me if I was sure. No matter how grown I thought I was, I was still only 17 years old, but, hey, the show must go on right? My attorney informed the judge that I wanted to be tried as an adult. The judge asked me a few questions about knowing what some of my rights were, and if I was making this decision with sound mind. Now, after reading about my life thus far, I'll let you make that call.

The judge found me fit to stand trial as an adult, and didn't waste one second before sending me up to the adult tank in the Criminal Courts Building in downtown Los Angeles. I was sent upstairs to the adult tank in my juvenile hall outfit, a pair of tan khakis and a light blue sweat shirt issued to all inmates that enter Central Juvenile Hall.

It was time for the big leagues, the Los Angeles County Jail, the place where my friend and mentor, Chinese, had been killed, the place my homeboys had described as a city within a city. I finally would have my chance to make my mark as a gang member there, as so many other Crips, Bloods, Black Gorilla Family members, Black Panthers, Slausons, Business Men, Mexican Mafia and Aryan Brotherhood had.

On my walk up to the tank, I thought the deputies were going to place me inside a juvenile tank then transfer me to the county jail and process me in with the other inmates, but no such thing happened. They took me straight to the adult tank and what I witnessed my first minute there blew my mind in a way that I thought wasn't possible. Inside the L.A. County Jail the inmates are issued dark blue jump suits, so when I entered the tank it was clear to everyone there that I had just come from the juvenile tank. I wasn't afraid of the men in the tank because most of my life I had been around the baddest dudes in Los Angeles, The East Side Crips. I never had a fear of the situation I was in, but what I hadn't seen in my entire life on this earth was what I witnessed inside that tank.

I saw scores of homosexuals, and regular guys not wanting to claim their homosexual traits, having sexual intercourse, literally laying on the floor before God and anyone else that could see out of their eyes, kissing one another on the mouth. I couldn't believe my eyes. When I was younger I knew about homosexuals, in fact I grew up with one that everyone in the neighborhood was close to and didn't discriminate against, Jackie Davis, Mug from 59th Street, brother of Jeffrey, Stanley, Dennis, Percy, Lisa and Tooty. Jackie was as homosexual as they came, from childhood. There was no mistaking what he was and he ran with another homosexual named Pee Wee, who lived across the street from the crime I was accused of committing. So I was familiar with homosexuals. Plus, when I was in Y.A. there were dudes that had oral sex with other inmates for cigarettes. I never witnessed it personally, but it was understood who the dick suckers were.

But this was different. I actually witnessed men, grown men that were claiming to be Crips, engaging in homosexual activities. I was shocked beyond any words that I could put together. Immediately, I was on the defensive because of my juvenile outfit. I put my back up against the wall, and prepared to die inside that tank if anyone approached me with any of that madness that I was witnessing.

I heard the keys rattling outside the door of the tank, indicating that it was time to be transferred to the L.A. County Jail, somewhere I had never been. In my mind I was thinking if these men carried on like this inside the holding tank, they must be out of control inside the county jail, where I was sure was no supervision whatsoever.

Once we reached our destination, the Central Jail, I never looked at men the same way again. I was taken to a different area from those that had been in the tank with me, because I had to be booked into the jail. I got fingerprinted, stripped naked, searched, and sprayed with something they claimed was good for you. I knew this probably wasn't one of my greatest decisions, but for the reputation I was in search of, it was the best choice I could've made. That was my way of thinking.

Going through all the lines to be processed inside the County Jail was a task in itself. This line is for this, that line for that. I listened to all the talk for what line meant what. When I heard people in line talking about getting a number seven I asked this dude, "What does the number seven mean, if you get one?" He told me a number seven meant you're going home. I thought, "Oooh, shit. I'm going to get a number seven and I'm not going to even make it back there to experience what I came for."

In my mind, I still knew that I was innocent, so I had to be getting a number seven. There was no way people went to jail for crimes they hadn't committed. I continued to believe that. They began calling booking numbers and the line numbers. Line's 1, 2, 3, 4, 5, 6 and 7 all meant something different.

No number seven for me. I was going in. Once the process was completed, I was sent to 3200/3400 Module, full of Crips, BGF, Mexican Mafia and other organizations. This most definitely wasn't juvenile hall. Instantly I knew that I was in a dangerous environment and I could see how Chinese had been killed inside the county jail. There wasn't any supervision whatsoever, just as I expected. If one was to survive the county jail madness, he was going to have to do it on his own merits and with the help of his homeboys.

I was sent to Charlie Row, the last cell on the tier. It was four men to a cell, on a tier that had 12 cells, and the tier beneath it had six men to a cell. There were two more tiers on the opposite side, identical except for the names, and we had access to each of them. There were four tiers to a module, two for 3200 and two for 3400.

I went inside the cell with Mad Dog (aka) Smokey from Atlantic Drive Compton Crips. Smokey was 6'2", 190 lbs, light skinned, and he wore a small afro and sang all of Smokey Robinson's songs, as good as Smokey himself. He had many of Smokey Robinson's songs tattooed on his body. Needless to say he was a Smokey fanatic.

Then there was Clarence. He wasn't a gang member, but he was from Compton and his brother was a legendary Crip out of Compton who I had been dying to meet, Bitter Dog Bruno.

AMERICA'S CONDUCT

Then there was Q-Ball from Avalon 116th Street. Q-Ball was a big youngster, 6'3", 240 lbs, brown skinned, short hair, who had clearly lost hope of ever going back to the streets. There, I got the chance to see what lost looked like. I wasn't the only person running around proclaiming my innocence. Many people were saying the same thing, but scores of people were saying it to protect themselves from informants getting hold of information they didn't want anyone to have.

They asked me where was I from? This was my language, I immediately told them 6-Duece Neighborhood East Coast Crips. I had several homeboys on the same tier but in different cells, Big Duck from 89th Street Neighborhood East Coast Crips was there. He was just like Big Bubble, Big Casper and Big Quake from 62nd Street, the only difference is that he was from 89th Street East Coast. He still had seniority over me, and all the East Coast Crips in 32/3400.

Then there was Big Marstien and Ice Man from 69th Street East Coast Crips, Rat Tone from 89th Street East Coast Crips, Big G-Man from 118th Street East Coast Block Crips, Winbone and Big Trick from 89th Street East Coast Crips.

I was in the company of people from my neighborhood in 32/3400. When they opened the cells for us to come out I walked down the tier to Marstien's cell. I had no idea he was in jail. I asked him what was he in jail for, and he told me that one of the young ladies in the hood claimed that Big Popa, Ice Man, Big Vamp and he had taken her pussy which wasn't hard to believe. That crew was death on a piece of pussy, and now he was looking at some time in conjunction with her allegations. He asked me what was I doing in there, and I told him that I just had come from juvenile hall. I told him that I had told the judge that I didn't want to be tried as a juvenile. He told me, and I quote, "Cuzz, you're crazy as a motherfucker, don't you know it's better to be tried as a juvenile?" I responded, "Shit, I'm going home, so it doesn't matter one way or the other." He asked me what was I in there for. I told him for five counts of attempted murder. He asked on whom, and I told him the police claim that some Villains got shot on 56th and Ascot, but I didn't do it. He asked me did the homies do it, and I told him that I didn't know.

Marstien, Duck and a few more homeboys told me all about the dos and don'ts. Following those rules was going to be an undertaking for me, because I was looking for some complete madness to get involved in. I wanted to take my frustrations out on somebody and the opportunity came in no time at all.

I remember going to the chow hall for the first time. It reminded me of Nelles, only it was full of grown-ass men that were the most notorious gang members throughout Los Angeles County. Crip, Blood, Mexican and all other forms of resistors you could think of were there. All I knew was I was going to survive it, and stand out while doing it. But first I had to learn which Sheriffs were intolerant, and which ones were a little flexible, because they were truly the most vicious people I've ever been around in my life. They would beat people about the heads for simply stepping out of line, causing many riots amongst inmates and Sheriff's deputies, which they welcomed.

As I walked through the dining hall, I glanced around to see if I saw any adversaries to my neighborhood, Blood or Crips, because I had no intention of getting jumped or taken by surprise. I saw many of my old partnas from camps, juvenile halls and Y.A. I saw some of the infamous Crips I had heard of only by name and reputation, but there they were in the living flesh. I thought I had made it to Crip paradise.

I was really still a baby to those who were in charge of running the county jail. One of the most aggressive of all the Crips was Big Ant from Compton Crip Grandees. He was a true warrior in hand to hand combat, and whatever game anyone wanted to play with him, he welcomed. The Sheriffs respected him as well. I told myself I had to keep both eyes on him because something wasn't right about him; I could feel it in my bones. The entire time I had known Big Ant, I had never once heard him use the term cuzz.

We made it back from the dining hall, and I was able to get on the phone to call my mother. She asked how was I doing, and if I was going to be alright. I told her I was fine and that I would be alright, and not to worry about me because I had her and my father inside of me. I also called Jackie, and told her that I was in the county jail and that I had been arrested for 5 counts of attempted murder, but that I didn't do it and should be out soon.

Jackie knew all about the street life of the inner city gang rivalries, because she lived in the heart of the rolling 30's Harlem Crips and one of her brothers, Big Bob, was a prominent member. In addition, plenty of her childhood friends had experienced the same encounters as I had in their lives, so she wasn't shocked that I made a call to her about being arrested for such a crime.

I asked her was she going to wait for me, and she said that she didn't know. I don't know what made me ask her something like that, because we weren't really together in that way. I guess my intuition was telling me that I wasn't going to be getting out soon, even though I truly believed that I would. One thing I knew, I was truly innocent, beyond a shadow of a doubt.

Getting back to the cell after making the calls, I was happy that I had the chance to talk with my mother and Jackie. Being in the county jail had many advantages over being in juvenile hall. The phones were one of the advantages, because in the county jail we were able to use the phones every day. In juvenile hall, we were not allowed to use the phone unless it was some kind of emergency, so that was a relief. We also were able to raise so much money in the county jail that people wouldn't believe it unless they witnessed it themselves. I witnessed people walking around with tens of thousands of dollars, winnings in cards, dice, chess, and other gambling. Any kind of gambling you could think of went on inside the county jail, and people would literally bail themselves out from their hustle.

They called day room, which meant everybody on the tier got to go inside what is called a dayroom to watch TV and play games. All the gang leaders, Blood, Crips and every other movement you could think of, were in the dayroom. As I met Crips from other neighborhoods, I intended to find somebody who my neighborhood didn't get along with, to continue my journey to hell. While we were inside the dayroom, my homeboy Big Duck was talking with these notorious Blood gang members from Neighborhood Family 89th Street Bloods. There was Junior Bridges (aka) Rag Times, and John Sawyer. My neighborhood was in direct conflict with theirs, and I wanted to get them, but Duck grew up with them and didn't want to take advantage of them because they were at a disadvantage by being surrounded by so many Crips in the module. Because Big Duck was calling the shots on the East Coast Crips in 32/3400, I had to respect his orders. I never had a problem with that, because soon I would be in his position, so I respected the game. Just as I thought the day would be coming to an end, in came a young active Blood from 89th Street Neighborhood Family Blood, out of the juvenile tank within the county jail 31/3300. He was allegedly fighting every Crip he had the chance to; that was the word on him. His name was Curtis, and as soon as he walked in the day room, Big Duck and Big Trick from 89th Street East Coast knew just who he was. They told John Sawyer, "Look, your homeboy, Curtis, has to get down with my little homeboy, La La!" They didn't object; in fact, Curtis was so hard with his banging he came in the day room looking for some Crips to fight. I guess like me he was looking to further his ranking with his hood. I can assure you he had come to the right place that day. Duck came to me and said, "Cuzz, this young motherfucker's from 89th Street Family, and I want you to beat his ass. Do you want to get down with him?" I said, "Hell yeah." Duck and John talked and told us to go ahead and get down. Curtis was born to be a Blood, if such a thing makes sense. He looked like a Blood, with a reddish brown complexion, sandy colored brown hair and reddish brown eyes. He was a little taller than I was. He was 5'10", and weighed about 160 lbs, but on that day he was outmatched. I had been groomed just for this shit.

I was frustrated and agitated about being in jail for a crime I didn't commit, so I didn't see any way Curtis, would gain a victory over me. Before we got it cracking, Duck walked over to me and said, "You know what to do!!" Rag Time and John were telling Curtis likewise; he was one of their young soldiers. We walked over to each other without any words. In the day room everybody took their ringside seat, and make no mistake about it, everyone who fought or stabbed someone in there was always looked at for their skills, strengths and weaknesses. I was prepared for this stage, and Big Duck knew this wouldn't be a match for Curtis.

We collided into each other's force and began to strike each other with crushing blows, but mines were more violent. I could tell Curtis was out of his league, fucking with me, and I was going to make a statement out of his weakness. I looked at the expression on his face. He looked directly into my eyes, asking for a pardon and communicating to me that he wasn't as bad as he tried to make himself out to be. I couldn't help him, because I was as bad as advertised, and I intended to bloody him up. I busted his lips, nose and ears. Then Curtis did something I had never seen anybody do in fighting; he grabbed me tight, pulling me close to him and whispering in my ear that he had enough, that he was cool. I was trying not to hear any of that shit. It was Do or Die on both ends of the fence, ours and theirs, so I continued to beat him until blood started oozing out of his ears and he became limp. John and Rag Times pleaded with Big Duck stop it. Duck had some compassion for his old friends and told me that was enough, so I spared him. They had all once gotten along, before Barry, Rag Time and John all had turned Bloods, but I was a young East Coast Crip, ready to be like Crazy Quake. I had seen how he destroyed anybody who stepped in front of him. I had every intention of taking 62nd Street Neighborhood East Coast Crip on the road, and I knew that within me, I had the abilities to survive the Los Angeles County Jail. One down and many more to go.

This went on for the entire time I was in the county jail. I finally got the chance to meet my state appointed attorney. I can't recall his name, but I do remember thinking he had my best interest at heart, based on the kind of questions he asked me. He also informed me that the District Attorney was willing to offer me a plea bargain for 4 years recommitment back to the California Youth Authority. I told him I wasn't taking 5 minutes back to YA because I hadn't committed a crime, at least not that crime. It took him sometime to actually believe that I hadn't committed the crime I was charged with. I remember one day I was visiting with him he said, "I believe that you didn't do this, but we have to prove it, and I believe that we can."

I came back from my visit with him and went straight to Big Duck and Big Marstien's cell and told them what my lawyer had said about the deal the prosecutor was offering me. Both of them told me to take the deal. I told them that I really didn't do it. Big Duck said, "Cuzz, it's not always about if you actually committed the crime yourself, you have to look at if you think you can beat the case. Can you prove that you didn't do it?" I told him, "Hell, yeah! I was at home watching a hockey game, cuzz." He said, "Do you have witnesses?" I said, "Yeah, my mother was home at the time." He said, "That might not be enough because they're going to look at it like your mother is covering for you." None of what Duck told me made much sense, because I was innocent and there was no way on this earth I was going to take a deal for some shit I didn't do.

I started meeting a lot of Crips my age. I was hanging around with two people in particular, Big Turtle from Avalon Garden and Big Popa, from Rollin 30's

AMERICA'S CONDUCT

Harlems Crips. Both were in for murders - Turtle had two and Popa had four counts.

We became really close with one another while I was there. At that time the black and Mexican inmates were constantly fighting each other, simply because of race. We all had shared that experience together from the streets, so it wasn't anything new to us. We took delight in those encounters. The county jail always became overcrowded, so they sent inmates out to an extended part of the system, like other jail outlets. One place in particular was Wayside, which was dormitory living where most of the riots amongst Black and Mexicans inmates took place. Each dormitory easily housed 150 to 200 inmates or more. A lot of inmates tried their very best not to be transferred there; some were scared and others didn't want their visits with their family to be interrupted after being directly involved in the riots and placed in the hole for days on end. Others welcomed the chance to wreak havoc on each other. In the county jail we were locked up behind bars, as opposed to Y.A. where we were locked up in a room.

I began to recognize, as I had when I was in Y.A., that Black people were killing each other at a rate that was staggering. Even though White people didn't have to kill Black people themselves any longer, i.e. physically with their own hands Black people they still viewed White people as their enemy. The seed that they had sown in Black people's conscious mind, to hate themselves, had taken root and fully blossomed.

If we looked at what was happening to us without sugarcoating things, it was clear that just as with my grandfather and the Black people that came before him, we did not have all the rights we thought we did.

We were guilty until proven innocent. The Eighth Amendment was being egregiously violated with most of the inmates in the county jail that were poor.

AMENDMENT VIII

Bail-Fines-Punishments

SECTION 1. Excessive bail shall not be required, nor excessive fines imposed, nor cruel and unusual punishments inflicted.

Proposed September 25, 1789; ratified December 15, 1791.

The majority of the inmates inside the Los Angeles County Jail were dirt poor, with bails that were so outrageous it was laughable, if one could muster up the courage to laugh at himself. My bail was $100,000. I hadn't ever seen that kind of money in my life, so I knew that I was never going to be bailed out of jail. That was another way for the judicial system to tell us we were stuck in jail until a resolution was reached in our cases.

I continued my journey to hell when I met two dudes from Watts. One I went to school with when I attended 92nd Street Elementary School. His name was Blue, from Grape Street. The other one was Cisco from Grape Street Watts. Blue was a superb fighter; I watched him beat down men twice his size and Blue wasn't a small dude himself. He stood close to 6'3", 200 lbs; dark skinned and wore a small afro. He was a pure ass kicker, and the entire time I was there he was undefeated, until a Mexican he was beating half to death inside his cell stabbed him in the arm, damaging some of his nerves. He won the fight, but his arm was damaged for life.

Cisco was 5'10", light-skinned, 160 lbs and everything nasty about the east side, he was. The rules of barbarianism were embraced by Cisco, fully, so if you were looking for a pass in the gang life after violating a rule you could forget about it. He was surely going to punish you. I liked that about him. He didn't stay long, since he was only in there for traffic tickets.

Crazy as it may sound many people in the street purposely accumulated as many tickets as they could, and turned themselves in to visit their homeboys. Others did so to come inside the county jail to make money, because whatever the price of drugs was in the streets, you could make ten times that inside the jail.

I found my way around there and built up a reputation as a supreme fighter. Fighting I loved to do. One day we were on the top of the roof of the county jail where they allowed us to go to play basketball, lift weights, and use the telephones. That was as close as we were going to get to freedom without being released, so many prisoners went whenever they called roof. While up there, I decided I would play a game of basketball with the fellows. I got tired and wanted to rest so I went over to the telephones where there was a line of prisoners waiting to get on one of about eight telephones. I chose to wait in a line where one of my homeboys named Doc Roc, from 89th Street Neighborhood East Coast Crips, was. He was next to get on the phone, and out of nowhere this dude named Tony Jake, from the Rolling 30's Harlem Crips cut in front of him and told him that he was next. Doc Roc told cuzz that he had been waiting for a long time and that he had to go to the back of the line like everybody else. Tony Jake said to him, "Cuzz, I was next, I won't be long."

I jumped in immediately because I didn't feel like he was handling the situation the right way. I told Tony Jake, "Cuzz, fuck that bullshit. You gotta get in line like everybody else, plus I was next." Tony Jake told me, "Cuzz, you don't know who I am." I told him, "I don't give a fuck who you are. You gotta get in the back of the line, cuzz." Now a lot of people came around the phones to see what was up. My homeboy, Big Duck, was up there and he asked me what happened. I told him, and he told me not to trip up there, to wait until we got back to the day room to address the matter. I told Duck, "Cuzz, I want to get down with cuzz." Tony Jake was much bigger than I was; he had a reputation for being cruel and he was counting on me knowing about it and being scared because of it. He said to me, "Little cuzz, you better go somewhere before I hurt your young ass." But what he didn't know about me is what was running through my mind, and he proceeded to get on the phone and laughed the entire time doing it. Duck knew I was mad, but I followed orders and always respected my OG homies.

I did tell Tony Jake we're going to get down when we get back to the module. He told me, "Cuzz, I'll beat your young ass." I noticed the word young kept coming up in his language, but on this day he was sure to learn a valuable lesson about fucking with me.

When we got back to the module everyone went to the dayroom in anticipation of the unknown, but there was never any doubt in my mind what was about to happen. I knew I wasn't about to become nobody's victim.

Big Duck, Big Trick, and Big Winbone, met with Tony Jake's older homies, Big Perv, Don Don and others. Big Perv was doing all the talking for them. He and Big Duck went off to the side to assure one another it was a head up fight between Tony Jake and me. I was ready to get down. I told Tony, "Cuzz, I'm going to beat your ass for disrespecting my homeboy." Tony Jake really thought he was going to destroy me. He stood 6'2", 200 lbs easy. There I was 5'9 160 lbs so in his eyes this was a cake walk. But he was about to learn what I taught everybody who stood in front of me, that I kicked ass, sun up and sun down.

Once Duck and Perv assured everyone that win, lose, or draw, this was a head up fight, we were good to go. But Big Trick didn't like the fact that Tony Jake was much bigger than I was, so he tried to convince Duck to let him fight Tony. Trick was an ass kicker as well. I felt disrespected by Trick trying to take my fade, so I told him, "Cuzz, get the fuck out of the way. I got this cuzz." Trick said, "La La, don't let cuzz whoop you." I told him, "Just watch how Six Deuce does it."

Tony Jake and I went at each other and it was bloody from the start. We clashed like Pit Bulls. Tony Jake knew he had underestimated me and that I was in it for the long haul. We got down until everyone in the dayroom started saying the police were coming. After that fight, Tony Jake and I became the best of friends out of respect for each other. As for Tony Jake, I'll let him tell the people reading this book who won that fight.

I started focusing on my case because it was getting close to trial. I learned they had arrested another dude from my neighborhood named Effrom Alexander. He lived on 62nd and San Pedro and drove a blue station wagon like the one described by the victims. He allegedly was the driver and I allegedly was the shooter, but what was strange to me about this fabrication was that he and I never went to court together, not once, even though we were codefendants. That was some more legal shit that flew over my head at the time. I asked my attorney how much time would I get if the worst case scenario took place. He told me 9 years and tried again to get me to take the deal of 4 years back to Y.A. I told him he was crazy if he thought for one minute that I would contemplate taking a deal.

I went to the hole for something, I can't remember what. While I was in there, they brought this dude named Rick, from Hoover, to the cell I was in. He had been accused of killing three or four people out in Pasadena. He had two other crime partnas that had allegedly committed the crime with him, Tony Stacy, who was a notorious Hoover Street Gang member and Holly Ray. I met them all and because of this crime it was a big war in the county jail between the gang leaders out of Pasadena and the Crips. Allegedly Doc Holiday and Ray Ray Brownie, two infamous gangsters, were behind this war, and the Crips obliged them.

When I was released from the hole I was sent to another module 36/3800. This is where I met some of the most notorious Crips in Los Angeles County. I was sent to 3600, to the cell with Big Treach, from Raymond Ave 120th Street, Big Snake from Avalon Garden, Maestro from Rolling 30's Harlem Crips, Atlas from 190th Street Delamo Block East Coast Crips, and Sutter Man from Raymond Ave 120th Street Crips. Many of Los Angeles County's street gang leaders were in this module: Tony Stacey from Hoover, Big Heroin from Compton Crips, Ronnie Bam from East Coast Crips. But none stood out like Big Treach from Raymond Ave 120th Street Crips.

Big Treach was facing the death penalty, for allegedly committing a double murder, execution style. His alleged crime partna was Big Evil, from Raymond Avenue 120th Street Crips. Big Treach was 3 years older; I was 18 and he, a very mature 21 year old. I had been around most of the Original East Side Crips at a young age myself, and he struck me as having their maturity, and in many cases he was mentally and physically stronger. I respected him a lot. Late at night he and I would stay up and talk. I would ask him many question about his circumstances facing death, questions like what it feels like to be facing death. He wouldn't blink when he responded; he was always a matter of fact responder; very blunt. He stated, "I don't care one way or the other, because Black people in America are already dead." He told me that the District Attorney wanted him to turn state's evidence on Evil, to spare his life, but that he loved Evil too much to betray him. I admired that in him and the entire time I stayed in 36/3800 he carried himself like a true Crip.

I remember one day I came back from court and as I walked down the tier back to my cell, something didn't seem right above the tier. I noticed Big Snake from 88th Street Avalon Garden and other Crips standing on the upper tier watching me walk to the cell. Big Snake and I were in Nelles together, and he wasn't superior to me in any way. I didn't know if he was trying to act as if he was, because if he thought that, I was prepared to show him that he wasn't. Out of nowhere, this dude walking in the opposite direction fired on me in the chest as hard as he could. I didn't waste one second; I whooped his ass. Everyone on the upper tier was screaming, "La La, cuzz is just playing." But I didn't let up; I continued to beat him like my mother used to beat me. Then I told Snake, "Cuzz, I want to get down with you, I don't know who you think you are." Snake knew he couldn't whoop me. He said, "La La, I didn't have nothing to do with that, I told them that you was going to beat cuzz ass." Big Treach told me to leave it alone, that I had proven my point. Treach took a liking to me. Each night he would wake me up out of my sleep, calling me, "Little East Coast, get up so we can talk, cuzz." We talked about all the things we hadn't done in society at our young age and all the things we wished we had done. So many people in the county jail were facing the death penalty. I wondered how I would feel if I was facing the death penalty. I knew one thing for sure - the life we led in the inner city was common to most of us. But the way America had judged Treach and others like him was completely off track, because he wasn't the monster they were making him out to be. I would have trusted him with my children without a second thought. I thought, here America goes again with a license to commit crimes continuously and get away with them, and yet with no reservation or hesitation to charge us for crimes of the same magnitude. Talk about a double standard in the judicial system. A lot of people literally didn't care any longer, and it was a sad sight to behold. My homie, Big Sadd had been arrested for all sorts of shit. He had been in jail most of his life, so it was like a vacation for him. I remembered telling him what I was in jail for and the circumstances surrounding the crime. He told me without hesitation to take the deal. I couldn't believe how people could be inclined to take a deal that would send them to prison, because I knew I wasn't going be one to do it.

 I started to see the dark side of the county jail, where people were being raped. I just didn't understand how men could be attractive to other men. I watched men claiming to be Crips and Bloods pretend to be homosexual. They dressed like they were gay and walked down the hallway to find a Sheriff and tell him they were gay and needed to be placed with the other homosexuals. Like clockwork, I witnessed these infamous gang members acting like they were homosexual in order to be with another man. Those that weren't able to manipulate the Sheriffs into moving them in the tank with the homosexuals had the homosexuals sneak out of their module and come to their cells. I remember asking Treach about why the homies did that. Treach put it as blunt as anyone was willing to. He said, "Because they're homosexual themselves, but people are scared to call them on it. Treach wasn't scared to; he was respected and feared and was willing to die for what he believed in. I met one more dude like Treach that I admired, Leg Diamond from 83rd Street Gangster Crip. Diamond, (aka Lonely), was a man amongst boys and he loved his neighborhood the way that I loved mines; I recognized that in him early on. He was also known for his skills as a Crip walker. I knew that was something that would draw us together because I thought of myself as being one of the best in South Central Los Angeles. Crazy Poke who was from 52nd Street Broadway Gangster Crips was one of the best Crip walkers in Los Angeles. He was also there when I was in 32/3400 module. We had to meet at some point in there, to put our feet together to express our feelings and our experiences. I had so much on my mind. I wanted to scream to the world "FUCK OFF!"

I went to the hole for something else and when I was sent back to 36//3800 the most astonishing thing happened. I was sent to a cell with one of my enemies from 52nd Street Broadway Gangster Crips, Insane, who I had known from Nelles. When I got inside the cell I asked him what he was doing there. He told me something I can't recall, but he asked me what I was in for. I told him 5 counts of attempted murder. He asked on who. I told him that I really didn't know because I didn't do it, but they say some Blood Stone Villains. He said, "My hood is at war with them right now too."

A few days later I was telling somebody in the cell about the circumstances of my case and Insane said, "Cuzz, we did that shit you're in here for, me and my homeboys. How did they get you for it?" I said to him, "Some crazy-ass bitch was lying on me, talking about I used to date her sister, somebody I never met, and several Villains testified against me, claiming I was the shooter." Insane asked me to contact my lawyer, so he could tell them I was innocent and that he was responsible for the crime I was incarcerated for.

I contacted my appointed attorney and told him about my new discovery he told me that he would come down to the county jail to visit with my cellmate to determine if there was any truth to his claims.

When my attorney came down to visit with Insane he determined that he was being truthful and was convinced that he had committed the crime. However it was his belief that that wasn't enough to get the District Attorney to drop the case against me. He believed Insane would have to give up the others that were involved before the District Attorney would even consider such a confession.

I told Insane about what my attorney said; he was reluctant to give up the others involved, which I understood. He told me that he had to talk to some of his homeboys that were locked up in the county jail at that time. Three of however many people that were allegedly involved in that particular crime were in the jail at that time. Insane introduced me to them and asked them if they were willing to come forth and admit to the court that they committed the crime. To my surprise, all three of them agreed to confess to the crime themselves without giving up the others involved. I was surprised, because we were sworn enemies, but they were willing to set me free because they thought what had happened to me was wrong.

AMERICA'S CONDUCT

I thought that was more than enough for the D.A. to investigate, and surely enough to convince them that at the very least they had arrested the wrong person in me, but that still was not enough. It was clear that I would have to stand trial, so we started to prepare for it. My attorney began interviewing all of my witnesses. Big Erin, who would testify that Big Vince, he and I were together that night at Big Vince's little brother's Dray's birthday party. Mrs. McGowen would testify that I was at her house just before the shooting allegedly happened. Dray whose birthday it was would testify that I had attended his party that night.

I had scores of witnesses; there was no way that they could convict me of this crime. I had a foolproof alibi.

It was time for trial, and Big Duck asked me before we started, was I sure that I wanted to go forth with it and not consider the deal. I told him I wasn't guilty! He asked how much time I would get if I was found guilty. I told him my attorney told me 9 years.

The trial began and the D.A. started his opening statements by telling the jury how he intended to prove that I was responsible for committing the crime, and how he was going to call in eyewitnesses to testify that they identified me as the assailant who had fired a shotgun into a crowd of people. In my mind I was thinking the complete opposite, that when these witnesses comes walking through that door they would testify that they had made a mistake and like in the Perry Mason movie, the judge would tell me I'm free to go and there would be no hard feelings. The system would've worked for me. I would've gone back to playing cat and mouse, trying not to get caught. But I had become worse off by that experience, and I had grown so much in the few months that I had been in the county jail because of the violence, maturity, and corruption surrounding me.

After the D.A. finished his opening statement, my attorney began his own by telling the jury the complete opposite of what the D.A. had told them. How he would show that the witnesses made a mistake in identifying me, because he knew about Insane and his homeboys. The D.A's. first witness came through the door and sat on the witness stand. I can tell you I wasn't worried about any witness he had coming through the door, because I knew once they saw me for the first time in person they would realize they had made a mistake in identifying me, if they really had.

One by one most of the D.A's. witnesses identified me as the shooter. This went beyond making a mistake, these people were outright telling lies, knowingly; I was convinced of it. One girl who was shot said she knew me because I had once dated her sister. I told my attorney that she was lying, to find out who her sister was, and call her in to testify to this bullshit.

This went on the entire trial. The D.A. told the jury that I left the party and went on to shoot the people on 56th and Ascot, and then went home to watch a movie on the On TV cable station. Once he felt he had convinced the jury that I was personally responsible for committing this crime, he rested his case. Then it was our turn to prove my innocence, which I couldn't wait to do.

I sat there thinking these people are crazy. Here it was, they had a process where all these people were responsible for carrying out justice for all, yet there I was being crucified. I looked at the judge, thinking to myself, are you people serious? Is this really happening? There was no stopping it now; it had begun and an innocent man was standing trial for a crime that I was convinced they knew I didn't do.

All of my witnesses testified to what they witnessed that night, one after the other, but I couldn't wait to get up there myself to straighten all this bullshit out. The time came for me to take the witness stand. I didn't have any worries about the D.A. catching me in any lies, because I wasn't there and I wasn't the shooter. So I was confident that I could assure them of this fact with my testimony.

My attorney called me up to the witness stand to testify on my own behalf. I remember thinking finally I would be able to tell these people the truth and get the fuck out of there. Eleven months was long enough; I had met more Crips than I could have ever dreamed of. I had seen every crime in the streets committed right there in the county jail. I had witnessed corruption in the Sheriff's Department, officers to be specific. I had seen the betrayal between Crips that I didn't think existed amongst them. I had seen another side of the men that represented what I had been hollering out of my mouth since the age of 10, engaging in homosexual activities and not thinking of themselves as being homosexual. In fact they thought it more manly to take another man's ass away from him.

I had had enough. I had survived the craziness of the L.A. County Jail. I was ready to go home and tell my homies about all the fights and stabbings I had been involved in and how I had represented the set. I wanted Big Quake to know he had taught me well.

I took the stand and testified to my whereabouts the night and time of the shooting. I told the jury that I was at home at the time of the shooting, watching a hockey game on cable, On TV network, during the time the D.A. alleges the crime happened. I told them that I didn't know any of the people that had been shot, and I definitely didn't know the lady's sister who testified that I had. I asked for the D.A. to bring the girl in for the jury to hear her say we dated. I knew he wouldn't because it was a lie, and my attorney told me he couldn't because the county only gave them so much money to investigate a case, and he didn't have any money saved to pay an investigator to go out and investigate the girl. Now ain't that a bitch for a poor man in the inner city?

AMERICA'S CONDUCT

The D.A. kept questioning me about whether or not I was watching a hockey game. I continued to say that I was. He again asked me and I quote, "Mr. Davis are you sure that you were watching a hockey game on On TV that night around 8:30 p.m? I said, "Yeah." He said to me, "Who was playing that night if you can recall?" I said, "The Edmonton Oilers and some other team." It was a playoff game. He asked me again, "Are you sure that you were watching a hockey game Monday night, April 12, 1982 at 8:30 pm?" I answered, "Yeah." In his mind he was setting me up to prove I was outright lying to the jury, because he could prove that there wasn't any hockey game scheduled to be played that night on On TV network programming. I had no idea he was going to bring in the On TV subscription programming book to verify that. He asked me again, "Are you sure that you were watching a hockey game, Mr. Davis?" He asked me the question like, "Come on, I got you trapped in a lie and you are the only one that doesn't know it." I again answered, "Yeah I'm sure."

He asked the judge if he could approach the bench. The judge gave him permission to do so. Dianne Wayne was the judge, and I will never forget her name as long as I live. He told the judge he had an On TV programming book that he would like to hand the defendant and direct his attention to Monday, April 12, 1982, at 8:30 p.m. and read to the jury what it said. I looked at it and realized immediately why he was asking me if I was sure that I was watching a hockey game that night. There was no mention of a hockey game in the book, but I wasn't troubled by that because I knew I had watched a hockey game. I proceeded to read what the book said. It was a movie whose name I can't recall, but it definitely wasn't a hockey game listed in that 8:30 p.m. slot. The jury looked at me like, "Damn, you almost had us fooled, but there was no way this book could be wrong, because it was in black and white." However I knew it was wrong and that a movie wasn't playing that night at 8:30 p.m. The D.A. turned to the jury and told them, "Ladies and gentlemen of the jury, there is no possible way that Mr. Davis was at home Monday, April 12, 1982, at 8:30 p.m. watching a hockey game, because there wasn't a hockey game on that night." I wasn't fazed by any of his subterfuges, because one thing I knew to be true is what my mother taught us. When we lied to her, we couldn't hide the truth. We could lie but the truth was still the truth and could never be hidden. I knew the truth was on my side that day. And the District Attorney had no idea he wouldn't be able to hide the truth that day from the jury.

My attorney objected, saying something about the book being verified. The judge sustained his objection and the D.A. said he was finished with his direct questioning of me. The D.A. walked back to his side of the table looking at the jury like he had just slain the lion. The judge looked over at me like, "Damn, Mr. Davis, you have the nerve to come in this court room and tell a bald face lie." I remember looking at her, thinking about my father and the reasons why he hated most white people. There they were, attempting to judge me and I was innocent as could be.

They wanted me to feel bad for myself, but they were the corrupt and rotten ones. I didn't care anything about them, and I damn sure wasn't feeling sorry for myself, because I already knew about most white people. My parents had told us how they were treated when they were children, and to me, nothing had changed from their childhood to ours. I just made the same mistake that Kunta Kinte had made a century earlier - getting caught by them.

My attorney looked devastated; he looked at me on the stand and in his eyes he was communicating to me. His eyes said, "Why did you put me in this situation?" I sat there looking at him like "Do your job, motherfucker. You all prosecute innocent people every goddamn day, and I'm not the only person sitting in a witness seat innocent. It's a possibility that the D.A. is wrong, and it's your job to prove that he is."

He proceeded to ask me, "Mr. Davis, the prosecutor handed you a book and you read from it, is that correct?" "Yeah." "When you read it, it didn't say a hockey game was playing that night is that correct?" "No it didn't." "Are you sure you were watching a hockey game that night?" "Yeah I am." "Now is it possible you maybe have the days mixed up?" "No."

He now doubted my alibi and he was giving me a way out. I looked at his sorry ass and thought to myself, "Now I know I'm dead. My own attorney is selling me out."

He asked the judge for a moment, and came to the stand and said, "Are you sure?" I told him, "Man I don't care what that book says! I know I was watching a hockey game that night." He was confident in me again, and asked the judge for a recess to call the On TV station and verify what they were showing the night of April 12, 1982 at 8:30 p.m. The judge granted his request and looked over at me almost as if she felt sorry for me, like, "Come on, Mr. Davis, you're going to go on with this lie? You're busted. Don't continue to humiliate yourself." I looked at her like, "Fuck you, bitch!!!"

They all came back from the recess and called me back up to the witness stand. I saw joy and happiness in my attorney's face. The judge told the jury that the D.A. had to correct some of his previous testimony. He got up there and told the jury that they called the On TV program station and asked them what they had scheduled the night of April 12, 1982, at 8:30 p.m. They told us whatever the movie was that I had read to them, but the station didn't play the movie because of an unscheduled playoff hockey game, which replaced it in the schedule.

The judge looked at me this time like, "You dirty motherfucker! How dare you come in this court and make us look like fools!" I thought to myself, "This bitch is crazy." She should have been looking at the D.A. and the lead detective like,

AMERICA'S CONDUCT

"How dare you all bring a man in my court knowing that he is innocent." However that wasn't the case. The show must go on, right?

My attorney got up and addressed the jury. He was sure I would be acquitted in light of the newly discovered supporting evidence. I remember he asked the jury, "How on earth could Mr. Davis tell you all about a hockey game that wasn't scheduled anywhere in the world? He couldn't have made it up, and no one could have told him about it, because the On TV Station manager didn't know they were going to show the hockey game at the time the program was printed."

The D.A. turned around and told the jury, "There's no doubt that Mr. Davis was at home watching the hockey game, but during the game he left to go out to shoot them people and came back home to finish watching the game." Now, just minutes before, he had told them that there's no way I was at home at 8:30 p.m. watching a hockey game, and then brought in the On TV program to prove a hockey game wasn't even scheduled, but after confirming my alibi he switched tactics. I knew then that I was going home; there wasn't any doubt in my mind. Their deceptions had been exposed and surely the jury saw right through their bullshit.

The jury took the case into deliberation. I recall feeling happy that this bullshit was over and proud that I had learned so much in the county jail. I became worse off as a human being but more mature as a man, and I didn't regret my decision to come to the Los Angeles County Jail.

During the deliberations, the D.A. once again attempted to offer me a plea bargain to Y.A. I told my attorney I wouldn't take time served, because I'm not guilty. I would never take one day in jail for something I didn't do; I didn't care how corrupt the system is.

I recall how Treach and I sat up talking during deliberations. He said, "Little East Coast, what are you going to do when you get out?" I told him, "Go kick it with my homeboys," whom I missed with all my heart. I sat up at night thinking about all the fun they were having without me, but that would change in a matter of days.

I also remember talking to my homeboy, Big Sadd, about the case and him telling me to take a deal. He had just taken a deal for 17 years, with 80% that had to be served before he was eligible for parole. I thought he was crazy. Big Speedy, Buster, and Wayne from Back Street took 40 something odd years as a deal, and felt that they had gotten a good deal. What the fuck was wrong with Black people's minds?

Here we were being punished for crimes most of us hadn't committed, and others loved giving their lives up to a system that hadn't paid for one day of its abuse against them. I knew for sure I wasn't going to be one of those who felt good about sending myself to prison. My mind hadn't been that destroyed, to imprison myself.

The jury deliberated a couple days as I sat in the court room tank waiting for them to reach a verdict. The bailiff came to the tank informing me that the jury had reached a verdict. This was what I had been waiting for. I had sat in the county jail with people accused of killings that were unbelievable. I had watched people surrender their lives out of fear of spending the rest of their lives in prison. They thought 50 years with 80% was better than a life sentence. This shit was ridiculous.

I walked into the courtroom feeling like today would be the day I went home to be with my little brother, who I had missed a lot. I recall looking at the jury to get a read on them, because I had heard so many people in the county jail swear they were innocent, as I had, but then be found guilty. For a moment I started having doubts about the process. I asked my attorney what he thought my chances were of being found not guilty. He said that he felt good about the evidence, and that all of my witnesses had corroborated my story. But as I watched the jury, my hope of being sent home diminished rapidly. They all turned their heads every time I tried to read their mannerisms. Still, my heart wouldn't allow me to believe they would send an innocent man to jail. I knew of plenty people in the county jail who claimed they were innocent, but I knew for sure that I was.

The judge asked the foreman of the jury if they had reached a verdict in the case. The foreman assured her that they had. The judge asked the foreperson to pass the verdict forms to the clerk and then to her. She then passed them back to the clerk, asked me to stand up and asked the clerk to read the verdict. "We the jury in the above entitled action, find the defendant, Larry Davis, guilty of the crime of Attempted Murder PC 664/187 as charged in count 1.

The clerk read that off five separate times. I looked at the jury and thought they were stupid fools who had just participated in a circus and still had the audacity to sit over there looking as if they had just performed their civic duties. At that moment, I became my father through and through. From then on, no one could tell me that America had changed and things were better for black people, because it had just been made clear as rice paper that America didn't give a fuck about fairness, and now I didn't either. From that day forth, my motto was let the chips fall where they may. One thing was for sure, I didn't want to see no human-being confronting me, acting like they gave a fuck about me. And I sure as hell wasn't going to go through the probation process like everyone does when they are found guilty. I wasn't guilty, and I sure as hell wasn't going to act like was.

Because I was 17 years old when the crime was committed, by law they had to send me to California Youth Authority to be evaluated to see if I was fit to be sent to prison. Now, whether or not you believe I was innocent, for the sake of argument let's just say that I was. I now had to go to Y.A. and act like I was a good person who wasn't fit to be sent to prison, and convince the people that would be evaluating me based on these principals. It was no longer about whether I was innocent or guilty; that ship had sailed and was long gone. Now, as an innocent person, what was I supposed to do? Was I supposed to feel grateful for the opportunity not to be sent to prison? Should I feel blessed to have been sent to Y.A.? What if I was really innocent?

I had already been to Y.A. months earlier and I knew the games they played there. Every single inmate in Y.A. had to admit to their crimes or they weren't going home until they finished every single day of their time. I wasn't going to play any of those games.

I was sent to Norwalk SRCC to be evaluated. Right off the bat I didn't care to be there. I was sent to Portullia Unit, where I ran into few of my Y.A. partners. Tank McGruder from Grape Street, Joe Joe from Front Hood Compton Crips, and my homeboy big Mont from 6 Deuce East Coast Neighborhood Crips to name a few. There were a few notorious Blood gang members on the unit who I suspected of shooting one of my homeboys on the streets. I told Tank and Joe Joe that when we lined up to go to the gym I was going to take off on the Bloods in line. They told me they were down and would follow suit. The Blood I had my eyes on was Wibble Wobble from Swans. He knew me from juvenile hall and he knew I was active, so he too was ready for a fight. I didn't make him wait long. As soon as they told us to line up, we came at each other. Wibble Wobble wasn't ready for my game. I beat him senseless while Tank and Joe Joe engaged in their own struggles. The unit became one big riot. After the police broke it up they sent Joe Joe, Tank and me to the hole, where the police claimed I started the riot, which I had, and never attempted to pretend otherwise. While I was in the hole, one of the counselors, a lady, came to my room for an interview about the crimes I had been found guilty of. It was part of my evaluation. She asked, "Don't you want to go to Y.A. instead of prison?" I stared at this woman like she was crazy. "Don't I want to go to Y.A. instead of prison?" I replied. At that moment, I knew what the slaves must have felt like. I was given a choice of which jail I would prefer to live in, and asked, didn't I want to go? If I kept fighting like I wanted to be free, then I would be evaluated as troublesome, an instigator, rabble rouser or a trouble maker. Doesn't that sound familiar? Even for my generation that psychology was still in place, the same mental abuses practiced on my grandfather in 1911 in Alabama.

I didn't cooperate in any of their hoaxes. I refused to act like I had done anything wrong and continued to get my Crip on. I was sent back to the county jail after being in Y.A. for close to two months. When I got back to the county jail, I immediately asked my homeboys what had happened to Big Treach? They told me he got the death penalty. I was sad for him, yet I knew he probably wasn't even sad for himself, because he was wise beyond his years. Treach understood that the system was still killing Black people the way that it had always done, only now they had legalized it through the judicial system and they had gotten a bunch of stupid ass Black people to partake in their fraud of equality.

March 4, 1983, Case #A378988, Los Angeles County Court. I appeared before Dianne Wayne for sentencing. She read about my activities in Y.A. during my evaluation process and told me that I wasn't fit to be sent to Y.A., therefore she was sentencing me to the California State Prison for 18 years and 4 months, and each count was to be served consecutively. I stood there and looked at that white bitch with hate, and with telepathy I communicated to her: Chitty Chitty Bang Bang, Nothing but a Crip Thang, Crips Don't Die, They Multiply.

Lost Souls

I was sent to Chino Reception Center to be processed into the California Prison system. When I arrived I could see it was different from the Los Angeles County Jail. Chino Reception Center was old and run down, like a building two hundred years old without any repairs. It was like warehousing cattle and it smelled awful. Cigarette smoke filled the building 24 hours a day, mixed with the stench of piss, bile, and musk from unclean bodies. The atmosphere was of death. It really was horrific, but nothing could be as bad as how I felt about what had just happened to me. There I was, being processed as if I had committed a crime, and nobody thought for a second that I was innocent. Where were all these Black Civil Rights leaders to protect the poor from these racist judicial servants of the people? They were nowhere to be found, and to be truthful, most of the inner city youth thought the Black Civil Rights leaders were in on the exploitation of Black people, so they could be accepted in the American system as white people's equals. People like me were collateral damage, and many of the so-called black leaders looked the other way, although they knew we were being wrongfully convicted.

I was placed on the third tier, in a cell with this older dude out of San Diego; he was only doing a violation but had experienced prison life in its totality. Before I could sit he told me that right before I arrived the White Nazi's Aryan Brothers and Black inmates had gotten into it over the tier, because a White boy had called a Black inmate a nigga. So the Blacks had planned to attack the white boys when they let us out for dinner later on that night. He asked me my name. I told him La La, from East Coast Neighborhood 6 Deuce Crips. He asked me; "Are you down for attacking the whites when the cells open?" He just didn't know how down I was; after what I had just experienced, I would be down for an eternity. At that point in my life, anything "normal" would've been unusual for me.

My cellmate was one of those militant dudes who hated white people. He didn't like Blacks saying nigga, and here I was, every other word out my mouth was fuck that nigga, nigga please!! I was a full-fledged super ghetto child, and as militant as my cellmate was, he couldn't stop me from saying nigga.

Right before dinner, my cellmate gave me military drills about how to come out of the cell, and how to stand up against the bars while other inmates passed. He was serious. He reminded me of that character played by Damon Wayans on *In Living Color*, in the skits dealing with inside prison life. He epitomized the so-called intellectual jailhouse-schooled convict, using big words that usually were out of context, but dead serious about his rhetoric and displeasure for the system.

I stood there listening to him, without disrespecting him, but I just had left Big Treach, Diamond, Big Ant, Big Sadd, Ronnie Ram, Big Heroin, Big Duck, and many other Crips who were aggressive men. When he finished with his lessons on combat, I told him that I was just going to attack the first white boy I saw. He had knives already made, and the Blacks were talking Swahili to each other. I thought to myself, where in the hell did these Black men learn how to talk in Swahili, American as they were? I was impressed to say the least. I learned right there, in that moment, that prison was completely different from any place I had ever been. This was going to be a challenging experience for me, but I was sure I could survive it.

I knew that I wasn't trying to get stabbed, so I wasn't going to play any mind games with the white boys. I was going to attack the way I learned in all the race riots with the Mexicans in the Los Angeles County Jail. When we waited one second too long, we were always attacked by them, so I learnt from that experience to attack first. I would later learn that prison and the county jail were two different worlds altogether.

When the cells opened, the whites had the same thing as I did on their minds. It was all out chaos, and despite the fact that my cellmate talked a lot of shit, he was a super bad man with a knife in his hand. He just didn't talk it, he walked it. When the smoke cleared, the correctional officers came in and took people who had markings on their hands or stab wounds to the hole. But a lot of people made it back to their cells with wounds, and others had patched themselves up.

My cellmate and I made it back to the cell unharmed. He said, "Youngsta, you got heart. Where did you learn how to get down like that?" I told him, "Cuzz, these white motherfuckers got me in here for some shit I didn't do. I'm mad as a motherfucker."

I oftentimes thought about my mother, and wondered how she was doing over her son being sent to prison for 18 years for something he didn't do. Who in this world cared about her feelings about having her child taken from her? What was she supposed to do about me being in jail, without any resources to fight for my freedom? Was she, as a mother, supposed to accept the capturing of her son as something legal, in a society that told Blacks things were different? Hell nah! She knew better; she told me there wasn't anything she could do, because she knew from her childhood experiences that scores of white people were cruel, and never wrong in their world. They protected each other's interests and prison was becoming big business. They needed their friends' prison beds filled and they were going to fill them by any means necessary. Men like me were only collateral damage that nobody would make any fuss over. But I intended to raise some hell for myself.

I stayed in Chino Reception Center approximately three months. Chino was similar to Norwalk Reception Center, in that they evaluated you to determine where you would be sent. So everyone who went there had to endure a battery of tests.

AMERICA'S CONDUCT

I recall they tested everyone's IQ, mine being 100 at the age of 19. I was so embarrassed by that number, because I didn't know what it represented. So when people asked me what my IQ was, I always said I didn't see it.

The Bloods and Crips at Chino fought, stabbed and insulted each other every chance they got. They even had it set up so that Bloods and Crips had their own separate units. We were being taught the tactics of divide and conquer, and had no idea we were being purposely divided and subliminally controlled, because we were completely ignorant, as most of our ancestors were.

I was sent to Folsom State Penitentiary where two of my partners were. Big Poppa, from Harlem 30's had gotten 98 years to life for the four murders he had been convicted of, and Turtle from Avalon Garden had been convicted and sentenced to 54 years to life for his double murders.

On the ride there, I recall thinking about all kind of things I had heard about San Quentin State Prison and Folsom State Penitentiary. Now, at the age of 19, I was being sent to this notorious place that had so much history, and held the most volatile men in the State of California. It was my turn to enter this place of horror.

My life was full of miseries, and I had no idea what was in store for me at Folsom. The ride there was quiet. You could just imagine what people's thoughts were in that atmosphere, a constant thought of the unknown. Everybody on the bus had heard about the killings and the riots there. I was thinking I would get the chance to meet all the Crips that had been incarcerated, and now I would meet them in the war zone no less. Cripping was still on my agenda; I didn't care where they sent me.

When the bus arrived at Folsom's gates, I couldn't believe my eyes. It looked like we were about to enter some old English castle, made of the biggest stones you could ever imagine. I remember thinking, what the fuck is this I'm about to enter? I was sure from the looks of Old Folsom that the most notorious human-beings in the world were housed inside those walls.

I waited for the gates to open so I could see what I knew was behind them - complete terror. As the bus drove slowly forward, I watched the guards give the bus driver the okay to proceed. The guards looked hateful and racist. I knew that look, from trips to Alabama, and from the Sheriffs in the Los Angeles Jail. I immediately recognized the look of overt racism in the faces of the guards at Folsom.

As we drove to R&R to be processed into the prison, I saw guards walking on towers three stories high, with mini-14's, ready to shoot at all times. I wondered if they really shot inmates, or if it was a ploy to scare the prisoners. It wouldn't be long before my question was answered.

LARRY DAVIS

In front of R&R we were ordered off the bus one at a time. Everyone on the bus was shackled down with chains, which were wrapped around our waist. It was the most uncomfortable feeling I had ever endured. At the time, I didn't know CDC could be much crueler.

When we stepped off the bus a prison guard took off the hand cuffs in front, and we went inside R&R where the other guards took off the leg shackles. We were ordered to take off all our clothes, until we were butt naked, and they completed a full body search. I stood in front of a guard who told me to open my mouth, stick out my tongue, and run my finger around my gums. "Lift your hands up over your head, wiggle your fingers turn your hands over on both sides, then take your hands and run them through your hair. Lift up your testicles," and for those who weren't circumcised, they pulled back the foreskin on our penis. I turned around, lifted up each leg, showing the bottom of each foot, and then bent over and spread my ass cheeks open so they could look inside my asshole to see if I was hiding anything inside my rectum. I squatted down, spreading my ass while coughing twice. Then I put the jumpsuit back on.

We were fingerprinted and given all the other instructions that came with being processed into prison. All of the other humiliating shit we went through wasn't new to me, because all authority figures, from juvenile halls to camps, Y.A.'s and Los Angeles County Jails, and now prison, got a kick out of seeing men naked. I was more concerned with the guards and the guns they carried every second of the day.

We lined up single file to be sent to the building where we would be housed. Since we had arrived close to five o'clock, the prison was shut down, and there weren't any inmate movements. As we headed to orientation, the guards trained their guns on us until we were inside the building. Once we entered the building, the guards inside followed us with their guns as well. Goddamn, what the fuck was this? Everywhere we went we had to have someone pointing a goddamn gun at us! We lined up alongside the gigantic stones in the building, and the guards ordered us to face the wall and not turn around. I was taken aback by the five tiers of cells inside the building, thinking somebody could easily be thrown off the fifth tier and killed. Just then, the prisoners in their cells started screaming at us, "Get the fuck off the wall." They were hollering, "Turn around! Fuck the police! They're trying to punk y'all." What the fuck was this? Were these motherfuckers really trying to punk us, or is this procedure? I knew I wasn't a punk, and I sure didn't want to start off my first day having the prisoners looking at me as one, so I was faced with a decision. Was I going to defy the guards and turn around with their guns trained on me? Of course I was. I turned around to look at one particular man I heard screaming like he had lost his mind. To my surprise it was my partner from West Side Harlem 30's Crips. When I caught his eyes looking down on me, we both smiled widely as if we had found our long lost friend.

AMERICA'S CONDUCT

Poppa was still as defiant as I remembered. His cell was on the second tier. He had what looked like a thousand blue rags, pasted on his wall with soap to make them stick, leaving no doubts to anyone that he was a Crip. Bloods assigned to the same tier had their red rags pasted the same exact way.

I saw bigger white boys than I had ever seen before, with Nazi tattoos, grown men both literally and figuratively. I saw stoned-eyed Mexicans with the look of warriors. I saw the hateful eyes of blacks, looking at us with disgust. I knew how black people functioned; I was prepared to defend myself against them. It was the looks from the Whites and Mexicans that caused me to wonder where these people had sent me.

We were assigned to our cells on "fish row," for the new inmates. We stayed there close to a month, until we were classified by a committee, which consisted of counselors, Lieutenants, Captains, and a Psychologist. The committee determined if we could be assigned to the prison program, or if we had other needs to be addressed, such as enemies. They had to safeguard themselves from lawsuits, so they asked all of those questions. Many people would falsely claim to have enemies in certain prisons, so they would be sent to prisons that were more convenient for their family. Then they would tell the person who they had named as their enemy that they used their name, and for them to let their counselors know that they aren't enemies and have them to sign a marriage chrono (a write-up) stating this fact.

I was sent to the fifth tier, on the opposite side of the building from Poppa. I told him I would see him later, during chow or any other movement they gave us. I was assigned to a cell with this dude that was in Fred C. Nelles with me in 1980. When I was at Nelles I was 15 or 16, and this dude was 24. He had been sent there from Y.T.S., a Youth Authority for older prisoners, 17 to 25. When he came to Nelles, we wondered how he made it there. We later learned he had been sent as a barber for the institution.

He had been convicted for a murder now, and told me he was innocent and should be going home on his appeal soon. I looked at him for a minute, thinking he was under the same illusions as I had been. America didn't care about him being innocent. I was innocent and sitting in a cell in Folsom State Prison at 19.

I didn't know much about the Appellate Courts and how they worked. But I learned quite a bit about the process and procedures of the court as I studied the opening briefs filed by my appellate attorney.

Here's an example of how the appeal process works from the book *The Prisoner's Guide To Survival*, by L. Powell Belanger.

CHALLENGING YOUR SENTENCE AND CONVICTION

One of the key issues on the minds of many prisoners is "When am I getting out of here?" A confinement to prison is generally based on two things: a conviction and a sentence. These are two different legal procedures. The conviction was the result of a plea or trial. The sentence, on the other hand, may have been determined in part on past criminal conduct, recommendations by a prosecutor or defense attorney, calculations made by a probation officer, application of state or federal statutory language and/or interpretation of sentencing guidelines by a judge.

In each of the steps involved in conviction and sentencing there is room for error. If you or your attorney can identify any errors made during these resulted in an unfair or illegal sentence or conviction, you have a chance of having your sentence or conviction changed for the better.

There are several ways to challenge a conviction or sentence. The circumstances of your case will determine which options are available to you. The most common methods for challenging a sentence or condition are through direct appeal, habeas corpus and petition for writ of certiorari to the U.S. Supreme Court. A brief overview of each process appears below.

APPEALS:

Appeals are often the first step for many criminal defendants. A direct appeal involves asking a higher court to review the decision of the court that convicted or sentenced you. Some important aspects of an appeal include:

- An appeal must be based on issues contained in the court record (the written documentation of the legal proceedings).

- An appellate court will examine the court record for errors of law.

- Criminal defendants filing their first appeal will have counsel appointed to represent them if they cannot afford to hire an attorney. A Notice of Appeal must be filed in a timely manner or the right to appeal is lost. The filing time is generally within a week to ten days of the entry of judgment.

- A defendant may base an appeal on errors that occurred during the plea bargaining process, at trial or sentencing.

If you pled guilty in exchange for certain promises made by the government and those promises were not kept, you may have a legitimate issue of appeal.

HABEAS CORPUS

Habeas Corpus is a challenge to the legality of your conviction or sentence. Individual states may have habeas corpus proceedings, however, this book concentrates on federal habeas corpus which involves asking a federal court to review decisions made by a state court or other federal courts. Unlike a direct appeal, a habeas corpus action is not limited to only those errors in the court record. It is a review of conviction or sentencing proceedings to determine if there were any violations of the U.S. Constitution or federal laws. Some important aspects of habeas corpus include:

- Habeas Corpus actions are subject to strict filing deadlines. You generally have only one year to file your action.

- The method for filing a habeas corpus action is slightly different for state and federal prisoners. State prisoners file a petition for writ of habeas corpus while federal prisoners use what is called a 2255 Motion.

- In addition to challenging a sentence or conviction, habeas corpus actions may be used to challenge the way a sentence is being administered by a prison or penal institution.

- It is possible to appeal when your habeas corpus petition or motions is denied.

PETITION THE U.S. SUPREME COURT

The highest court in the nation is sometimes the last stop for prisoners wishing to challenge a sentence or conviction. The U.S. Supreme Court accepts only a small number of cases for review, but over the years there have been a fair number of prisoner cases selected. The high court is most likely to review cases involving conflicts between lower courts or presenting new or unique legal questions. Some important aspects of petitioning the U.S. Supreme court include:

- When you ask the U.S. Supreme Court to review your case, you file what is called a petition for writ of certiorari. If the court decides to hear your case, they grant certiorari.

- The U.S. Supreme Court has special rules for individuals who cannot afford to pay court fees and costs. You cannot be denied access to the U.S. Supreme Court because you do not have the money to pay for an attorney or court fees.

- They will deny you for being ignorant of the law and missing the time restraints causing someone with a life sentence that may be innocent to stay in prison for the rest of their lives. Just think about it for a minute say that you were completely innocent something that America wants most of its citizens to believe never occurs and you can't show that there were technicalities made in your case. The courts will uphold your conviction because you couldn't show any technicalities were made. That doesn't mean that you were guilty of the crime you were charged with, all that means is that they didn't make any mistakes in the process of prosecuting you therefore the Appellate Courts affirm the conviction. It doesn't have anything to do with whether or not you're guilty or not. So for many people in prison when they are denied their first level of appeals often and in most cases do not have the legal minds to continue forward and their appointed attorneys informs them that they are forbidden to represent them any further. So I disagree strongly that if you cannot afford to pay court fees and costs you cannot be denied access to the U.S. Supreme Court. You usually will be denied based on your ignorance of the law. The chances of someone getting this far in the process before being shot down is slim and none, because the system usually will decide much earlier on that your appeal does not have the merit in which to proceed.

- If the U.S. Supreme Court accepts your case, there is a good chance that an attorney will be appointed to represent you.

Now, really, what chance does someone growing up in the inner city, like scores of young men and women, have to understand the law the way so many lawyers who went to law school and studied for many years do?

My cellmate and I hadn't been on fish row three weeks before he received a letter from his attorney informing him that his case had been overturned on direct appeal, meaning the appellate court judges agreed with his attorney that there were mistakes made during the trial process. Again, that doesn't mean that he was innocent or guilty, only that the trial judge allowed an error or errors to occur during his trial, so the appellate court judges agreed to allow him relief, and he was released.

It was about a month before I was allowed to go to the yard with all the other prisoners. Before we could be let out, prisoners on fish row had to go to the laundry to get our state-issued clothing. Correctional Officers escorted us to the main line, in a single file line through the prison yard, in between hundreds of unfamiliar faces looking as malicious as they could. I took great pleasure in making sure I didn't break eye contact with anyone who looked into my eyes. I wasn't going to allow anyone to misread my heart.

Walking over to the laundry room, I noticed that the Bloods and the Crips wore their rags on their heads, out of their pockets, any and everywhere they could find a place to put them. I thought, *There are quite a few Mr. Low's around here.* I could see I would need to start back lifting weights, to build up strength to survive in hand to hand combat, because these dudes were much bigger than I was. I hadn't seen so many big men since I stood around and watched my cousin Big John lifting weights at his house with Baby Alton and the other Crips.

The prisoner working the laundry window asked what size I wore. I needed to get a big shirt to make myself appear much larger than I actually was. The process went like this:

"What size shirt?"

"Hmmm, 15."

"What size pants?"

"Hmmm, 32/34."

"What size shorts?"

"Hmmm, Large."

"What color rag do you want?"

"What?"

"What color rag do you want?"

"Blue!!"

"What size shoe?"

"8 1/2."

"What size T-shirts?"

"Large."

"Next."

I walked away from the window, the blue rag in my top pocket to be sure no one would be able to miss it. "Chitty Chitty Bang Bang, Nothing But A Crip Thang."

It didn't occur to me at the time that CDC was promoting the gang life by identifying all the members of the Crips and Bloods with the blue or red rags. We all went to the window often, to make sure everyone knew what we represented. This was complete foolishness on our part, and over time, it came back to haunt us all. Just as our ancestors had been hoodwinked, we were being outplayed intellectually. We thought we were soldiers for our causes, which we all loved profoundly; however, the causes we were representing were CDC's. They controlled everything we did and knew about all things that everyone did.

Once back in the cell, we were allowed to go to the yard with the general population. I went with my blue rag hanging out of my left back pocket. Poppa and Turtle greeted me, and we talked about all the things we all had been through since we last saw each other, and that Big Treach had gotten the Death Penalty. They told me about the dos and don'ts around there, and how a group of Black prisoners called The Black Guerrilla Family was at war with Mexican Mafia over something I didn't think made any sense. From my childhood to the present time, my experience with Mexicans had been combative, because many of them didn't like Blacks. So in my mind the war was about race.

The Crips and Bloods weren't involved; it was strictly between those two groups. I asked why it was like that. The Blacks from juvenile halls, camps, Y.A.'s, and county jails, always fought together. But in Folsom it was different, because The Black Guerrilla Family had been attacking the Crips since they began coming to prison in the mid 70's, alleging that the Crips were a destructive movement in the Black communities, causing separation. The Black Guerrilla Family wanted to eliminate the Crips by any means necessary, so the Crips didn't support them.

When I reached the yard, it was like being introduced to the Super Bowl starting lineup, psychologically insane as that was. I had finally made it to where most of the Original Crips were, and in my mind there could be only good that came out of that situation.

I wanted to be like all the legendary Crips I had heard about when I was a little boy. I met Big Bam from 83rd Hoover, Vertise Swan from East Coast Crips (one of the founders of the Crips), Bitter Dog Bruno from Compton Crips, Zig Zag from 112th Street Hoovers, Trouble Man from 118th Street, Chili from Main Street, Bull Dog from 83rd St. Hoover Crips, Larry Don from 43rd Street Avalon Crips, Big Ant from Compton Crips, Big Choo from 52nd Street Broadway Crips, Big Satan from Harlem 30's, Big Mumphy from Rolling 60's Crips, Big Bebop from Santana Block Compton Crips, Big Speedy from Back Street Crips, Big Buster from East Side Crips, Big Frog from 43rd Street Crips, Big Foster from 62nd Street East Coast Crips, Big Lavell from 120th Street Raymond Ave Crips, Big Zoom from 53rd Street Avalon Crips, and many others.

Folsom yard was quite small for all the prisoners it housed. Every time I went to the yard it felt like something awful was going to happen. Folsom, true to form, housed some sick-minded individuals. Big Foster had been incarcerated for murder since 1979, so he was anxious to hear what was happening on the street. We talked about what he had missed and what I was about to miss myself. I told him that I had been convicted for 5 counts of attempted murder that I hadn't committed.

Big Foster wanted me to move into his cell in 3 building as soon as I came off fish row. I told him I would, but before I was able to, I was moved to 2 building with a brother named Marvin out of Compton. Marvin wasn't a gang member, but he hung amongst Crips. He was laid back, while I was out of control, going nowhere fast. We were different in every way.

Marvin also gave me the rundown of the joint. He said, "La La, in a little while there's going to be this punk coming to the cell asking you if you need anything. Tell him no, you don't need nothing." I asked Marvin how the guy knew that I was there. Marvin said, "He's the clerk in the building, so he knows when everybody comes and goes." Sure enough, before I could finish my inquiry of Marvin, here came the punk. He said, "Hey youngsta, you need anything? Soap, lotion, toothpaste, anything?"

In prison, in the 60's, 70's, and 80's, one of the rules to follow to be on the safe side was to not accept anything from someone you didn't know, because usually the person offering you something wanted something back in return - sex, or monetary returns with the prices inflated 1000%. They knew you couldn't pay the debts back, which put you in an unfavorable position. These were the same men that thought the Crips were dividing the Black communities in the inner cities. How ridiculous was that? It was awful for the Crips to fight amongst themselves, but constructive for the BGF to extort and rape other Blacks? Go figure. They felt like their ideals were law, and should be adhered to. But many other Blacks didn't feel that way.

Before I said no, I laughed so hard I almost cried a river of tears out of my eyes at the sight of this man who stood before me. He was an older man, approximately 60, blacker than night, bald, 5'7 in height, 190 lbs and no facial hair. In the face he looked like an old brute. He wore his pants so tight you could see the imprint of his testicles and penis. I think he's the first person I ever saw in skinny jeans. I stood at the cell door in disbelief that someone's grandfather was far away from home, soliciting sex from somebody's child. I thought, *This has got to be a damn joke*. But I knew scores of Black people didn't care about what others thought of them, and he was one of them. He just wanted to be pleasured, but it wasn't going to be by me.

I couldn't pass this one up. I said to him, "Nah man, I'm cool. What's your name?"

He said, "Sergeant."

I said, "Sergeant, like Sergeant At Arms?"

He said, "Yeah youngsta. I'm gonna come back and talk to you later."

I said, "Hold up! Sergeant, look, I don't fuck around with men. No disrespect intended, but don't come back to this cell for nothing!!"

Sergeant looked at me and swayed off like you don't know what you're missing. I told my cellmate, "That's somebody grandfather!" We laughed up a storm.

Marvin told me that Sergeant was no joke; he be pulling knives on people, taking their dicks from them. I told Marvin, you can't take no man dick, they're giving it to him, saying that he pulled a knife on them as an excuse to engage in homosexual activities. I knew if he pulled a knife on me, he'd have to use it, and still wouldn't get my dick. Sergeant never came back to my cell.

It was basketball season and the Los Angeles Lakers were playing the Philadelphia 76ers, the Malone and Doctor J years. My cellmate and I watched the game and laughed about the one-sided affair. The 76ers were a bit too much for the Lakers, sweeping them in the series, 4-0. We also talked about the street and the things we missed most. I found myself thinking about my little brother a lot. I thought it was unfair that I had to spend one day in jail for the shit I had been convicted of. I also thought about my mother. I missed her a great deal; she had always been my favorite person in the world, so I knew she felt bad for me. But the strangest thing of all was that I started thinking about Jackie as if she was my girlfriend, and we had never had a relationship like that. Because of that, I learned that someone may believe people are together because they see them with one another, but that doesn't make it so. Jackie and I had never been together intimately at that time, but I thought of her as my girlfriend. I shared most of my concerns with her about wanting to be freed, and what my plans were when I got out. Jackie shared in my dreams, making me believe she was inclined to further our relationship. We started what I thought was a meaningful relationship, and I began thinking she was my girlfriend. But reality and illusion aren't that different from each other. I later learned that people may believe some things that aren't real, and they may carry on in life believing in that illusion. I was one that believed in the illusion. Deceptive as my relationship was to Jackie, I still felt that loyalty was important and that she should honor that request towards me, but I didn't have to honor that towards her.

I was too young to recognize that life goes on, and that people in society have lives to live and they don't sit around suffering with those that are convicted, as many of us in prison think they do. Jackie wasn't suffering. I didn't know it, but she had a boyfriend named Raymond, from Harlem 30's. I knew Raymond from the street. He ran with Killowatt from Harlem, and we kicked it together on a few occasions. But I didn't know Jackie was talking to him at that time. I learned that many years later.

AMERICA'S CONDUCT

Marvin couldn't get over the fact that I kept saying that I was innocent. He kept asking me was I really innocent, or just saying that I was. I told him every time that I was innocent, but he just couldn't believe it. I found it strange that many of us who were Black in America, knowing the history of America towards Blacks, still couldn't believe America would send innocent people to jail. Marvin did his time mainly by making wine and drinking himself into a false world of blissfulness. I had stopped drinking and smoking cigarettes in the Los Angeles County Jail when I got in that brutal fight with Tony Jake from the 30's, so I didn't share in his indulgence.

I eventually told Marvin that I was going to move in with Big Foster. Big Foster was an angry man. He also said he was innocent of the crime he had been convicted of, and he acted like he was. He talked about his innocence more than I did mine. He tried to tell me to study my case, and go to the library as much as I could, but I felt like that process would take care of itself. I wanted to go to the yard to meet all the Crips I hadn't met. Big Foster used to tell me that when I found myself stuck in there ten years from now, I'd wish I had started studying law. I didn't even think that was a possibility, ten years. I was thinking next year I would be out on my appeal, and there he was talking about ten years from now.

I met Big Mumpy from Rollin 60's Neighborhood Crips. He was one of those Crips who always stayed neat, his pants and shirt pressed, shoes shiny. He wore a blue rag in his top shirt pocket, one on his head, one in his back pocket, and he carried one in his hand. If he was drinking coffee, one would be tied around his coffee cup. There would never be any mistaking what was in Mumpy's heart. He walked deliberately slow, talked ice-water cool, and was fun to be around.

Then you had Bebop, from Santana Block Crips. He stood 5'7, 130 lbs. I was 19 years old, so he had to be 30 years old at the time. Bop was draped in black and blue rags. To this day I have never seen anyone wear more rags at a time than Bebop. I met Butcher and Little Billy from Grape, Crip Dog from Q102 and Doc from Harlem. Doc was one of a kind in so many ways. Devil, from 107 Hoover Crips, was the same Devil that the Underground Crips thought I was when I took Vivian home for the first time. There was Bobby Mason, aka Big Satan from Harlem 30's, Lil Bam from 74 Hoover Crips and Big Bam from 83rd Hoover Crips. Bam was one of my instructors on the history of the Crips. I questioned him to death about the history of the Crips. I thought he would get tired of me, but he never did. In fact, he welcomed my questions. He often said I was one of only a few youngsters who wanted to know what it was I was representing, so he loved talking to me about the creation of the Crips. Big Rider from 60's, he was a shit starter, through and through. I wasn't mad at him, that's just who he was. Big Tim from 43rd Street Crips was a true East Side Crip. He had a fight with Bull Dog from 83rd Street Hoover. Bull Dog was one of the original East Side Crips who was with Raymond Washington when he started the Crips at Fremont High School. Bull Dog was known for his brutality and ass-kicking skills. Tim stood his ground with Bull Dog, and I was impressed and started liking Tim a lot after that.

I eventually moved in with Foster in Three Building. Foster was truly different from all the other Crips. One day he'd be Mr. 6-Duece, and then the next day he'd be a pimp, walking down the tier in his long cotton shower robe and a pair of low cut leather house shoes, swinging his hand from one side to the other while he secured the robe with his off hand. I just laughed at him. He really cared about me, and never wanted me to be sunk by what was going on in prison. But I wanted to be sunk by the unknown goings-on in prison, because I wanted to be known for something in my life. Many black people were vilified by the government, so I wanted to stand for something, and be known for what I stood for. Foster had been there long enough to know that the very people I admired weren't worth admiring or respecting. But, as I had done 9 years earlier with my mother, I rejected his wisdom because I felt I had to make my own way in life.

Foster and I didn't stay cellmates long because the institution moved prisoners to buildings according to what kind of jobs they had been assigned to. I hadn't been assigned to any job, so I was moved to 2 building, with Mumpy from Rolling Sixties.

Abyss

The rest of my time at Folsom State Penitentiary consisted of madness. In there, anything you had done on the streets didn't count for nothing. You had to show in the prison that you were who you claimed yourself to be, whatever that may have been. I started volunteering to stab people who violated rules that we as Crips abided by.

One morning, I was supposed to stab this dude from Watts, because he had murdered one of Cisco's homeboys from Grape Street. Cisco didn't want to stab him because he felt like it would cause chaos between the gangs out of Watts, so he asked me to.

The night before I was supposed to stab the dude, he got wind of it. I was walking down the tier he lived on, and he asked me was I going to stab him. I was shocked that he asked me something like that, because if he truly believed I was, he could've stabbed me without warning. I told him hell nah, and where had he heard something like that from. He said he didn't believe it. Now, while he was questioning me about whether I was going to stab him, he was inside his cell wrapping magazines around his torso area with plastic wrap. I thought I was convincing enough to have deceived him so I didn't bother to think he would stab me.

The next morning on the yard I was going to stab him, so it didn't matter anyway. For breakfast, Big Mumpy wanted me to walk with him. I wanted to concentrate on the job I had to do that morning but Mumpy eventually convinced me to get up.

In the chow hall I looked for the victim. I spotted him sitting several tables away from me. I didn't think anything of it, because I knew a few hours later he would be nice and stabbed up. As I took my seat at the table, Warlock, from Main Street Mafia, sat with me. I told him to watch the dude and let me know if he got up at any time, so I could keep an eye on him. I wasn't concerned with him doing anything to me, but since he had questioned me the night before, he bore watching.

Before I could sit down good enough, I saw an impression on Warlock's face that was clearly a sign of distress. As I looked in the direction that Warlock was looking, it was too late. The victim that I had deemed mines, made me his instantly. I felt an impact to the back of my neck, like when I was in junior high school and the kids would walk up behind each other and slap their necks, playing. But this was a bit more serious. I immediately jumped up and began doing what I knew how to do quite well, kicking off into his ass. While we were fighting and he was stabbing me, I noticed that he had tied two bed springs around his wrist so that he wouldn't lose his weapons.

Cisco and Mumpy started beating this dude with their metal trays, but it didn't stop him. He continued to swing and we continued to beat him about the head, until the prison guard fired enough rounds in there to bring this battle to a halt. When the smoke cleared, I had small puncture wounds to the back of my neck and in the upper part of my chest. Cisco had suffered a puncture wound, I believe to his chest area, and the victimizer had several deep gashes over his eyes and head. Mumpy didn't have any wounds, and he never got discovered for his involvement, which shocked me because everybody in the kitchen saw who was directly involved.

Cisco and I went to the infirmary for an examination. I was asked to undress and then looked over by the physicians. It was determined that my injuries were superficial and didn't need treatment, but Cisco needed several stitches. The victimizer was treated for abrasions about the face and given stitches over his left eye.

Cisco and I were led off to the hole, a security unit where prisoners are housed for rule violations or housing concerns. I was placed in a cell with Bear, from Grape Street. Before all of this happened, Cisco and other Crips had tested me to see if I would stand up for myself by having Bear go into my cell and steal all of my property. As I walked up to the cell door, I saw Bear placing all my shit into a pillow case. I thought he had mistaken where he was at. I told him, "Cuzz that's my shit." He told me he knows who shit this is and that he was taking it. I had been through this shit in Y.A. and I knew what the outcome of this would be. I told him, "Cuzz you must be crazy. I'm going to beat your ass." I walked into the cell closed the bars behind me and commenced to beating Bear senseless. I knocked him to the ground, where he was semi-conscious. I started jumping off the toilet onto his head repeatedly. Cisco showed up telling me to stall Bear out, but I refused. I told Cisco, "This mf was trying to steal my shit." Cisco told me Bear was playing, that they had sent him in there to see what I would do. I still didn't care about any of that bullshit; I continued trying to kill his ass. Cisco continued to plead with me to let up off Bear. I finally did when I felt I had taught him a lesson and not the other way around. Bear and I hadn't said one word to each other after that incident.

Once inside the hole, out of nowhere my body gave out from the assault to it. I grabbed the end of the bunk to hold myself up until I was able to regain my strength. Immediately, Bear saw an opportunity to get me back for beating his ass senseless. He jumped up and grabbed my arm. I knew it was over for me; I couldn't win this battle. I was too weak. I would've given my all, but a victory wouldn't have come that time around, I'm sure of that.

But instead of jumping me, he asked if I needed help to get up onto the bed. I was relieved that this wasn't going to be one of the moments where I had to test my heart. I never worried about the roughness of any other man, because in my heart I have always believed in myself. And I had learned to battle under the supervision of Big Quake, so I had it in me to survive and never give other men recognition over my neighborhood under any circumstances.

Bear helped me up on top of the bunk. Once I lay down, he got up and said to me that he hadn't forgotten about me jumping on top of his head. I told him I didn't care if he forgot about it or not, I bet he wouldn't steal my shit again. It didn't matter to me that I was wounded; I wasn't going to turn into a punk.

Bear said, "I think I could get you right now, LaLa."

I told him, "You probably could but it's not like I'm going to stand there and let you do it."

I didn't want to fight and was hoping he didn't either. He said he was cool, that he shouldn't have done what Cisco and them put him up to.

Once I settled in, I started receiving kites messages, salutations from Crips that I hadn't met because they were in the hole for rule violations. Some of them said "What's up, comrade? I hope that you and the loved one, Cisco, are okay. Don't worry about cuzz that hit ya'll. We will take care of him as soon as he hits the yard." The only thing that caught my attention in the entire kite was the word "comrade." This was the first time I ever saw the word. I immediately asked Bear for a dictionary to look it up.

Comrade: a close friend; close companion; person who shares interests and activities in common with others.

I thought then that I had met some real loyal Crips, who were brought up like Raymond and the other Crips, who had each other's back when one of them got themselves into situations. They were always there for one another and that act of concern reminded me of that. The kites kept coming. "What's up comrade? This is such and such. I heard what happened are you alright?" These were dudes I didn't know, showing their interest in me. I wasn't in the hole for a rule violation. They had me down as a victim so I wouldn't be staying back there for a long period of time. They just had to take me to classification to see if I wanted to go back out there or not. The kites never stopped coming, "What's up La La? Do you need deodorant, toothpaste, soap, or anything to read?" When I was a young boy, far away from ever coming to prison, I had always been told not to ever accept letters or other materials from people you didn't know because the BGF's did most of their recruiting this way. They would send their constitution to someone's cell, having the person believing they're going to be given something else and when they get the constitution, they are members of the BGF. 99% of the people didn't have the courage to tell them to fuck themselves, because they had abused so many people in prison. They had established a reputation for being brutal, so the fear was there. But surely the Crips weren't scared of them; I knew I sure as hell wasn't. This one particular dude asked me if I needed something to read. I told him yeah. Now all the time I had known this dude I always thought of him as being a Crip, and one of the baddest I had ever encountered. This would be one of the lessons I would take with me the rest of my life. The dude sent me a magazine with an envelope inside. I thought it was more of this Crip love, but that wasn't the case. It was something I couldn't accept, just as clear as rice paper. Without hesitation, I threw it outside the bars onto the tier. The person that sent it to me asked if I had seen the envelope inside the book. I yelled I had, and that I threw it on the tier. He came close to losing his mind. He yelled down at me, "Fish it in!" Fishing was when the prisoners tied together string, torn sheets or whatever else they could assemble with a weight of some sort on the end of it, to connect to the object you're trying to retrieve. In this case it was something they didn't want the police to get their hands on. Now, the love, that moments earlier I thought was genuine, had instantly turned into hate. They all started yelling at me "La La, get that envelope off the tier." Mind you, these dudes were supposed to be Crips, but they weren't; they all were imposters pretending to be Crips. Because of that I learned to believe little of what I heard, and none of what I saw. I started yelling back at them, "I'm from East Coast Crips 6-Duece." I meant every word of it. Whatever tactics they were using on the other dudes weren't going to work on me. I was a real Crip in my heart. Now that I knew these dudes' secrets, I would forever be their enemy unless I came over to their side, which was never going to happen.

I think I stayed in the hole no more than seven days before they released me back to general population. In seven days I had gained many enemies, because I wouldn't pretend to be a Crip and deceive other Crips into becoming what they were, as many of these dudes were doing.

When I went back to the main line I found Big Foster and told him what had happened while I was in the hole. He told me to leave that shit alone, and just do what I was doing before. I asked him, did he know anything about that. He said yeah, that's why he wanted me to concentrate on getting out of there, but for me not to worry about it, because he was riding with me.

I wasn't satisfied with that response. I wanted him to feel like me and put all of these dudes out there for all the Crips to know that they weren't Crips. But the strangest things were happening. These very dudes were calling the shots on the Crips at Folsom. I told Papa and Turtle that I wasn't going to listen to shit they said, I know what they are.

Meanwhile, there was actually a war going on with the BGF's and the Mexican Mafia. I watched, along with the rest of the Crips, as the Mexican Mafia took down one BGF after the next. To me it didn't matter because they weren't Crips, and I had always believed if the Mexican Mafia got into a confrontation with the Crips there was no way they could defeat us. Well it wouldn't be long before that belief would be put to the test.

After I got out of the hole I was moved into a cell with Lavell Player from Raymond Ave. 120th Street Crips. He was one of those cellmates who constantly practiced some sort of defensive maneuvers, so we stayed at it in the cell. Lavell would roll up newspaper so tight it looked and felt like a police billy club. He would take a pencil, then shave all the lead of it off, dip the end of the rolled up paper into wet lead. He'd give me a billy club, himself one, then we came at each other as if we were stabbing one another. If you had any markings on you, it would show that you weren't able to defend yourself. Lavell would have a thousand markings on him, but would swear to God I hadn't touched him once.

The BGF was being dismantled by the Mexican Mafia. In fairness to them, the administration had locked up their warriors, and left the most inexperienced of their organization out there on the main line. They did have some members that would've eaten the Mexican Mafia's members head off for breakfast and lunch, but they were in the hole. Finally, the dudes pretending to be Crips couldn't stand by any longer and watch. They had orders from their superiors to act.

Several of these fake Crips had gotten out of the hole and were mingling with the Crips on the mainline, with every intention of getting involved in the war. But they couldn't say anything to the actual Crips on the main line, because the Crips hated the BGFs with a passion, and wouldn't have allowed their members to fight on the side of the BGF.

One day we all were on the yard and you could tell something was not right, because certain dudes kept huddling up. But since there were Crips amongst them, it was not so alarming. Of course, the Crips with them were fake Crips, and the real Crips had no idea they had been hoodwinked.

This group of men all walked off the yard into the building, and the next thing we heard on the yard was an alarm. That always meant something had taken place that required the police attention. When the alarm went off, the entire population had to get down. We laid out on the yard in the prone position, waiting to find out exactly what had happened. We didn't have to wait long. All five of these men were escorted by correctional officers in handcuffs. We knew they had been involved in something, but we just didn't know what.

The police started clearing the yard making us all go back into our assigned cells. On the way in, we learned these dudes had stabbed an elderly man of Mexican descent. That meant one thing - the Crips were going to see what they were made of because it was now war. I always wanted to test our strengths up against the Mexican Mafia, because our numbers were overwhelming compared to theirs, but I would later learn numbers don't mean anything. It's what's in a person's heart that counts for everything. We didn't stay locked down long at all. They released the 3rd tier first in Three Building, and the alarm went off as quickly as they opened the doors. The Mexicans didn't waste any time; they stabbed a Crip immediately and very badly. After the first Crip was stabbed in the war, the institution was placed on modified program, which meant the authorities controlled all movement, going and coming. When it was time to release the inmates to chow, they would come by each cell and strip out the Black and Mexican prisoners. I had seen many of the Mexicans' tricks during the war with the BGFs, so I knew how fearless they were, and I wasn't trying to be victimized by any of them.

I wrote Straw, and told him to put his knife inside his shoe and we would attack the Mexicans inside the chow hall. Straw wanted to wait until we got back on the tier. I told him we might not have time to make it to the chow hall let alone back to the tier, but he was convinced that we could.

Straw and I made it to the chow hall with our knives, the same chow hall where I had been stabbed not long before. I remember telling myself after that day that I would never allow someone to get off first, so that was heavily on my mind. I told Straw, "Look, cuzz, I'm going to go ahead and get off now. You just get down after me." He was adamant about waiting until we went back up the tier. I told him, "Cuzz, don't you see those Mexicans looking at us? They're thinking about the same thing we are, cuzz. I'll wait til we get out of the chow hall, but as soon as we get to the stairs, I'm getting off." I took my knife out of my shoe inside the chow hall but Straw still hadn't got his out when three of them came at us. Lucky for me, I was ready, and all the practice with Lavell paid off. When the smoke cleared, Straw had been stabbed in his arm, and two Mexicans had been stabbed in their upper torso. The police saw the incident, but didn't know who stabbed who, so they sent me and Straw to the Emergency Housing Unit, the EHU. This unit was for all the prisoners they could identify as Crips or Mexican Mafia members. When I arrived, there were at least two hundred Crips and Mexican Mafia members. Straw went to the hospital and came later. Everyone was informed of what was expected of them, and how not to make any mistake walking to and from our cells during showers or on our way to the yard.

The Crips leadership was always in direct communication with the Mafia leadership. What was weird about all of this to me was once we got over there in direct contact with the Mexican Mafia, the war seemed to stop and all sort of rules were given to us by the Crip leadership as to what we could and couldn't do. But all of the rules appeared to be not to our advantage. For instance, we were told we couldn't stab one of them going to the shower, which we were more than capable of doing. We were told that in EHU the war was off, and that we would handle our business when we were released back to the main line. Many of the Mexican Mafia members were still in general population, stabbing as many blacks as they could while we had been negotiated into a stalemate. For me that was the turning point. I vowed never to listen to anyone not directly from East Coast Crips, because it was clear that the Crip leadership was either scared or respected the Mafia too much. The shortest time an individual was housed in EHU was six months, so we were out of commission for that period of time without any fighting. But every single time we heard an alarm go off and looked out the window, we saw a Black being carried off. Sometimes they were stabbing innocent Blacks, and then telling us that they'd made a mistake. It was clear to me that the Mafia had negotiated their safety over in EHU, where the core of their leadership was vulnerable to being hurt by Crips who would have attempted to kill them given the opportunity. But it wasn't so clear back then, as it is today, that the Crips leadership was under direct control of these imposters, and all of us who were genuine street thugs, East or West Side Crips didn't have a clue we were being played by these traitors. My entire time in EHU I hung out with Q-Tip, from Raymond Ave Crips. We lifted weights, boxed some and talked about how we were going to destroy the Mafia the first chance we got.

The administration had begun releasing prisoners of both sides back to general population without warning, so everyone had to be ready. It was crazy in prison. Everything is secretive; it's important to never allow anyone of the other race see what you're doing, because it could be the difference between life and death. But the strangest thing started happening over there. Everyone stopped caring about practicing discretion, and began openly making and sharpening knives for everyone to see, making it understood madness and murder was in full effect.

We had some of the best knife makers in the prison, I was certain of that, and they didn't fail us. They were sending out, to each and all, 9 inches of pure iron, with points that were clearly intended to do one thing.

Before someone was released to the main line, they would leave the building, telling others "I'll be back in five minutes", indicating that they were going out there to get their man, so they wouldn't be on the main line for long.

I was always down emotionally, because I felt like we were clearly losing the war. But one of my favorite moments was when they released some Hoovers from EHU, and they all were soldiers for this Cripping. Big Devil, Boo, Art, Swallon, Cat Caesar (EC) and Chris from West Coast Long Beach Crips they all went out there. The police used to take bets on who would stay out there or who wouldn't. I hoped they had made a wager against them. We all stood by our cell doors waiting to hear the alarm go off, hoping it wasn't going to be them being carried off to the hospital.

We didn't have to wait long before the alarm sounded. Everyone looked out of the windows down on the yard to see who the police would be carrying off the yard. Someone on the fifth tier starting screaming out Crips CA, CA, CA, CA, CA, CA, CA, RIP!!!! Then the entire building sounded off Crip, Crip, Crip, Crip. The

Hoovers had pumped life back into our movement and that was a turning point in the war for us.

Early one morning Big Sadd yelled down to me that he was going back to general population. The night before we had thought it was our turn, so Ty Sticc and Boss Hog from Neighborhood Crips in San Diego sent us two 9 inch knives. I had hidden mines where the police would never find it. Big Sadd is my homeboy from East Coast Crips, so I was worried that he was going out there without me. I told him, "You know what time it is, cuzz." Minutes later the police came by my cell informing me that I too would be going to the main line with Big Sadd. I was elated, and Sadd was also, because he knew he would be with someone who would stay all the way down with him.

On our way out, the Crips in EHU were telling us to make them proud. Without question, I had every intention of doing just that, even though I knew most of them weren't really Crips. But for the real Crips, I would stand up. When we left the building, Sadd and I were told we would be going to Two Building, but in separate cells. I was moved to the first tier and Sadd was moved to the second tier directly over me. Sadd worried about me because of my lack of concern about the danger I was facing. We both left EHU with blue rags on us everywhere. The mainline was on modified program, meaning everything was controlled by the administration, all movements.

When I came to the cell, there was this dude named Dallas. He claimed he was from Texas. He had Red rags hanging all over the cell; since the Bloods weren't involved in the war Dallas attempted to align himself with them. I asked him, was he a Blood? He said no. I told him to take them rags down and put these up. I gave him just as many blue rags as there were red ones up. Dallas asked me did I know that the Crips and Mexicans were at war. I asked him who was on the tier. He told me that it was only elderly Mexicans. I didn't want to stab an elderly man, even though the Mafia was stabbing elderly black men.

I started tying blue rags on the outside of the bars so when the Mexicans in Three Building walked past they wouldn't be able to miss seeing them. This was suicidal, Dallas thought, but I didn't agree with that. It would've been suicidal if my heart wasn't into it, but I was quite serious. From childhood I had been fighting this battle, and I knew from the streets they couldn't stand up to this Cripping if the Crips fought them. But because these dudes had compromised their beliefs in the Crips, and mixed an idea different from Raymond Washington's in our movement, this is what we ended up with - fear.

They had released Three Building for chow. As they passed by Two Building, every single prisoner had to pass by my cell. I stood in front of the cell bars and noticed Dallas was hiding his face under the covers. I told him, "Cuzz, you're a scary mf." He began telling me how the Crips on the mainline were acting like they were Christians and Muslims because the Mexicans were stabbing them. I told him they aren't Crips, that a Crip would never do any shit like that. As the Mexicans in Three Building passed my cell, they all were doing a double look, like they couldn't believe what they were seeing. They were so accustomed to seeing this cell filled with red rags, this couldn't be the same cell. One thing I can say about the Mafia, they done all of their homework and they took care of their business.

They began doubling back to my cell, but knew they had no chance of getting me because they only released one building at a time. This was more to identify who I was. When they doubled back, I'd be standing in front of the cell with my 9 inch knives out, telling them that I was going kill one of you mf's as soon as the cell door opened. They couldn't contain themselves; they couldn't believe I was bold enough to display my rags outside the bars and had the nerve to be standing there threatening them.

They started talking Spanish to a Mexican right above me, who I knew from my cellmate, Dallas, ran the building for them. I immediately told Sadd that he was on the tier with the shot caller, and that's who I want to get at chow time.

Unfortunate for me another Black had been stabbed in Three Building on his way to chow, which caused the prison to go back on lockdown. While we were locked down, I was transferred to Tracy State Prison (DVI). The administration had put most of us in EHU up for transfer, so I didn't stay out on the mainline longer than five days, and we were on lockdown the entire time. The night I was leaving, Dallas was happy to see me go, and sad to see me go.

He told me, "They don't have any Blacks out there that will stand up to the Mexicans.

I said, "You can't worry about the next man. Every man is different, you have to worry about yourself. You can make a difference."

While I was on my way out, the Mexicans tried to spear me with a rod, which I saw a mile away. They didn't get close, but it showed their determination and I respected that. I sent Sadd my knife, and told him to be careful. I learned later he had transferred on lockdown to Soledad State Prison.

The two years I spent in Folsom was something no young man should ever have to experience. I was an innocent man sent to the depths of hell. And I started to emulate the behavior of it.

Gladiator School

1985. We arrived at DVI-Deuel Vocational Institution (Tracy). Tracy was the complete opposite of Folsom in two ways that I noticed instantly. First, Folsom was much more sophisticated in plots against other prisoners. At Tracy, it was basically black and white; what you saw was usually what you got. Two, in DVI there were often stabbings, but none like the stabbings in Folsom. Folsom prisoners had been dipped in savagery, and weren't looking to be corrected. One more thing I noticed at Tracy, the security was a bit relaxed. The guards weren't always following us around with guns, so it gave the appearance that we could get away with more than we could at Folsom.

Tracy was notorious for the Blood and Crips war against one another. When I got there, the war was not as active as it had been, because the Crips had removed most of the Bloods off the yard. The ones that remained disclaimed their neighborhoods, and pretended not to be gang members. One of my close friends, Pee Wee, from 69th Street East Coast Crips, had been murdered there not long before I arrived, so I thought that I would be able to get more information about how he was killed and who had actually killed him.

Now that I was at Tracy, I didn't have to worry about being stabbed every minute on the minute, so I felt much more relaxed and focused on getting out of prison. My appeal on the direct level had been denied, which I was told I should expect. But I hadn't expected it; even though I was in jail myself, I refused to believe innocent people went to jail. I still believed the system would do the right thing and that they would eventually recognize their mistake and I'd be on my merry way. No such thing happened at Tracy. I lost my last appeal and would have to do the complete sentence that was given to me by the judge, because my family didn't have any resources to pursue my arguments of total innocence.

I came to Tracy with several Crips who were older than I was, and people I was in the Los Angeles County Jail with that were influential members from their neighborhoods. One dude in particular was a shot caller in the County Jail out of Watts. I won't disgrace his name, although I should; for the sake of decency I'll spare him. When we were in the county jail, he was one of a very few that gave orders to attack the BGF's and one alleged gangster out of Pasadena named Ray. He was allegedly a king pin and quite ruthless. I saw the two of them meet up in D-Wing, a housing unit. Ray Ray saw my homeboy and approached him. I already knew who Ray Ray was and was given a knife to stab him if he attempted to attack my homeboy. Ray Ray was supposed to be extremely good with his hands, so I was warned to be careful. I thought to myself, how good could he be if he had no idea who I was, and no clue to what my intention was? Nevertheless the two of them approached one another and this is how that encounter went.

Ray Ray, "Say man don't I know you from the county jail?"

My homeboy, "Yeah I was in junior high power."

Ray Ray, "Oh yeah, you was sending your homeboys at my people on the mainline."

My homeboy, "Nah man, it wasn't like that."

Ray Ray, "Yes it was. I couldn't get at ya'll like I wanted to because I was in high power." High Power is a unit that houses prisoners the deputies feel are too dangerous to be housed around other prisoners. And junior high power is a step below high power.

My homeboy, "Cuzz, that was in the county jail, I'm not trippin down here. I came down here to kick it."

Ray Ray, "Fuck that shit man, you and I can get down head up. We don't have to involve anyone else in our shit."

My homeboy, "Nah man, I'm cool."

Ray Ray, "Okay blood, you know what time it is."

Now just stop to think for one minute. Ray Ray didn't know I was in position to stab the shit out of him. And he wasn't worried about that possibility at all, to call out my homeboy who instructed me to post up in security for him. In my presence, he punk the game by being challenged by Ray Ray and declining to get down with him. I walked away, thinking to myself Ray Ray was a man willing to get down for his anyplace, anytime, with whoever. But for my homeboy, I lost all the respect one man could give another human-being. I told him immediately he needed to step back and I would run all this shit around here. He agreed, and I was the captain of the ship at the tender age of 21.

All of us that had been sent down to Tracy from Folsom were sent to East Hall, which is an orientation building for the newcomers. There I learned that Tracy was filled with BGF's members, and favored the Bloods over the Crips. Go figure. The Bloods and Crips represented the same things; the only difference was the color of the rags, which we wore to distinguish which side we were on. Many people believe that the Bloods and Crips fight over colors, which isn't true. The colors only identify which side you are representing. But the BGF's were closer to the Bloods.

There on fish row I ran into Big Bubble, one of the co-founders of my neighborhood. When I saw him, he was being Mr. Willie Majors, the second coolest dude on the planet, Big Sadd being the first, bar none. Bubble's wife had just been killed on the streets in what many of us believed to be retaliation for a dispute with a rival gang. He was hurting, but he had to push forward because of where he was. As bad as he felt, it was impossible for him to show any sign of weakness around people who had no sympathy to give. Big Bubble and my homeboy Big T, from 89th Street Neighborhood East Coast Crips, were cellmates. I knew T from the streets. Lil C, Co Co and I were at his house when we were arrested for allegedly shooting the Mexicans. So I was happy to see them both.

Tracy is up north (Northern California), and the BGF have always had their foot dug into the foundation of that institution. When I got to Tracy, I had already gotten older mentally. The Mexican Mafia forced me to grow up faster than I would've liked.

I moved in the cell with my big homie, Mr. Major. Now this was an awkward situation for me to be in because I was literally Big Bubble's little homeboy, but now I was in charge of running a prison of Crips which included him.

On the flip side, I had grown up in the 3 years I had been in prison, being exposed to the madness and evil that lay in grown men's hearts. By force I was subjected to it, and I was compelled to embrace it in order to survive. That is what I truly believed.

I was now a 30 year old man at the age of 21, and was confident I could handle the position given to me, or should I say taken by me. I was now the man I wanted to be. I thought about Big Quake, Big John and Baby Alton how they would be proud that I had become somebody in life. I was now a gang leader, responsible for rebellion against the system. It was my duty to be my father's child, and I intended to represent it fully. I had seen grown men crumble under pressure, get weak and refuse to come out of their cell during wars against other prisoners. I had witnessed men in power engage in homosexual activities, lie, cheat, manipulate, deceive, and abuse the human spirit. I had lost complete trust in everyone except myself. I knew I wouldn't let myself down. I was obligated to love myself and stand on my own two feet like a man, the way I had witnessed Ray Ray stand on his with my homeboy. I refused to become weak like those around me. I was going to make my father proud of my heart.

Bubble and I sat down and talked. I told him I knew my place from 62nd Street. I knew that he was my big homie, and I would never forget that, but I trusted myself and I ran my own life. I told him prison was different from where we come from. I refused to allow men from other areas to run me, and since I wasn't around our immediate homies, I had to represent me. He understood, and was proud to see one of his lil' homies from 6-Duece come to prison and not transform into something he wasn't.

AMERICA'S CONDUCT

I told Big Bubble, "When I was younger growing up, I watched everything they did. I remember those speeches they gave us, and took them to heart. I believe in 6-Duece and I believe in the cause Lil Oscar died for. I believe a man should have the courage and strength to stand up for himself under any circumstance. Win, lose or draw, a man should at least have the courage to try. I refuse to depend on anyone other than myself to carry out that conviction. I will do it without fear or hesitation. I believe fully in what the Crips stand for; I believe in it differently than many others did. I had never mistreated anyone outside of the rule that governed the Crips. I had never rat packed anyone; all of my battles had been toe to toe. My heart isn't like the rest of the people around me. I believe I can do great things for the movement of the Crips, and I will strive to accomplish it. I refuse to become anything like the people I met in Folsom State Prison. Many of those men had betrayed Raymond's love and ideas for the Crips. I, on the other hand, am not about to betray his legacy." I told Bubble I wouldn't allow those serpents around me to stop me from teaching the young Crips what it meant to be a Crip.

Bubble understood, "You little mf, you got all these mf's listening to you in here. I ain't trippin." I told him, "Cuzz, don't take it the wrong way. I know my place with 62nd Street. This ain't the Hood, this is prison, cuzz. I'm not going to let these serpents get me killed in here, cuzz. I have to push the Hood the way I was taught by Big Quake in order to survive."

Big Bubble was cool with it. Every time I came off the yard into the cell, I would let Bubble know I'm still his little homie, and I didn't treat him as if he was beneath me. Bubble knew I was still his young homeboy and never attempted to pretend otherwise. I would always question him about the beginnings of our neighborhood, and this is when he would remind me that I came after him. I took joy in watching him shine and be the leader that I knew he was.

Tracy was run quite efficiently by the Crips that were already there before us. They were winning a war with the Bloods, but had lost two Crips in death for reasons that hadn't been explained to my satisfaction. I truly believed that the Crips were some bad motherfuckers, so to me it was crazy to see our enemies try us in this way.

With all the Crips there, getting an understanding on how we were going to function on the line together was a balancing act, because scores of other Crips felt as I did. There were gang leaders from other neighborhoods that were equally qualified to run the prison, and were revered by their young homies, so this had to be done with respect, yet a firm hand, making sure everyone knew it was Crip business and not mines I intended to carry out. Meeting after meeting, we finally understood it was us against everyone else and we would do it together.

The BGF had been supporting the Bloods on the under, but it didn't help them any; we obliterated them. I have always been one to give credit to any person that has it coming no matter what they're representing. When I was at Tracy, the Bloods didn't put up a fight. They would come to the main line to get stabbed as opposed to fighting for themselves as the Crips did.

Now, how was self-hate manifesting itself thus far? How had it come to this in America? How had we forgotten the way America was treating us collectively as Black people? Why did we have so much dislike for each other, and take so much pride in harming one another like it was a sport?

There were many Crips that had been reputable: Big Turtle, Bird Doc, Ron Ron, and Bebop from Santana Blocc Crips. K-Rock, Pretty Boy, Warlock (from Shotgun), G-Man (69th Street), Loco (190), N-Dog (30), Lil Looney, and G-Bob from Rolling Sixties Neighborhood Crips. Dennis Johnson, Ali, Andy D, Capone, Hilly, Lefty and Big Jimbo from Harlem 30's Crips. Big Diamond, from Eight Tray Gangsters. Mudd from Menlo Crips. Kiko, 40 ounce, Doc Roc, Bamps, E-Man, Mr. Low, Ron Ron (Rest In Peace), Big Bubble, Malibu Mike, Big Tee, and Cat Ceas, from East Coast Crips. And so many other Crips there it would be impossible for me to name them all.

There was one youngster by the name of Law, from Raymond Ave 120th Street Crips. I hear he is a Christian now, however, before he became one he would stab anyone he thought was a Blood. The Bloods should thank God for that because Law was awful. I had to literally have Jimbo assign people to guard him from stabbing people. Law was outrageous and there was plenty more Crips on the yard just like him.

One Blood that ran with Big Sugar Bear, from 83rd Street Hoover Crips, was Cloudy Clay, from 92nd Street Bishop. He was a hard core Blood that was on my unit, D-Wing, so I met him through Big Sugar Bear. Clay was allowed to stay only because of Sugar Bear, but unlike the rest of the Bloods that didn't put up a fight, that wasn't going to be the case with Clay. We may have had to kill him. He claimed his neighborhood the entire time he was there.

Although my appeal had been denied, I never gave up hope that I would be released. But I hadn't done anything to make that a reality. I thought foolishly that these people would finally realize that they had made a mistake. I hadn't seen my family in over 3 years, so I missed my mother, lil brother, sisters and Boxco.

I finally was able to use the phone and call home to talk with my mother. I recall our first conversation. She said, "Larry?"

I said, "Yeah Momma."

She said, "Boy you sound like a man! How are you doing?"

I said, "I'm fine momma, I miss you. I'm ready to come home!"

It didn't matter how grown I had gotten, I still was my momma's little boy. She heard in my voice her child scream for help, and said to me, "Larry, pray to your father. Ask him to help you."

I asked about my lil brother Terrence. She got really excited telling me all the things he was doing; it killed me to talk to her. I would've given anything and everything to have her strength and courage as a man. She is the strongest person I have ever known. She is my world, and I needed her, but she knew the only thing she could do for me was to remind me to stay being the man that I had always been no matter what I was going through. She knew I was still a young man in an environment of wolves, and the role I was playing never went over well with her. I would always be her baby. Before I hung up with her she said, "Larry, I love you. Stay strong. You will be out of there in a little while, okay?"

I said, "I love you too momma."

Back on the yard, with all the human-beings who had been rejected from society, a thousand things were going on. Tracy had so many activities it was literally like being in a university. Every trade you could think of was there for the taking.

Legs Diamond had come down from Folsom also. I was elated to see him. I hadn't seen him since the Los Angeles County Jail, so we had much to discuss. We talked and walked a few laps. A lot of things had changed at Folsom. The SHU 2 prisoners, the deceivers, had been carrying out attacks on the Crips throughout the prison system under the pretense of bringing about law and order. But really all they were doing was recruiting for the BGF and instilling fear in those that were frightened by their tactics. I needed to know where Diamond stood on the issue.

The deceivers hadn't gotten their feet in Tracy; it was still 100% Crips there, and many had never been exposed to their trickery, so they didn't have a clue these dudes even existed. But I knew, because they had tried to recruit me two years earlier.

Crips on death row organized a movement called the Blue Notes to combat these dudes. The Blue Notes' purpose was to defeat the SHU 2 characters, and allow Crips coming into the system to move about freely and claim their neighborhoods, which they were being denied under this fake movement.

Diamond associated with these dudes, and couldn't believe what I was telling him, because he was a true Crip from 83rd Street Gangster Crips, and wouldn't have ever mixed his Cripping with such a movement. The strangest things started to take place with these dudes. They fell out with each other over power and positions within their organization. Many of them became disappointed in their positions, so they started revealing their secret existence to real Crips who they had a lifetime of friendship with. Once Diamond learnt the truth about what he had once refused to believe, he joined the rest of us in our efforts to defeat these clowns.

I received a letter from two prominent Crips on death row, soliciting my membership in the Blue Note Organization, which I respectfully declined. I wrote back, informing them that I felt as strongly as they did about what was going on, and I was down to act, but only as an East Coast Crip. They accepted my conditions and asked that I assist their comrades with organizing the front on these dudes in Tracy, and I was happy to oblige.

Big Jimbo, from Harlem 30's, was given the General position of the Blue Notes in Tracy; while my buddies from Menlo and Long Beach were second in command. Everyone in Tracy thought I ran the Blue Notes, but it actually was Big Jimbo. He was the top dog of that vessel.

Crips from everywhere were getting fed up with these dudes' brutal actions. They had started acting just like the BGF, stabbing Blacks, mainly Crips, raping them and taking their property for so-called violations, which they made up.

Anyone we could identify as associated with them wasn't allowed to stay at Tracy; they were either stabbed off the yard or left voluntarily. Either way, they weren't welcome and were going to leave. What does that say about our mentality, deciding which human-beings we would welcome into prison? That alone shows how mentally sick we were.

Word had gotten around to other prisons that Tracy was off limits to these dudes, but they weren't having any of it. They were out to prove to everyone that they ran CDC, and that they were the ones who would make all the rules for the Crips to follow. Only they were sadly mistaken; it wasn't going to happen there in DVI.

They also learnt that I was behind the insurrection against them, so word was they put a hit out on my life. I went from being convicted of a crime I hadn't committed, to being thrust into madness in Folsom State Prison, and now there was a death threat against my life because I refused to allow a group of men I didn't know to run my life. All of this in a three year period. I was up for it. Big Quake was the baddest man I had seen at that time, and I hadn't seen anyone like him running around there. I surely wasn't going to let him down by allowing these dudes to scare me.

We set up areas for the dudes who managed to slip past our security, which was rare. On maybe two occasions it did happen, once when Big Ant from Compton Crip made his way down to Tracy. Big Ant is the aforementioned dude who was one of the meanest men I had ever met. He was with the dudes in SHU Two. When we heard he had made his way down to Tracy we all knew he had come down there for me, because he had no business being in Tracy at all. Immediately we set up an ambush against him, with the Compton Crips leading the way. Ant had betrayed many of them, and they wanted to be the ones who took him down. He had no idea he was in for a hurting.

Big Ant understood the functions of prison. He was senior to most of us, so he knew better than to walk out into a trap, and he sent his cellmate ahead of him. His cellmate came to the yard looking for their comrades. We had it set up where prisoners walked around proclaiming to be representing the deceivers, so other prisoners would feel safe to reveal that they also were members. Once that happened, it would be over with for them. Big Ant's cellmate did such a thing; he walked to the yard asking for these dudes and was pointed to a certain area, where he was stabbed in his neck with a rod. Big Ant learned of this and never made it out to the yard.

I was approached by Big Sugar Bear, from 83rd Street Hoover Crips, who I respected immensely. He told me that he and Big Ant had gone to school with a sergeant there, and that the sergeant wanted to speak with me.

"I don't want to talk to the sergeant."

"It's cool, just listen to what the sergeant has to say, and then make a decision about what you want to do."

This was the first time I learned that prisoners and C/O's had direct interactions with one another and that the C/O's ran all the groups in prison - every single one of them. Many people refuse to believe this, but I know it to be true.

The sergeant called me to the office. "I went to school with Big Ant and I have learned that his life is in danger. We go back a long way, and I want you to spare him."

"I'm not responsible for his safety; he has to protect himself."

"I understand, but I want you to go down to East Hall, where Big Ant is housed, to talk with him. We can't let him out; you'll have to talk through the door."

I said I would. When I walked down there, Big Ant was standing at his door. I walked up and asked him why he had the sergeant call me to the office. He said he didn't have anything to do with it, which I found unbelievable. I would learn many years later these dudes were much closer to CDC than what anyone would ever imagine. All the things thugs grew up believing regarding principles, morals and values were only a dream. It was dirty pool here in prison, and it got classified under the Art of War, by any means necessary, all kinds of metaphors to justify snitching. The things they were doing, if any civilian had done them it would've been considered snitching, but for them it was tactics. The shit was crazy, and if anybody challenged them, they would take a solid dude's name and destroy it with rumors and filth. The dude wouldn't have done anything wrong to justify his name being destroyed, other than refusing to agree with them. Then you have those scary mf's that didn't want to be punished agreeing with everything they heard. They would type up fake reports on individuals stating that they were informers, getting them stabbed. And the real reason they were removed was because they couldn't control these men.

Big Ant asked me if he could come to the main line. I told him; "Yes, why wouldn't you be able to?" He said he was only coming down to program, and that he didn't want any problems. I told him it was okay. Just that fast he forgot that he was one of the dudes in SHU 2 that sent that shit to my cell.

I left and went back to the building that I was housed in (D-Wing) where Sugar Bear asked me what happened. I told him about the sergeant and the meeting with Ant. He asked me was Ant coming out, and I told him he said he was. But he never did; they found a knife sitting on top of his mattress and sent him to the hole.

Things stayed the same around there. Everyone would be on the yard like we were at a festival, with radios blaring, so they decided all the Crips would have a Crip walking contest. I loved this; it would be like back at Bethune Park dancing days. All the Crips gathered around: Bebop, Legs Diamond, Hoover Mack, Hoover Spook, Ta Ta, Big Jimbo, N-Dog, Mudd, Bird Doc, Harlem Hilly, Big Turtle from Santana Block, Lefty, from Harlem, Dennis Johnson, Ron Ron 97 EC (RIP), KiKo 118 block, Bamps 76 EC, Mr. Low 62nd St., E-Man from Q102, Bug from Long Beach and so many other Crips. At that time, Mr. Low and Legs Diamond were known for their artistic foot work. I was good but I hadn't reached their level. Still, I would never refuse to tell any story with my feet. I wanted to take on Legs Diamond, the notorious Crip-walking machine. One by one, Crips started to perform. Everyone wanted to see me and Legs get down. I went before Legs and thought I had done quite well until Legs took his turn. After he finished there wasn't a doubt he was the very best there. I admired Legs, everything about him. He was what I always thought a Crip should be, and how one should carry himself; he represented that to me.

I checked into school and started doing what I failed to do when I was younger. I still had some of the same phobias that I had when I was younger, not wanting people to see my weaknesses and clowning around a lot. I eventually took the GED and passed, but I never truly felt right about it, because I cheated. I had all the answers to each test. At the time I felt, "Fuck the system," because I knew it wasn't fair. After all, I was sitting in prison for something I didn't do. Therefore, fuck honesty and all the other pretty words that define anyone as righteous. I didn't give a fuck about any of those things. I was going to cheat the system every chance I got.

The Crips at Tracy were a well-oiled machine, and threatening to the BGF. We had wiped out the Bloods on the main line, and I had become aware that I was no longer a little boy, at least physically. Mentally and spiritually I was basically still a teenager. I didn't realize until years later that I was stagnated in my mental growth.

When I first came to Folsom State Prison I was 5'9, 165 lbs, 15 inch arms, and my chest, well, I can't even say, I was so fragile. Now in Tracy, some 3 years later, I was still 5'9, but my weight had increased to 185 lbs, and I had 19 inch arms and a 50 inch chest. I was bench pressing over 400 pounds. I was an angry man and lifting weights was how I spent my time, expressing myself, just like Legs did with his feet. My homeboy Ron Ron, from 97th Street East Coast Neighborhood Crips (RIP), and I were light in weight and used to take down anyone in our weight class on the bench press.

One day I was laying down in my cell and the C/O told me they needed to see me. I didn't know why. It could've been anything because I violated most of the rules there every day. When I came out the cell they told me I was going to the hole for extortion, rape, trafficking, weapons, and some more shit. The only thing that stuck in my head was the word rape. Who in the hell was I supposed to have raped? A police officer woman? When I got to the hole and saw the people they had locked up with me, I knew the rape charge was real. These were homosexual loving men. The question now was how my name got involved in this mess. Like the case I was in jail for, I was also innocent of the charge of rape. All the rest of the charges could've stuck and I wouldn't have said one word. I would've fought it but I wouldn't have cried wolf.

Going to the shower one day I saw the homosexual and asked him, "Why the fuck did you put my name in that shit?" He told me that my homeboys had been raping him for awhile and he was scared and went to the BGF for protection. They told him to go to the police and tell them I made him carry knives from building to building, and that I, along with others, had raped him. These are the tricks the dudes used to get rid of people they deemed threats to them in prison. If you practice these sorts of tactics on the streets, you'd be considered a snitch, but in prison they classify it as tactics of the Art of War. That's some straight bullshit. They wanted me out of the prison. I screamed for a rape test; I refused to allow CDC to label me with any kind of homosexual conduct.

Going through all that bullshit, I ran into one of my close homeboys named Bruce Millsap, aka Loco, from 190 Street East Coast Delamo Block Crips. While back there in the hole, he and I learned so much together. One thing about prison that is amazing is that you have people there that know about everything and can build or make anything. So whenever prisoners were at war with one another somebody, was going to suffer. We learned how to make knives, bombs and spears.

Loco would get carried away after he learned how to make bombs. There was no holding him back. He would write me kites telling me that he heard a white boy use the word nigga, so he planned to deal with it. This went on so much I started to doubt it because no one else was hearing it, but when Loco came out of his cell you would always hear that explosion, and the white boy screaming for dear life.

The white boys used to write me kites telling me that Loco was making up stories about hearing them say the word nigga. So we all set Loco up to see if he was fabricating this information. I had one of my homeboys close to Loco listen for one of the white boys to use that word. Loco would fish me a line telling me that he heard somebody down there say the word. Before he was able to throw a bomb in one of their cells, I would send a line down to one of my homeboy's cell, asking if they heard any white boy there use the word and they would tell me no! So I stopped Loco from blowing up the building. He didn't like it, and he wanted revenge.

While back there in the hole together we had some memorable good times. One of my next door neighbors, a Northern Mexican named Angel, didn't get along with the Southern Mexicans and Tracy at that time was predominantly a Southern Mexican prison. Angel was combat-ready; he taught me some tricks on how to spear other inmates while they were walking down the tier. One day he placed shampoo out in front of his cell as a Southern Mexican was walking to the showers. The dude slipped, and Angel told him the next time he doesn't watch his step he's going to stab him in his neck, in essence letting him know he could get him any time he wanted to.

I ran into Big Ant on the yard; he claimed he didn't want any problems and had actually came down there to kick back. I didn't buy any of it. I knew if he had been on his stomping grounds he would've tried me, but he wouldn't have survived that attempt there.

I was found guilty of the write up, and put up for a 13 month SHU Program at San Quentin State Prison. Before I left I ran into my brother Boxco; he came there for a minute. He and I were happy to see each other. Boxco looked good and healthy, he was telling me about my little brother Terrence, how he had been growing. I was extremely happy to see him, and to hear about my little brother's growth in the world.

I completed my SHU term there in Tracy, so I wasn't going to go to San Quentin State Prison. I was sent back to Folsom State Prison general population, the home of the SHU 2 deceivers, where I was on the most wanted list. <u>GLADIATOR SCHOOL!!</u>

Reunited

I returned to Folsom a wanted man for all of my transgressions at DVI. This was the SHU 2 deceivers' headquarters. I was sent directly to fish row to be classified. I stayed on fish row approximately one week before I was released to general population.

Scores of people were elated to see me and just as many wanted to see me taken down for various reasons, some because I stood in their way of accomplishing the big takeover of the Crips and others because they thought that I saw myself as something special. Many Blacks can't stand to see other Blacks succeed in anything, and they are quick to condemn their accomplishments for no reason at all other than just pure hate.

I didn't give a fuck. Literally, everything I did came from my heart, and I was willing to represent it all over again. One thing I had learnt during this period was that no matter how many people belonged to an organization, it took one man at a time to build it. I saw the deceivers as individuals, and didn't focus on how many of them there were. I realized that each man had a responsibility to represent himself, and I was willing to do just that. If they had a hit out on me, I wasn't going to walk around scared. I could do just as much damage to them as they could me.

It was ridiculous to me; I knew Crips who ran with them that were tougher and smarter men than their leadership was. It never made any sense to me that these Crips allowed ordinary men who hadn't proven themselves, in either the streets or prison, to control them. It was obvious to anyone who paid attention that the Crips couldn't possibly be in control of their own affairs. Everything that was going on was the opposite of what we stood for, yet everyone acted like they couldn't see that these traitors had attempted to turn The Crips into some militant movement, against the will of Raymond's spirit. They attempted to take ownership of something many of them hadn't really been man enough to represent. The Crips were being dictated to and manipulated into carrying out another organization's agenda, by men who had only become their leaders by getting book smart.

I wasn't going to allow that to happen to me. Big Quake was the only leader I'd known, and that wasn't going to change, in or out of prison. When I returned to Folsom I wasn't the young man who had left two years earlier. I was now 185 lbs, 19 inch arms, massive chest, strong as a bull, and literally didn't give a fuck.

When I went to the yard the first person I saw was Poppa, from Harlem; he was as happy to see me as I was him. The first thing out of his mouth was, "I heard about all that shit ya'll did down there in Tracy."

I told him, "Yeah, what happened to ya'll here? I heard you got stabbed by your own homeboy for them dudes?"

He said no, that it wasn't his homeboy. However, he was stabbed simply because he wouldn't join them. Now how scary is that? How was that Crips loving Crips and carrying out the best interests of the Crip movement? The Crips on death row weren't having no parts of these dudes' actions, and continuously praised me for my willingness to stand up against them. In me, they saw themselves, and were proud to call me their comrade.

I told Poppa, "Cuzz, fuck them dudes." I still feel the same way right now.

Poppa said to me, "Cuzz, we went through it up here. They hit me in the back."

I said to him, "Shit, cuzz, you knew they were going to hit you. Why did you wait for it to happen? You let them do it."

Poppa said, "What do you mean?"

I said, "You waited for them to hit you when you knew they were going to make an attempt, instead of you stabbing one of them first."

Poppa acknowledged that I was right and swore it would never happen again. I told him I hope not.

I ran into a few more of my immediate homeboys from East Coast Crips: Rocc (RIP), Big Sadd, Lil Sadd, Baby Bubble, and Key Boss. They had just finished the war with the Mexican Mafia. I could tell, because I saw a million blue rags on the main line once again. When the war was going on you couldn't spot one, but now that it was Black on Black, Blacks weren't afraid to show their stupidity for all to see.

Big Foster was sitting back on the wall letting me finish being a celebrity. I went to him, because he sure as hell wasn't going to come to me. Foster was one of my big homies and I never thought I was above him, so with pride and honor I walked over to where he was and greeted him. He said, "What's up, big head, you picked up a lot of weight. I can't call you my little homie anymore, huh?"

I told him I needed to talk to him, that it was serious. He told me that he knew, so we walked and talked. I began by telling him I knew he had heard about Tracy, and what happened down there with the dudes he ran with. He again said he didn't run with them. I told him it didn't matter to me because I would continue to oppose them. I didn't want to bring my problems to his front door steps, but I refused to follow these dudes' rules under any circumstances. I told him that I was a Crip, and I knew these dudes weren't.

He told me he understood, and that he was still with me, but wasn't anybody trippin on me, so kick back. Big Foster just had no idea what we had done to these dudes down there in Tracy.

Folsom had just built three more new facilities called New Folsom A Facility, B Facility, and C Facility. They needed prisoners in them and somehow I was chosen as one of fifteen prisoners to be sent to B Facility. I hadn't been in Old Folsom a week before I was transferred and I hadn't been approached by any of those dudes. I caught death stares, but eyes hadn't ever killed a man.

I had been called to trans pack (transfer pack) all of my property and was sent to B Facility, where there wasn't a single prisoner. The only Crips who had been trans packed to go were Devil, from 107 Hoover Crips, and me. Once we got, there the administration used our dumb asses to move all the mattresses into all the buildings. Everything that needed to be done to prepare that prison for the next busload of prisoners, we did, without so much as a clue we were being exploited.

AMENDMENT XIII

Slavery

SECTION 1. Neither slavery nor involuntary servitude, except as a punishment for crime whereof the party shall have been duly convicted, shall exist with the United States, or any place subject to their jurisdiction.

SECTION 2. Congress shall have power to enforce this article by appropriate legislation.

Proposed January 31, 1865; ratified December 6, 1865; certified December 18, 1865.

Prison life doesn't wait on anyone and we had a prison to run. Devil and I represented the Crips so we met with the Mexicans and whites and decided where the Blacks would be on the yard and where they would be. Before all the other prisoners made their way over there, we established the boundaries each race would honor and respect. Once that was done, I asked Devil was he comfortable with our choices. He said he was, so we moved forward.

For a while, we had the run of the place. They didn't move anybody else over there until we finished moving shit around, so when they ran committee, we had first choice of whatever jobs we wanted. They called me in and asked me where I wanted to work. I declined a job because I was upset about that rape shit at Tracy.

That would be on my record, so I wasn't ever going to work. I didn't give a fuck about no job.

Plus I was angry about having to do all this time for a crime I hadn't committed. In prison you still had to go through all these processes as if you had done it, and the people aren't concerned with whether or not you did it. In their minds, you're there, so you're guilty.

They started bringing other prisoners over and we were given yard and other activities. Then the strangest thing happened. Before I left Tracy, I had filed a 602, which is an appeal procedure for prisoners to file when they're dissatisfied about something that may have taken place. I filed a 602 about the rape, and the way they carried out due process in the matter.

One day, I was on the yard and was called to an emergency classification hearing. I had no clue what this was about. It couldn't be anything good, that was for sure. When I sat down, Lt. Joyce told me that this hearing was about an appeal I had filed. It had been ordered reissued and reheard by Sacramento, and he didn't see enough evidence there to find me guilty, so he was dismissing it. I almost jumped through the ceiling of the building. I didn't mess with men, and I didn't want anybody to ever think that I had, so I was overjoyed with happiness.

Because Lt. Joyce had dismissed the write up, they had to send me back to a level 3 institution. They put me back up again for Tracy and Richard J. Donovan. Two weeks later I was sent to R.J. Donovan.

Masquerade

I arrived at Donovan eager to start anew. I knew one thing for sure, it wasn't going to be anything like Folsom or Tracy, and I intended to take full advantage of everything Donovan had to offer. I was sent first to the Three Yard, where everyone got classified then sent to whatever yard the administration felt best suited their needs. I had no idea what I wanted to do, so I signed up for I believe Auto Mechanics.

I was then sent to the One Yard, where that trade was located, and placed on a waiting list. Donovan was a new Level 3 prison. Before I got there, something had happened. One Yard was at war, with the Bloods and Crips going at it but now there weren't any Bloods allowed on the One Yard. I had been used to Black on Black crime by that time, so I intended to follow suit with the Crips agenda.

The One Yard was a fun yard. It wasn't like Tracy or Folsom with their sophisticated systems; it was like a schoolyard of a junior high school. I knew I would be able to manipulate the administration there into believing I was a changed man, and not the animal they had made me out to be. But I knew also that I was full of rage because of what they had done to me by sending me to prison for 18 years and forcing me to actually do the time as if I truly had committed the crime. No one knew what was going on inside me - I was destroyed. I knew the system wanted everyone to believe it had our best interest at heart, but this heart was torn to pieces and wasn't capable of being repaired.

There weren't any shot callers with egos there, just the ordinary gang members wanting to be bad, as I had when I was younger. I didn't know what bad was until I went to Folsom State penitentiary and got a firsthand dose of what bad was, and it wasn't me. I had seen the worst bad could ever be, so the ordinary bad was nice to me and I could live with it.

I started playing basketball again with other prisoners. My game was close to Larry Johnson's, former UNLV and NBA star, and I had Magic Johnson-like passes. Christmas, Fatso, Don Juan and a few more prisoners at Donovan had once played at Nelles, so we were all excited to play again with each other as grown men. I thought it was funny that we all met up like this.

I had an opportunity to start teaching the youngsters about what complete madness was, because I knew they had no idea. When I was their age, I had no idea, until I was sent to Folsom and witnessed retardation. I thought I could shortcut their experiences of knowing what total chaos was, because if and when they hit Folsom they would be in for the shock of their young lives. In Folsom I witnessed the bad get taken down. I witnessed the bad put up fights that were to be applauded but at the end of the day they were stabbed seven or eight times badly. Death came to some, paralysis came to others, and severe damages were incurred by most. There wasn't a man I met there that liked anything about Folsom State Prison. I sure as hell didn't. When they witnessed three or four dudes on one dude stabbing him until he became lifeless, while everyone looked on with no intention of helping save his life, it would make them think about their own abilities to survive. They would have to question their skills against such attacks. And the answer would be they'd hope God was with them on that day.

Donovan gave me a chance to relax and I planned to take advantage of every second I was there. I moved in the cell with my homeboy Lil Doc, from 69th Street East Coast Crips. I've tried to describe everyone in this book with great accuracy, as best I can. Doc was different from everyone I had ever been around. I knew him from the streets already; he had been a victim of a shooting that left one of his legs paralyzed. Doc stood 5'7, 160 pounds with not a drop of sense. Doc was absolutely insane and the funniest person I have ever seen in my life and that doesn't exclude any of the celebrity comics. Doc is the funniest man alive, hands down, and I love him to death.

I used to carry Doc around the yard on my back and he loved it. Sometimes many of us would be standing around talking and decide we were going to go somewhere else on the yard, and we'd be walking too fast for Doc. He would say to me, "Hey bastard, give me a lift." He would jump on my back, I would walk him to wherever we'd be going.

Doc is also one of the elite East Coast Crip members, despite his leg situation. He is a top gun who is respected and feared in the inner city of South Central L.A., so don't let that leg fool you. Doc is the real McCoy. It's funny that I use that terminology, when oftentimes we don't have any idea where these terms come from. It wasn't until I came to prison that I found out where this terminology "The Real McCoy," originated. In 1882, Elijah McCoy (1843-1929), African, patented a machine called the McCoy Graphite Lubricator. Before McCoy's machine, trains had to stop periodically because their engines would overheat due to friction. The engines had to be lubricated by hand. McCoy's lubricator did this automatically, and the trains no longer had to stop. Managers of the railroads settled only for his lubricator – the real thing, rather than shoddy substitutes. The term "The Real McCoy" arose from the success of Elijah McCoy's invention. I thought that was fascinating. Doc was that real thing, "The Real McCoy."

Doc was crazy - he worshiped the Devil and laughed about it. The way people worship Christ, he felt just as strongly about the Devil, and didn't care who knew. Doc had a girlfriend who had started dating one of our homeboys; he didn't like the thought of some other man touching his girlfriend and couldn't take it much longer, so he told me he was going to do harm to my homeboy because of it. At this time it was unheard of that East Coast Crips would inflict harm on each other for any reason, let alone over a woman.

I didn't take kindly to Doc telling me that, so I told him that he needed to reconsider his position or there were going to be consequences for his actions. He stood his ground, but his heart was broke over my position on the matter, as well as mines over his statement to me. I told Doc that I was going to discipline him. He couldn't believe that I was coming at him like that because of his rank in the East Coast Crips. I called a meeting with all the East Coast Crips who were there in Donovan: Big Pie 97th Street, Wiggles 69th Street, Dead Eye 190th Blocc, Choo 62nd street, Baby Boy 118th Blocc, and many more. I told them that none of them were allowed to talk to Doc until he apologized to each one of us for making such a statement about harming another East Coast Crip.

Doc couldn't believe that everyone went against him because of what he had said. He took it as a joke and walked off saying, "Fuck all you bastards, I'm Lil Doc." When Doc left I told everyone I was dead serious, and they were not to talk to Doc. Most of them couldn't believe this was happening to Doc. Some of them came to me later saying, "La La, don't you think you're being too hard on Lil Doc?"

I told them, "Hell nah, I'm not being tough enough, if it wasn't Lil Doc it would've been worse off for somebody else. He's getting a break."

It hurt all of them not to be able to talk to him. They adored Lil Doc and loved him with all of their hearts. I did as well, but Cripping ain't never been easy. Somebody had to be able to enforce the rules without shedding any tears, and I was the man for the job.

Before we put Doc's discipline into effect, I told him "Cuzz, if you were able to get rid of cuzz you still wouldn't be able to control what that girl does with her body. She's doing what she wants to, cuzz, why can't you respect that?"

He wasn't having any of that. He was furious at cuzz, and at me for calling a meeting on him but with me, he knew there wasn't anything he could do about it. I was really the boss.

Doc thought it was funny until about the third week had passed and nobody said a word to him. He'd try to find one of our homeboys alone and talk to him, but they all knew that if they did, their discipline would be much more severe than little Doc's, so he couldn't get any of them to talk to him.

Doc was my cellmate and all of this transferred over to our cell. Doc started acting in his devilish ways. I would come back to the cell and he would have drawn 100 pictures of the devil all over the wall, and be chanting something crazy about his father, the Devil, getting me for going against him. Well, my father won that battle. Finally Doc couldn't take much more. He told me he was ready to apologize to everyone, so I called a meeting and this is how Lil Doc's apology went.

"Dam, cuzz, I can't believe that ya'll weren't talking to me. I'm going to kill all of you bastards the first chance I get. And you, Wiggle, you're from 69th Street, you know better. That shit was killing me. I thought that ya'll were going to say something, but you mf's stayed strong."

Coming from Doc that would be the best we were going to get. Eager to talk to him, everyone accepted it as an apology; my homeboys were more excited about talking to Doc than he was to them. I was elated it was all over as well. When we got back to the cell Doc started in on me, "Hey bastard don't ever do that again, because my father is still going to get your black ass." He started laughing up a storm, telling me how much he missed talking to me.

It was time for Lil Doc to go home; he didn't want to leave me behind. When the day came, he decided he wasn't going to go. I told him, "Cuzz, get your ass out of here. I'll be out soon. You just keep your crazy ass out." We hugged and he walked off into freedom. I missed him the second he disappeared from my sight.

I still was in communication with Jackie but our relationship was riddled with conflict. Jackie was less than truthful with me the whole time. She was always attempting to mislead me about her love life. I found out that she was dating several men, so I didn't take her seriously, as I once had.

I started dating two ladies, Peaches and Libby. First Peaches, whom I met through my new cellmate Big Snap from School Yard Crips. Snap was a Big Youngsta, 6'3, 220 pounds, light brown skin, long hair, and built like a body builder. Peaches was dating his younger brother, and Snap loved his brother to death and thought Peaches felt as he did. In his mind, Peaches would never talk to another man, so he never had a problem letting me talk to her when he called her. We began having feelings for each other and one day when I was talking to her I told her that I liked her a lot and that I wanted to date her. She felt as I did, but was concerned about Snap and I being in the same cell together, because she still was dating his brother. I told her not to worry about Snap; I'll handle him. She just had to know if this is what she wanted also. If this was in her heart, I'd do the rest. Peaches was 5'2, 125 pounds, light skinned with long hair; pretty as any woman I had ever seen in my life. She was beautiful.

Our relationship had become serious; it was time to let Snap know. I told Peaches it was time to tell him, because I felt like I shouldn't have to hide shit from him. She agreed, but she wanted to make sure that Snap played a role in us getting together. She told me to get her number from Snap, so if his brother found out that she was talking to me she could always say Snap was the one that gave me her number.

One day I came back to the cell and I asked Snap about Peaches even though I had been talking to her every day. He said something slick, and I asked him to give me her number so that I could talk to her. He said, "Cuzz, she talks to my brother La, she ain't going to talk to you."

I said, "I don't care who she talks to. Let her tell me that."

Snap said, "Cuzz, she's crazy about my brother, I bet she won't talk to you".

I told him I'd take that bet; little did he know she was already mines. It was all a game. With Snap not knowing the truth about our relationship, she had already got her visiting slip approved to visit me. Snap had been dating Peaches' friend Tanisha, so when they came up to visit Snap they would always ride together. But on the next visit, Peaches would be calling me out and not Snap. I knew they were coming up to see us that night. Snap's girl even knew Peaches and I were dating and never mentioned it to Snap, because Peaches had asked her not to.

That night they called us out for a visit and Snap asked me, "La La, who's coming to see you?" I told him Peaches.

He said, "You're lying, cuzz."

I said, "Nah, cuzz, she is."

He started laughing like I was crazy, and obsessing over Peaches. He said to me again once and for all "La La, Peaches is in love with my brother, cuzz."

I said to him, "That might be so, but she's coming to see me tonight."

We walked out to the visiting room together all the way there Snap still not believing Peaches was coming to see me. He thought it was Jackie or my older sister Debra, anyone but Peaches.

God works the way he does for the reason he does. This particular night, for unexplainable reasons, the visiting room staff made some sort of mistake and Snap's visits were placed behind glass, meaning he couldn't have contact visits. He had to visit Tanisha behind glass. I, on the other hand, walked right out there with all the other visitors. Looking on, Snap saw Peaches out there waiting to visit me. He was in a trance and couldn't believe what he was seeing. His brother was his hero; there was no way she could betray his brother. Peaches and I had already discussed that when she came I wanted her to kiss me in front of Snap, so he would know she was my woman and he could finally get over thinking that she was his brother's girl. I would make him see that she was my girl, and he needed to respect that.

When Peaches and I embraced I could tell she was nervous because she kept looking over her shoulder trying to see if Snap was looking at her. I told her, "Don't worry about him. I told you that. Just give me a kiss. I can handle Snap." She finally worked up the nerves to kiss me. When we kissed, Snap lost his mind - you would've thought Peaches was his girl the way he acted. Snap hit the window with his fist as hard as he could, causing Peaches to jump in my arms. I told her don't worry about Snap; he would apologize for being disrespectful to us. I told her to relax and trust that I would handle Snap. After that, we had a good visit.

The minute I got back to the cell I told Snap he was going to have to apologize to Peaches for his actions, that Peaches is with me so he doesn't have anything to do with what she does. She ain't your woman so stop acting like she is. He agreed that he was out of line, and called her to apologize. He still was hurt, because he looked at himself and his brother as men that women just wouldn't cheat on, so he was stunned that Peaches chose me in his presence. I told him it's all game; don't take it personally.

Peaches continued to visit me faithfully for close to two years, until she got pregnant by someone and the gig was up. It's all game, and I enjoyed myself with her and appreciated her taking the time out to come to visit me.

Then I started seeing this older woman by the name of Libby. She was really too much for me with all of her life experiences. I came to jail at 17 years old and was now 24, but my life experiences were still of a teenager, no matter how old I had become in prison.

Libby was any man's dream because she had everything you could dream of wanting. I met Libby through one of my homeboys she was dating, Trouble Man from 118th Street East Coast Blocc Crips. I used to call her when Peaches didn't have a way to come visit me and she allowed Peaches to use one of her cars without so much of a word to me. Libby would always say to me, "Why are you dating those little girls that can't afford to take care of a man? You need a woman in your life and let that little girl go."

I would tell her Peaches was enough woman for me. And she would tell me as soon as I finished playing with Peaches holla at her. Now in my mind if Libby wanted to kick game I had no problems with it. Libby was too much for me of course, but I would never concede that to her or no one else. I had a grown up role to play and I intended to play it to the max.

I remember one day Libby kept pressing me about wanting to be with me, and I told her that I couldn't mess with her because she was with my homeboy. She told me that they weren't together and that she chose who she wanted to be with. I never thought she and I would ever be together. I had 4 years left on my sentence, and to be honest Vivian was who I thought of mostly.

It was rare to see a relationship succeed in prison. There were exceptions, but for the most part they failed because of deceit by both parties. Men in prison live in a state of illusion, thinking that their women somehow are going to be faithful to them when they have 20 to 30 years to do. It just doesn't make any sense. Most of the men I know can't stand the thought of another man or woman touching their woman, so when they put that added pressure on their women they're asking them to lie to them. Being truthful is almost impossible in those situations, so the simplest way to cope with each other is to continue to lie about who you are until you can't take it any longer. Usually the women are forced to leave the relationship, because they can't continue to pretend to be somebody they're not.

Libby was 35 years old, with four children, and all the experience in the world over me. Now if she needed to learn how to run a prison, I was her man, but if she was looking for a man to guide her in society then I may not be the man she was looking for. In fact, I'm certain that I wasn't that man. I hadn't paid one utility bill in my life. I had come to prison straight from living with my mother, and I hadn't learned anything in prison conducive to productivity. All my experiences centered on trying not to be killed inside prison, and thus far I managed to succeed in that, through the grace of God.

Libby used to tell me not to make any decision about what I wanted to do until I came home, and then we would decide what we would do together. That was too much good sense for me. I had to play like I was grown. "Nah baby, I know what I want. I want to be with you."

Libby knew me better than I knew myself. She would tell me, "La La, I have these children. Don't make any promises you can't keep. I have to think about these children; if you don't want to be with me, it's okay. We can take our time."

She'd say, "La La, don't worry about me going anywhere. I will still do for you as a friend, so don't tell me you want to be with me, then I start making plans for us and then you decide you want to do something different. I don't want to put my children through that."

But me being super slick I said, "Baby, look, I know what I want. I ain't no child. I always dreamt of having a woman in my life like you. If you're having any reservations, then express them, but don't be trying to speak for me." That was me attempting to be grown.

Libby still gave me a way out saying, "La La, just think about it, okay, baby?"

I continued to get involved in prison situations. I didn't have to stab anyone there, but I had a couple of fights that didn't last a minute. I recall getting into it with Art from Playboy Gangster Crips. I went to get Doc to watch the cell door while I went in Art's cell to beat his ass. For some reason he thought he could kick my ass. When I closed the door behind me, he was in a world of trouble and had the wrong person on the door. Lil Doc wanted me to destroy him, so I gave the Lil Devil what he asked for - Art was destroyed. I remember the entire yard came together and voiced their displeasure, thinking I abused Art. I assured every one of them who felt that way that they could take his place. I would give each of them a shot at the title. With no takers for that feud, everyone was cool.

I continued to participate in all the sport activities with Mo Man from Grape Street, a gifted athlete who should've been playing professional basketball or football. I recall looking at Mo Man and other young men like him thinking, *When will they ever have a chance to prove to people they aren't the same people they were 20 years earlier? How long will they be held to pay for their crimes? And when, if ever, was America going to be held accountable for the crimes it had committed and still was actively committing against Africans?*

AMENDMENT VIII

Bail-Fines-Punishments

SECTION 1. Excessive bail shall not be required, nor excessive fines imposed, nor cruel and unusual punishments inflicted.

Proposed September 25, 1789; ratified December 15, 1791.

There was always conflict of some sort around there. The administration hadn't completely been able to control the conduct of each individual thus far, so oftentimes madness spilled over onto the yard. There were several superb fighters on the yard, one being one of my partnas named Hoover Dee from 52nd Street. He kicked ass from sunup to sundown. Dee was 6'1, 210 pounds, black as night, with arms as long as telephone poles. He wasn't a skill fighter; he was more of a power puncher, and tremendously strong.

One day, Dee got into it over the weights with Blue from School Yard Crips. This was the first time I had ever seen Hoova Dee get down. I had heard about how he was a fighter but I hadn't seen any of his work. Dee got some weights that Blue wanted or felt like he should've gotten. Blue called Dee all kinds of names and Dee said to Blue, "Look, cuzz, I ain't going to be standing here arguing with you. If you want to get down, let's just get down." Blue was bigger than Dee and much heavier, so it was a fair fight in my eyes.

I knew Blue from Los Angeles County Jail, where I saw him lose every fight he got into, so I know he wasn't concerned about losing at all. He and Dee went directly under the gun tower, where I was sure they were going to the hole. Dee chose that spot for a reason. One, two, Blue was unconscious. I was impressed with Dee's work to say the least. Some of the other Crips on the yard walked over to where Blue lay unconscious and brought him back to life. Once Blue came back, he walked back to the weight pile and Dee asked him was he cool or did he want to get it again? Blue wanted round two, but it had the same outcome; one, two he was unconscious again. I watched Dee's style closely; I knew that one day he and I would cross each other's paths, because we were adversaries. Blue didn't want round three, so that was it on the weight issues.

I saw Dee get down once more, I was really impressed with this fight because I was sure he was about to get his ass kicked. One day we all decided we were going to play football East Side Crips against the West Side Crips. Dee and Slim from Avalon Gardens got into it over the game. I tried to get in the way of this one because Dee and I had gotten close and Slim was 6'9, 220 pounds, and could fight pretty decent. Hoova Dee wasn't having none of my interference. He told me, "La La, get out of the way and let me knock this big tall mf out." Dee had hit Slim during the game and Slim took offense to the hit. When they started exchanging verbal disrespects, I looked at both of them as being grown men and stood my distance.

Dee told Slim, "Man we're playing football what do you expect me to do tap you?"

Slim said, "Do it again and I'm going to show you what I expect you to do!"

Dee said, 'Hold up, cuzz, who the fuck you think you're talking to?"

Slim said, "Fuck all that bullshit cuzz, do you want to get down?"

Dee said. "Hell yeah! Let's go over here." I took my spectator's seat. The last person Dee directed to a location went to sleep, but this time around I knew it would be different. Slim was an East Side Crip, so of course I was hoping he would win one for the East Side.

Dee had chosen a worse spot then the spot where he and Blue fought. This time they were in a wide-open space on the track, with nothing covering them. I asked Dee, "Are you sure, cuzz?"

He said, "Yeah, this ain't gone take long." They clashed - one, two, Slim was dazed and stumbling for his balance. Dee moved in to destroy him but I didn't let him. I told him, "Nah cuzz, I ain't going to allow you to fuck him off.'

Dee said, 'La La, get out the way, cuzz. Cuzz asked for it."

I told Dee, "He's already out on his feet, I ain't going to let you fuck him off like that."

Slim was trying not to fall on his face, saying, "Oh, hell nah, let me go. I want to get down with cuzz."

I told Slim, "Cut it out, cuzz, you can't even stand up straight. It's over, cuzz."

Slim was persistent, saying, "Nah, La La, let me go, let me go." I did just that. Dee moved in on him - one, two, Slim was out cold. Dee tried to put feet to him, but I stopped him in his tracks.

Then you had Grand Dad, from Grape Street Watts. I was in the county jail with him when I was 18 years old. Grand Dad had to be at least 40 years old. He was a full-fledged gang member, running around with kids my age, jumping on youngsters, robbing them and everybody else he could pull a knife on. Grand Dad was one of a few individuals who constantly started shit, every single chance he got. I knew it would be a lot of fun with him there at Donovan, because in spite of his mischief, he was a loving man who adored all of us youngsters in his own way. I always took Grand Dad's conduct to be that he didn't like scary mf's. When he sensed that anyone around him was scary, he didn't waste one second attacking them.

Grand Dad was 5'7, 150 pounds, with a brown-skinned complexion and brown eyes, and he wore a small afro and a full beard. He loved to fight at the drop of a hat. Grand Dad would fire on some unexpected victim and wouldn't let up until somebody intervened asking him what the fuck was wrong with him.

Youngsters would gather together with Grand Dad entertaining us, telling us jokes about some of his experiences. Most of the youngsters regarded Grand Dad as their big homie, even if they were from other gangs.

One day on the yard an older Crip about Grand Dad's age named Poppa Smurf, from 4 Tray Gangster Crip, came to the yard and started hanging out with some of the youngsters. Most of them had taken a liking to him, the way they had with Grand Dad. This was my first encounter with Poppa Smurf. As I listened to him tell his jokes and watched the youngsters enjoy his company, I saw that Grand Dad didn't appreciate him stealing his attention away from him. We were Grand Dad's children, and he wasn't going to allow anyone to come on his turf and take us away from him. It just wasn't going to happen. Nobody but me saw what was coming. I was laughing up a storm inwardly, as I watched Grand Dad inch his way closer to Poppa Smurf by playing with anyone in front of him, clearing a path to Poppa Smurf's face.

Poppa Smurf was the life of the party. He had everyone in stitches, laughing until their sides hurt, when out of nowhere his face met Grand Dad's fist. Bang - Poppa Smurf went flying to the ground. He bounced back up quickly, putting his dukes up in the air, rushing towards Grand Dad but everyone was attempting to separate them. Poppa Smurf asked Grand Dad, "Mf what did you hit me for?"

Grand Dad responded, "Fuck you mf, you don't come up here acting like you're somebody."

Smurf said, "What the fuck are you talking about mf? I don't even know you!"

Grand Dad, said, "So fucking what, you mf, I'll fuck your bitch ass up."

Poppa Smurf said, "You ain't gone do shit to me." He tried to break loose from the people holding him and Grand Dad was doing likewise.

Finally they were able to keep them separated. I went over to Grand Dad and said to him, "Cuzz, you're trippin Grand Dad. I watched the entire thing go down man. You think he's trying to steal us away from you. Grand Dad can't nobody do that. We love you and they like him also, so stop trippin."

Grand Dad said, "You always were smart young mf. Fuck that punk; he better get the fuck out of here before I stab his ass."

In the world we were living in, everybody wanted to be loved. Those that experienced it were willing to protect it by any means necessary. Love didn't come our way often, so when we thought we had come upon it we were compelled to hold on to it for dear life. We didn't allow another man's ideas to determine what love should be to us or for us. I knew Grand Dad valued our love for him and our own love for each other. Because Grand Dad hadn't been loved in his personal life (we assumed) he wasn't willing to share our love with no one, he wanted it all to himself.

I didn't last much longer around there. One day my homeboy Dead Eye got into it with a Blood dude that had come to the yard. Somebody came in the building and told me what had happened. I walked out to the yard, found the dude he had gotten into it with, and beat his ass right there on the spot. I was the barber on the yard so I had some barber clippers with me, and I used the clippers as a weapon inside the bag, splitting his head open. The dude took off running inside the building.

It was yard recall, so in my mind I had gotten away with it until they called dinner. Once they released us for dinner, they also released the dude that I fought just moments ago. He was walking back from dinner and when he spotted me, he panicked, thinking I was going to attack him. He started running across the yard, and because I had no idea where he was running to, I thought he may have been trying to retrieve a weapon; therefore I took off after him. When I caught up to him, Dead Eye was on my heels as well. I didn't know why Dead Eye followed me; he knew I didn't like jumping on people. I was telling him the entire time to get out of the way. I caught the dude and beat him senseless. Because Dead Eye was involved, the administration viewed the altercation as a rat pack, and sent us both to the hole for assault and battery. Had he stayed out of it I wouldn't have gone to the hole.

LARRY DAVIS

In the California prison system, prisoners are given points based on their record and conduct. These point totals determine what level institution they will be sent to. Level four prisons for example started at 52 points and higher. Level three prisons started at 27 points and went as high as 51 points, and level two prisons started at 19 points and went to 26 points, and the level one prisons went from 0 to 18 points. I believe I had 60 some odd points at that time, so I was only at Tracy on an override. (When I was in Folsom in 1985, when the Crips and Mexican Mafia were at war, many of the prisoners there were transferred to lower level institutions on overrides.) So there wasn't any room for me to fuck up when I was sent Tracy. I couldn't get into any trouble or I would immediately be sent back to a level four institution, which at that time were only San Quentin and Folsom State Prison. So while I was in the hole, I was not under any illusion about my situation. I knew I was going back to the life of the misguided.

When I arrived to the hole, I was sent to the cell with Smitty from Harlem 30's. He and I were on the One Yard together. I kicked it with him and Cadillac Jim from Harlem 30's over there. Jim was one of my favorite Crips to be around ever. He reminded me of those old gangsters in the movies. Jim was Harlem Crip through and through, and I loved him the way I loved Legs Diamond.

One night Smitty and I were in the cell when we heard this dude come through the door screaming, "FUCK ALL YOU PUNK ASS CRIPS. This is Blood mf's. Yeah, I just came off of the One Yard. I fucked some punk ass Crip up. The One Yard ain't shit; they let me come over there and get off. And I'm coming to the Blue yard back here. I want to go to the Blue yard. Fuck all you Crabs. This is Pac Man from 5 Nine Brims San Diego Blood."

I couldn't believe my ears. I thought initially he was crazy on drugs or something, but as I stood at my door listening to him, I concluded that he hated Crips. I needed to get my hands on him, but I knew that wasn't going to happen because Crips and Bloods didn't go to the same yards together. So I played back what he was saying about what he had done on the One Yard. I couldn't believe that the Crips over there allowed him to come to one of their units and assault one of them. I refused to believe it, until I found out that it was true and that Pac Man was the real deal; he was a Crip Killer.

The entire time I was back there I used to tell Smitty, "Cuzz, I wish I could go to the same yard with that fool so I could beat his head in." One day, Pac Man spit on the police as they were passing out something to all the prisoners. The police got so mad they didn't give a fuck what yard any of the prisoners went to. Pac Man had an enemy in the hole named Wick, from West Coast Crips in San Diego. They allegedly had been trying to kill each other out there for years. The police had some history about the two of them and attempted to exploit it. They secretly were going around to all of the Crips' cells, asking them did anyone want to fight Pac Man on the yard, head up. Every single one of them said no. I couldn't believe it, because my partna Hoova Dee was in the hole, and I knew he wouldn't have turned down a fade. Then there was Wick from San Diego; all the shit that came out of his mouth there was no way he was turning down a fade with Pac Man, I was sure of that. But he had.

The sergeant made his way to my cell. He began by saying to me, "La La, I went to all your homeboys' cells and asked them did they want to fight Pac Man and all of them said no. You're the last cell. Do you want to fight him?"

I asked him, "Why are you doing this?"

He said because Pac Man disrespected them.

I said, "I'm down to fight him but not for ya'll, but because he came in here and disrespected the Crips. And I don't want a write up for the fight."

He told me that I would get a write up but I would beat it during the hearing. I agreed and it was set up for the morning yard, Pac Man and me. The thing is they had Pac Man thinking he was about to fight Wick, from San Diego. I said to my cellmate Smitty, "Cuzz when I come back to the cell I'm going to bring back his front tooth."

Smitty said, "Yeah right." Smitty knew I was known for kicking some ass, but he doubted whether or not I could be a sharp shooter.

It was time for the match, I stood at the cell door; respecting Pac Man immensely because it was our yard, designated for the Crips and he was being let out first, demonstrating he actually didn't give a fuck about none of the Crips back there and that included me. The Bloods yard wasn't until that afternoon so he knew he was going to enemy turf. He showed me a lot about his courage, but I also knew he wasn't ready for me, by any means. He trusted the police too much, even though in his heart he despised them. I intended to make him respect me as a Crip, if he didn't ever respect another one in his life. I was going to teach him a lesson about watching what comes out of his mouth. As he walked out to the yard he looked around the building, making sure everyone knew that he was a young hog. I saw it that way as well. Pac Man had no idea he was about to fight me. The whole building was on edge after Pac Man made his way out of the building to the yard. Then the police came to my cell, checked me for weapons and proceeded to cuff me up and escorted me to the yard. On my way out there all the Crips in the building started yelling, "La La, beat that fool's ass." I was thinking to myself, *Scary ass mf's don't know I know that the sergeant went to every one of their cells.* I told Smitty, "This won't take long."

As I walked outside, Pac Man was staring at me like *"Who the fuck are you?"* because he was expecting Wick. Instead he got me and that was the wrong lottery ticket to be playing. I went through the first gate where the police had to take the handcuffs off, and then I entered the yard that Pac Man was actually on. I walked out to where he was and told him, "Cuzz, let's get this out the way; Wick won't be coming."

Pac Man stood 6'2, 200 pounds, light-skinned with short hair and arms as long as tree branches, angry as a mf. He said, "Blood, who the fuck are you?"

I said, "I'm the Crip that's going to beat your ass."

He said, "Who you midget?" And then he started laughing. I told Pac Man to get himself together, that I was serious. He recognized it was no longer a game and that the police had set him up. His hatred for the police allowed them to challenge his bravery with someone they knew he hated, Wick. However, Wick didn't want to fight him. So they still made him believe he was going to be fighting Wick, but he got me. I was someone they prayed would beat him senseless, and they knew Blue versus Red was a guaranteed match of some sort. This one was for me and everything I stood for.

We squared off and I went right to work on him, first by knocking his front tooth out of his mouth. Pac Man went to the ground, covering his head as I continued to beat him viciously. As he raised himself up to his feet, I spotted the tooth on the ground so I picked it up and put it in my pocket. Pac Man knew at that point that he was outmatched, and I intended to take my time with him and literally beat him properly. He started swinging wildly, like when you put your head down and thrust your arms forward as if you are swimming in a hurry. One of those punches caught me and sat me on my ass. That was the first time I had ever been put down. I jumped up and didn't have any mercy on him. I beat Pac Man so bad the police ran onto the yard pulling me off his ass. Pac Man was screaming and holding on to me as tight as he could and hollering, "I'm cool, that's enough!"

I told him, "This is Crip mf, let's fight!!"

To his credit, he said, "This is Blood, Blood 5 Nine Brim, I'm cool."

When I walked back into my cell I threw Smitty Pac Man's tooth. Smitty said, "Damn, cuzz, you got that fool's tooth." I cleaned it and tied it on a string and used to wear it to the showers every time I came out of the cell. Pac Man used to see me wearing it and would say, "Damn, La La, you're going to do me like that?" He and I became cool after that.

He stayed on all the Crips over there except for me. He would say to them all the only Crip over here had the heart to get down with me was La La. All the rest of you mf's are scary as a mf. He stayed true to what he believed in, with one missing tooth.

I would later write him a letter telling him to be careful back here, because the police could've very easily allowed me to kill him, and I would've, not for them, but because of his disrespect for what I represent. He acknowledged what I told him and we were cool after that. I went to the 115 hearing, which is the write up for the fight we had, and just as the pig had said it would be, it was dismissed and I was sent back to Folsom State Prison.

Callous

I arrived back to New Folsom B-Facility, the prison Devil and I had opened up. This was my third time in Folsom in 8 years. In the two years that I was in Donovan, B-Facility had been filled with most of the SHU 2 deceivers. Their entire Heads of State were there. I had never seen all of them assembled at one time, but there they were, the top dogs.

This made for an interesting encounter, because I didn't give a fuck about any of them. There were grown-ass men walking around the prison literally thinking that these dudes were actually of some importance, the likes of Nelson Mandela or Malcolm X, when in fact they weren't shit but some manipulating convicts. I wasn't about to be hoodwinked. For those who thought of them as their Gods, that was on them. They certainly wasn't mines, and would never be. I wasn't impressed with any of the books they had read or could recite verbatim. I was now 26 years old, a completely different man.

My homies found out I was on Fish Row, and sent me all the things I needed to hold me over until I received all of my own property. I found out that the SHU 2 deceivers wanted to talk to me about where I stood on all the things that had transpired over the years. Many of us hadn't ever had the opportunity to be in each other's presence. For some of us it was the first time meeting one another as Crips. Most of them thought I was a member of the Blue Note Organization, so they were concerned with whether I was following orders from the Real Crips who were still on Death Row bleeding Blue.

My name stayed ringing with them, La La this and La La that. I wasn't a part of anybody's organization, with the exception of the East Coast Crips. I fought voluntarily with the Blue Notes because they were the only men willing to fight for the Crips while everybody else stood around and got abused. It's easy for these men now in prison who didn't have to live through that experience to say all the things they would or wouldn't have done if they were there. I saw strong reputable men, far stronger than many of these dudes today, get broke down. I saw many Crips swear they wouldn't let these dudes do anything to their homeboys and then stand by and watch them get stabbed the fuck up. I saw all these dudes who were supposed to be down with this Cripping stand on the sideline the entire time this fight went on and do nothing, but as soon as it was over they had everything in the world to say. I was one of those that fought for what I believed in and I was elated they took notice of my efforts.

Here I was still on Fish Row. Just to give the readers some perspective here, there was no way I was supposed to leave fish row until I was classified by the institution committee. But my cell door came sliding open before I had seen anyone.

AMERICA'S CONDUCT

The police in the gun tower told me that some people outside wanted to see me. I really wasn't trippin off those dudes that much because Big Sadd, Lil Sadd, Baby Bubble and several more of my immediate homeboys were there, and I knew for sure Lil Sadd would ride with me.

I walked outside and there they were, the group of individuals that had caused Crips to lose their lives, and had attempted to transform the Crips into something foreign while still pretending to represent the Blue Rag. I walked up to the table where they all stood around acting as if I held them in reverence, which I didn't. I respected Big Treach, Big Tookie, Big Evil and other Crips on Death Row and I wasn't ashamed to let it be known where my allegiance was.

They started the meeting off by saying to me, "What's up La La," then began introducing themselves. I knew most of them, but not the actual shot callers that I had heard so much about. When I saw these dudes, I was at a loss for words. I couldn't believe these dudes standing before me were responsible for the downfall of some of the most notorious Crips in the inner city. I couldn't believe they had convinced real Crips to harm other Crips with whatever the fuck they were telling them. Trust me, none of them were Big Treach, Big Evil, or Big Took. I was in the county jail when they were around Big Treach, and trust me, none of them ever challenged him.

They asked me where I stood on all the shit that had happened in the past. I asked them what they were talking about. They said the Blue Note, and C.C.O. Shit. I told them that I was a Crip and stand with the Crips.

They said, "We are Crips too."

I said, "That's what you're not, and by the way I'm not a Blue Note, I just rode with them."

One of the speakers there acted like he had all the information he needed to indict me. He said some stupid shit like they talked to Big Sparks, which didn't mean shit to me. They said "Look, we aren't trippin down here. We just wanted to let you know where we stand."

These dudes were agents; trust me, I knew exactly where they stood. I told them I'm not trippin, if ya'll don't cross my line then we don't have a problem. You would never guess who was sitting there - Mr. Malone, Big Ant; how surprising is that?

Isn't it funny how he just happened to be everywhere I was? You couldn't write a script like this to save your life. These dudes were some real characters. Trust me they were serious and don't take my lack of respect for them as a joke, because that's what they weren't. They had some real live slaves following them who would've jumped out of a 10-story window for them if told to do so. After this fake-ass meeting, I walked back to my cell thinking, *The police sure love these mf's.* They allowed these dudes to call me out of my cell off Fish Row to a meeting. This was the second time I'd had a direct dealing with Big Ant and the police. I went back to my cell immediately to write Big Sadd a kite telling him to send me a knife. Before I could make it back to my cell good enough, the sergeant came to my cell informing me that they were going to move somebody into my cell. I told him I didn't care who they moved in with me. I knew this sergeant from when I was 19 yrs old; so many of the C/O's there knew us from over the years. He knew these dudes were out to get me, and his alliance was with them. The sergeant's thinking, I assumed, was that I didn't understand the severity of the situation. The sergeant said, "It's not like that La La. We're moving Malone in the cell with you."

I told him, "I don't care who you move in here with me, Malone ain't gone do shit to me."

He asked me was I sure I was okay with the move, and I told him that I was. They had to get my consent before they were able to move Big Ant in the cell with me. My consent took the heat off the administration if anything happened to me. But the worst thing that could've happened would have been for me to say I didn't want him in the cell with me; they would've shouted to the mountaintop that La La is scary, that he is not a warrior. I can assure you that I wasn't scared of Big Ant or any other human-being running around there. I learned a valuable lesson during the war with the Mexican Mafia; the bigger they are the harder they fall. And I can tell you, I saw some of the biggest Black dudes fall, run and some other shit. I had just the plan for Big Ant. I saw my father perform it when I was a youngster, and I had just the maneuver to neutralize any threat that may come my way by way of Big Ant.

Big Ant was their super warrior; he carried out most of their hits. The Mexican Mafia even feared Big Ant, because when we were at war he destroyed them every chance he got. Big Ant wasn't one of those dudes that fought in just the Crips or BGF's wars; he fought in all the Black wars and he knew his business, so let me be straight about who Big Ant was. The SHU 2 deceivers decided they were going to teach me a lesson once and for all, so they were sending in the killer. Remember, just 10 minutes earlier they weren't trippin, and they didn't care that I had homeboys from East Coast Crips there. That's how arrogant these dudes were. But those that didn't know me were about to learn I didn't give a fuck about any of Big Ant's accolades; I was going to cut his ass up. I was one Crip that believed the Crips couldn't be fucked with by anybody, and that included Mr. Malone. I grew up around the boss hogs of the Crips, and I didn't see any of them running around there, only BGF loving mf's.

Before Big Ant actually moved in, I remembered my father was in an altercation with my uncle Norman, my mother's sister Reolar's husband. I recall them arguing about something and my father kept walking towards him, telling him to come forward, but my uncle kept retreating saying put those razors down. I didn't see any razors until I looked closely at his hands. He had razors lined up in the creases of his fingers, each one of them. I thought to myself, even then as a youngster, it wouldn't be a good idea for my uncle to walk forward.

Since I didn't have enough time to make a knife or send for one as I had intended to do with Big Sadd, and seeing that they gave us a million of them, I decided these razors would do the trick. I laced them between all of my fingers and waited for Big Ant to walk in the cell.

On cue, there he was. I watched how the gun tower kept eyeing the cell. I was laughing on the inside. Trust me, in prison you have these dudes that think they're somebody's boss and expect you to respect them the way they think they should be respected. I was from East Coast Crips and to this very day there's not one soul on this earth that could ever say they saw me get my ass kicked, or that I followed behind these dudes.

I have always represented what was in my heart in the midst of disagreements with other men. If they thought for one second that I was going to stand there and let Big Ant do something to me they had to be sick in their heads.

When he walked through the door, I was standing up in the back of the cell. I had one thing on my mind, teaching him a lesson he thought he'd never learn. Big Ant said to me, "What's up, Bro?"

I said, "Crip."

He said, "What's up, La La?"

I said, "Cuzz, fuck all that bullshit, what you come in here for?"

He said, "La La, why don't we get along."

I said, "Because I'm a Crip and you're not."

He said, "What do you mean by that, Bro?" (Remember, I had never heard Big Ant say "Cuzz," and I had known him since 1983.)

I said, "Has it slipped your mind that you sent me that bullshit in the hole?"

He was checkmated. The games were over. It really had slipped his mind that he had done such a thing, because many people that had crossed their path hadn't challenged them. So he literally had forgotten and was stuck in his habitual character, i.e. trying to intimidate everyone he came into contact with.

I told him, "Cuzz, look, I'm a Crip and you or nobody on this planet will ever change that fact. I'm going to die a Crip. All you mf's walk around here acting like ya'll are offended by the Crips. Scores of us don't give a fuck about what ya'll represent. At least we have the courage to represent what we believe in, yet ya'll pretend to be something you're not. And what's so cold is mf's like you are original Crips. We are following what ya'll started and continue to believe in it. Because most of ya'll stopped believing don't give ya'll the right to attack the homies. Ya'll act like you're so manly; at least have the courage to tell everyone what y'all are and let them choose the way y'all did. I have homies that died representing East Coast Crips; do you think I'm going to come to prison and let some mf I don't know stop me from Cripping? If I'm making a mistake let me make them the way you had a chance to make them, but I refuse to let you or anybody else tell me what the fuck I ain't going to do. This is Crip and Crips don't die they multiply."

Big Ant said, "I understand, Bro." Big Ant wanted to shake hands, but that wasn't possible without me exposing my intent. I told him, "I'm cool, cuzz." I knew Big Ant, and I saw in his eyes that he respected me and that he knew what I was saying was who he once was. Now we stood on opposite sides, yet the courage in all men is recognizable no matter the causes, so he was compelled to yield to that reality. I had been prepared to die or attempt to kill anyone that tried to control me. I would never have allowed any of those dudes in there to dictate to me because I knew their motives were insincere. But what's so sad is they were willing to harm, destroy or kill anyone that refused to accept their outright deception as truth, and they frowned upon those that attempted to save the vulnerable from their wrath. I refused then and refuse now to become victimized by cowardice. Big Ant left the next morning and I walked out right behind him, directly to where his comrades hung out and told them, "I don't know what Big Ant told y'all. I know y'all thought he was going to do something to me, but he didn't. I'm not worrying about him or any of y'all. This is still Crip!"

I don't know why they never attempted to stab me, because I saw other Crips that were more notable than myself taken down and defeated by them. I believe the difference for many of those other Crips that were in harm's way was that they foolishly joined their organization or sympathized with them, forfeiting away any protection they had as Crips. I truly counted on my upbringing and my belief in the strength of the Crip movement to prevail over these dudes' deceit. In addition, I expected my homies from East Coast Crips to back my play, but many of them had joined these dudes' organization as well. For the most part I knew I had to stay strong for my father, mother and myself.

Shortly after that incident they started backstabbing each other. Monster, from 8 Tray Gangster, was there also. Monster (along with Big Heroin) is the only one I've seen with the courage to say what he was, without playing games. Monster didn't hide behind the blue rag; he screamed from his lungs "Black Revolution." I respected him because he was true to his convictions. He and Big Ant became cellmates and they were comrades. This is when I saw the absolute fear in most of the Crips, who justified not taking a stand against these dudes by pretending there wasn't any proof that they were no longer Crips. When Monster first arrived there were still a few Crips that were inclined to challenge him and his beliefs, one of whom was Big Busta from East Side Crips. Busta was 5'9", 210 pounds, 20-inch arms. He wore an Afro, had a light skin complexion and walked wide-armed, like he was just too big and there wasn't enough room on the planet for him to swing his arms around. He walked deliberately slowly and hardly ever said a word to anyone. When he did speak, it was worth paying attention because it was so rare. He never smiled, always looking as if he was mad at the world, daring anyone to stare in his direction. Busta was crazy. He called a meeting on Monster and Monster agreed to come. When he finally showed up to the meeting there were approximately 15 Crips, but Monster by his lonesome. We waited for Monster a good minute, then this is how the meeting went. Monster came walking up to where we were all standing waiting on him at a concrete table in front of the prison canteen. Busta approached Monster and told him to have a seat because he wanted to ask him a few questions about his beliefs and whether or not he was still a Crip. I had known Monster since we were teenagers and I had never known him to be scared. He had always been quite aggressive, so this was going to be interesting. Monster's head was shaved completely bald. He wore murder one sunglasses and his clothes were creased up immaculately. Today there is so much controversy surrounding Monster that many people don't think he's entitled to any recognition, but I don't feel that way about it. I'm only recording history the way I witnessed it. Monster is one of the most intelligent men I have ever known and I have always respected that about him. I don't agree with a lot of things he has done, but he's entitled to his history. Monster sat down, took off his glasses and introduced himself to us by his new Swahili name, Sanyika. Then he stood, poker-faced, waiting to be questioned by Big Busta. Busta started in on him by asking him, "Cuzz, are you still a Crip?" Monster replied, "No, I'm not a Crip nor should I have ever been. It took me a long time to realize how foolish I was to claim a street I don't own. The government owns all of our neighborhoods and could take them away whenever it wanted to, so I'm happy to say I'm not a Crip. I am an African Revolutionary Freedom Fighter." Can you imagine the looks on my homeboys' faces when Monster told them the truth about who he was and what he represented? That wasn't good enough for many of them still. I wasn't shocked by what he said; I had been fighting against them for the last six years. As my homeboys continued to stand there dumbfounded, I sat admiring Monster for being truthful and having the courage to separate what he now represented from the Crips. The rest of his comrades were attempting to deceive the Crips that didn't know any better into believing they were still Crips. There wasn't anything else to be said; Monster had told them what they didn't want to hear. Busta had no choice but to end his questioning on the spot, but he fired one more round at Monster. "Cuzz, we're Crips and we ain't going to have that bullshit on this main line." Monster replied, "I'm an African Freedom Fighter. Someday I wish you brothers would join us in our quest to fight for our freedom here in America. The government owns the neighborhoods y'all have tattooed on your bodies and most of y'all don't even have a neighborhood to go home to anymore because the Mexicans have taken them over. I hope you brothers become conscious soon." This seemed like the worst interrogation ever, but to me it was the most effective because now all of the Crips that attempted to act like these dudes were still Crips could no longer claim that foolishness. Monster, with great clarity, made it clear to all of them that the SHU 2 deceivers weren't Crips any longer.

Monster got up, adjusted his murder ones, and walked off like the militant he claimed to be. I was impressed to say the least. Not long after that, Monster and Big Ant got into it over something, a hamburger or something food-related. This was a dream come true for me, because every time one of them fell out with each other they would always tell their secrets to outside parties, and I loved it. I knew about most of their secrets because of their internal conflicts, so when they called themselves, thinking they were deceiving everyone, I knew they were liars. This time, Monster was up against it. He was now facing their enforcers and he knew none of his comrades would ever go against Big Ant for him. He had to find somebody he could trust. He knew my dislike for Big Ant, so he came to me for a knife. I gave him a 9 inch flat that would've gotten the job done, and told him if he didn't use it I wanted it back. I had never seen Monster look so concerned as he did that day, but their conflict never reached its peak. They worked out their differences and moved out of the cell with each other.

I moved back to seven building with Big Sadd. We were both getting close to going home. Sadd had 18 months left of his sentence and I had 2 years left of my 18 year sentence. Sadd and I sat around and talked about all the things we were going to do once we got out. Neither of us had a dime to our name, but our dreams were large and we fully expected to fulfill them. I talked about all the cars I was going to buy when I got out. My mind wandered into another galaxy of the things I wanted to do. I hadn't learnt anything about the functioning of society rules the entire time I was in prison. My entire stay there was about just trying to survive. I felt like I was entitled, and that someone would realize they had made a mistake in convicting me and compensate me for being wrongfully imprisoned. Those beliefs of mine never ceased.

I was given a job working in the kitchen with one of my homeboys out of Compton, named Big Heroin. I met Big Heroin in 1983 when I first was sent to the county jail from juvenile hall. He was on the very row I was sent to, and one of the leaders on the tier. He was close friends with my older homeboys, Big Owl from 68th Street East Coast Crips, and Big Duck from 89th Street East Coast Crips. Big Heroin was with Big Ant's crew but, like Big Monster, he didn't hide it from anyone. He constantly told me not to ever trust his comrades because they were lying snakes.

He liked the fact that I stood on my own and couldn't be broken by his comrades. He also used to tell me that Raymond Washington would be proud of me.

Heroin was approximately 5'9", 200 pounds, and a fierce warrior like Big Ant. In fact he loved Big Ant to death, but would tell Ant he was wrong for the way he went about trying to recruit people. Big Heroin had a golden brown complexion, wore a sandy brown color Afro jerry curl and was built like muscle man. He and I worked out daily, harder than most human beings on Earth. What scores of people in society viewed as extreme, in prison we viewed as something simple. In prison, everything is intensified by a thousand, so we worked out until we were completely exhausted. Heroin taught me about how all the prison gangs got started and what all the conflicts between them were over. I learnt so many things from him. I continued to believe that my success in life would come through the path of me hollering Crip out of my mouth, which was in direct conflict with the African Freedom Fighters' agenda. I placed them between a rock and a hard place, because many of them still paraded around there as if they were still Crips. It was difficult for them to sell their lies to those that were actually Crips, although many of their homeboys accepted them either way. My position had always been once you leave you're gone and you shouldn't have any say in Crips business. The problem was that even though they had left, they were still attempting to voice their opinions on our business. People like Big Ant were determined to succeed at their mission, which was stronger than many Crips' desires to be Crips. I refused to go for any of their maneuvers. When the Crips around there got into it with other races I would represent the Crips. The SHU 2 deceivers knew they couldn't tell me shit, so they would go behind my back, attempting to undermine me with the Mexicans and whites every chance they got. But the whites and Mexicans would tell me the minute any of them did such a thing, because they also didn't like or respect how they carried themselves.

I recall approaching Big Heroin about how his people attempted to undermine me. I told him what the Mexicans and whites had told me and that I intended to confront this one mf that ran with Big Ant's crew. I couldn't figure out for the life of me how that dude was able to get anyone to believe he was worth one cent, let alone be a supreme leader of men that followed behind him. I knew I was tougher and just as smart as he was. But Big Heroin asked me to leave it alone, because it would start the blacks back to fighting and stabbing each other and he didn't like that at all. I didn't care because these dudes had gotten away with their bullshit for far too long. I was still in direct communication with Death Row, waiting on whatever mission they wanted carried out against the SHU 2 Deceivers. Big Heroin went with me to the Mexican and white shot-callers, and told each of them that I spoke for the Crips and they should disregard anything any of his cohorts had to say. That's the kind of man Big Heroin was - 100% genuine.

I became good friends with one of the Mexican mafia members there - he was one of the coolest human begins I ever met in my life. (I cannot ever mention his name because of an agreement we made with each other. I will always honor that trust.) One day some of the SHU 2 deceivers went to him telling him that they were the shot callers of the Crips and that I was under them. He knew better than to believe them, because he knew everything about each one of them from his own investigation of who was who and what everyone represented. So when they made their attempts to deceive him it caused him to distrust them further than he already did. Big Heroin had gone behind their backs and debunked their double-dealings ahead of them. My Mexican friend couldn't stand Big Ant, which had more to do with what Big Ant had done to the Mexicans over the years in prisons than the games they were playing right now. Nevertheless he wanted to confront Big Ant about talking behind my back, so I went to Big Ant and asked him if he was going to the Mexicans and whites telling them that I didn't speak for the Crips. Of course he said no. Them dudes wouldn't tell the truth if their lives depended on it. Prison had destroyed them; they had no principles. Their entire existence consisted of deception. If they could successfully mislead someone that was an accomplishment in their lives, and they celebrated that sort of stuff. No matter what the deal was I had to take the side of Big Ant because of the racial situation, but I also wanted Ant and his crew to stay in their own lanes. I went back to my Mexican friend and told him that Big Ant denied his accusation. He asked me to go get him and he'd tell him to his face. He asked me to give Big Ant a knife and he would have his own knife and take Big Ant on and may the best man win. Big Ant himself would've welcomed such a challenge from my Mexican Partna any day of the week.

My Mexican friend took a liking to me far greater than what's acceptable in prison because of race. He claimed to have witnessed me stabbing someone on the yard one day and told me that I held the knife the wrong way. He said he was willing to teach me the correct way because he liked my style and wouldn't ever want to see or hear about me being stabbed. He wanted to be sure I could use a weapon properly, and to teach me how to battle with the best of them. My friend could do whatever he wanted to around there; the C/O's allowed him that privilege. He arranged for us to practice knife-fighting with one another. He taught me the difference between stabbing a person once and stabbing him multiple times. He showed me how to take a weapon from someone attacking me. I got real good at it; he would come at me full-force and I learnt to disarm him with ease. He showed me how to continuously stab someone when they tried to grab at the weapon. That's what prison life was like for me - complete madness. After he taught me everything he felt I needed to know, he would just stare at me, sipping on his coffee, then he would say, "There's one more thing LaLa. Make some time for me. It's important." I found him on the yard one morning and asked him if he could talk. He said, "Yeah, this won't take long. I have a question I want to ask you." I said, "What's up?" I thought it was going to be something about one of my homeboys disrespecting his people, the shit that happens on an everyday basis around there, but that wasn't the question at all. He asked me, "LaLa, if we were to go to war out here on the yard, would you stab me?" I told him, "No." He responded by saying, "I'll kill you in a heartbeat." I was shocked because of how close we were with each other. He explained, "Don't ever take anything for granted in prison. Nobody is your friend in here. The minute you start trusting people in here is the minute you're going to lose your life, LaLa. Because you trust me the way that you do, my people will send me to kill you in time of conflict. Do you understand?" I said, "Yeah." He said, "I want to ask you again if we go to war out here, will you stab me?" I said, "Hell yeah, fast as a mf." He said "Okay, now you're a warrior, and if my people ever find out I taught you anything they will kill me. But before they do, you and I will have to strap up and may the best man win." I told him I would never tell a soul anything about who he was.

    Days later, Ice Man, from 69th Street East Coast Crips, and I went to the hole for allegedly stabbing Big Busta from East Side Crip. Busta tried to have one up on me because he was from Raymond Washington's generation of Crips. He thought he could manipulate me with information he believed I wouldn't have any knowledge of. He said to me, "LaLa, Raymond left word with me to get you and Big Sadd to start a new gang called East Coast Crip Elites." I took offense to him attempting to play on my intelligence. I told Big Sadd I thought Big Busta was with Big Ant and them because of the way he got at me with some straight up bullshit. Raymond didn't leave him any such instruction, for me or anybody else. Busta had to think I was stupid or crazy, or both. Busta didn't go down easy. To his credit he fought hard and long. While we were in the hole they couldn't prove whether Ice Man or I had stabbed Busta so they released us back into general population. While we were on fish row, Ice Man and I were moved directly next door to each other. Ice Man was a real skinny dude, 5'8", 150 pounds maybe, dark-skinned. He wore his hair short, and had brown eyes and a thick black mustache. Ice Man was wild and always into shit. Late one night I kept hearing somebody screaming, so I got up and went to the vent to check on Ice Man. I asked him if he was okay, and he said he was cool, for me not to trip. Ice Man can throw down, so I wasn't worried about him getting his ass beat. Later I heard some more rumbling, and again I got up and yelled over there, "Cuzz, are you all right?" They were over there fighting, without question. The next morning when the doors opened up for us to go eat breakfast, his cellmate came running out of the cell screaming, "Help, help, help! He's trying to kill me." I looked at Ice Man and just shook my head in disbelief. Before the police came to investigate I asked Ice Man what did he do to that man. He said, "Nothing, cuzz." They came and took his ass straight to the hole, pending investigation of some crazy shit I care not to even mention.

    I moved back in the cell with Big Sadd. While we were gone the blacks and Mexicans had arranged a basketball game on the prison grounds. I wanted to play so I got at the people running the event. All the rules and agreement on what the bets consisted of was ironed out. One of the major things was whoever was winning when they announced yard recall **WOULD BE THE WINNER OF THE GAME.** The bet was ten boxes of cigarettes. The losers were expected to pay up at the end of the game. This is the sort of shit people are killed over in prison and why wars are started between different races. Everyone agreed they understood the rules. The ball was jumped at half court and the game began. The lead went back and forth the entire game. We had some super ghetto stars on our team: Lefty, Fillmore, and Todd, who was from 89th Street East Coast Crips. He was a bad man with that basketball in his hand. At halftime I believe we were up by 2 or 3 points. The Mexicans also had some ballers that really could play, but their determination came from not wanting to lose anything to the blacks. They literally hated blacks like the KKK had in the 1960's. When the game started back up it went down to the wire. The game was tied and I had the ball in my hands when I heard the police just about to call yard recall. I was at half court when I heard the crackling in the speakers. He barely got the word "Yard" out of his mouth before I raised up to take the half-court shot. Before he could finish saying "Yard Recall" the ball went straight through the net. All the blacks on the sidelines jumped in the air so high, yelling and screaming. It was a spectacular shot - all bottom of the net. The game was over but the Mexicans didn't want to pay. They protested, saying the shot didn't count because it was after the man said yard recall. They wanted to play one more quarter the following day. But the blacks weren't having any part of such a thing. We wanted to be paid. The dude that ran the yard for the Mexicans I knew quite well. His people had already told him a different version of the bet so he asked me what the bet was. I told him "The bet was whoever was wining when the man called yard recall wins the game." He asked what did we bet. I told him, "Ten boxes of cigarettes." He asked his people what they were protesting. They told him "The shot LaLa took was after the police said yard recall." He told them right there on the spot, "The shot LaLa took was right before the man said yard recall. Go get the ten boxes right now and pay them." They did just that in record time. That is one of the major differences in our race versus other races here in America. You couldn't pay blacks to have orderly conduct like that. Black people would've been offended that this black was talking instead of that black. Always something stupid. I even heard somebody ask who the fuck did the Mexican dude doing all the talking think he was. They said he acted like if he didn't tell them to pay us they wouldn't have.

Soon after that I was on the yard and the program lieutenant called Big Sadd and me to the office. Once we made it to his office he told us they had received kites stating that we were forcing inmates to traffic weapons throughout the prison. Doesn't that tactic sound familiar? The lieutenant knew us fairly well, and he knew some prisoners wanted us off the mainline yard. He also knew both of us were under two years to the house, so he told us either he had to put us in the hole or send us to the modified program they had in Building One and Two. Modified program is where they house prisoners that were deemed program failures. We were allowed to stay on the facility but we weren't allowed to be around the other prisoners on general population. We were sent to 2 building. The lieutenant told us, "Don't make a big deal out of it. Go over there, get some rest and go home. Prison is a mess."

Unsociable

Modified program is where I would be until CDC called me for parole. All the crazy shit I had to go through distracted me from thinking about my innocence most of the time, so I concentrated more on how I was going to survive in that mentally sick institution.

Big Sadd and I remained cellmates once we arrived over there. I knew most of the prisoners there. Sugar Bear from Hoover, who had been at Tracy with me, would become my cellmate before I left as well. He is one of the smartest men I have ever had the pleasure of knowing. Mr. Henry Wilds, Big Kill Kill, from Raymond Ave 120th Street Crips, and many others were there, so it wasn't like being sent to a foreign country. All we were was recycled inmates. I didn't waste any time trippin on those dudes and their politics. They were going to be who and what they were, no matter what. I just knew I wasn't going to join their rotten asses.

Modified program gave me a chance to think about the possibility of actually going home. It was weird to me how society operated. I was completely innocent of the crime I had been sent to prison for, yet I was feeling fortunate about the possibility that I could really go home. It had to be similar to what the slaves felt when they came to America. First and foremost they didn't have any business being in this country at all, but once that they were in America, when one of them survived being brutalized or raped during one of white people's hate-filled excursions, they felt extremely fortunate and blessed. There I was, feeling like the slaves – extremely fortunate that I was close to being released for a crime I hadn't committed, instead of being outraged and furious that I was there in the first place.

Psychologically, America mastered these techniques a century ago, and continues to practice them on us still. Whenever I sat before any counselor or committee in prison, they would not entertain the thought of anyone being innocent, so I was unable to think about bringing up the fact that I shouldn't be sitting in front of them at all. You have to sit before them and listen to them tell you how awful you are, and how the severity of your crime warrants you being there. They tell you about how your history of committing crimes, crimes you may or may not have committed, has resulted in your placement in an unfavorable category in prison. When the administrative people constantly tell you how bad you are, you start to believe what they are saying about you, and before you realize it they have created a programmed robot that acts as they tell it to, when they tell it to. You, like the many that came before you, have become a walking zombie.

I met another one of my homeboys in modified program, Dirty Red, from 190th Street East Coast Del Amo Block Crips. Dirt was athletic, built like a body builder, and I grew to like and trust him. He was only there for a violation of his parole, and having come recently from the streets, he told me what I should expect once I was paroled. I had a few homeboys who sent me money anytime I needed it while I was in prison, so money wasn't one of my concerns. Fitting into society was my chief concern, because I knew the things I had been exposed to in prison had affected me mentally. I was already an outcast from society, but what I had evolved into in prison was horrifying to say the least, even to me.

Libby and I had become serious with each other; she visited me for two years when I returned to Folsom State Prison. Jackie, on the other hand, didn't feel obligated to visit me, and she barely did. She and I had grown apart because of my immaturity. I judged her actions too critically, and as I got older, I understood better many of my own faults as opposed to judging other people's flaws.

Peaches and I stayed in touch also. She was always going to be cool with me. I truly appreciated all that she had ever done for me. But Libby was the one that had my attention. She knew how to take the lead and it made me feel like I had grown up from being a teenager into becoming a man. She was the final piece that was missing from my empty world. With her I could have easily made the transition any man needed to succeed on the outside of prison.

Libby started bringing her children with her to visit me. She had four children but only brought three of them to visit. Her oldest son, Joseph, was a teenager; I believe he was 18 years old at the time. The other three, JR, Ivory and Ebony, weren't more than ten years old. I wasn't ready to have a woman like Libby in my life. She was too independent. She owned homes and other properties and I was only a survivor of a prison camp of mentally ill patients. I hadn't accomplished anything in my life. Subconsciously I didn't even believe I deserved her, but she felt differently. She believed I needed her to have a chance to succeed in this life. She understood better than I did what I needed.

I hadn't heard anything from Jackie in close to six months. My life was moving forward in rapid speed. The reality was upon me that I was about to be let out of prison. I had approximately six months left to go when I talked to Jackie again. I told her that I was about to come home and that I wanted to see her. For whatever reason, she and I argued about everything. Out of all the women I've ever been with in my life, Jackie and I argued about any and everything. However, I learnt the most from her about veracity. She taught me a lesson that I will never forget about truth, honesty and deception, and other women will suffer because of it.

When Big Sadd finally went home it was one of the saddest days in my life. We had been through some difficult times together in there and now he was gone. I knew I was next; I just needed to hold on a bit longer.

Dirty Red had 30 days left before he was going home, so I wanted to make plans for us before he left. I asked him what his plans were out there when he left. Dirty was a thug through and through, so his intentions were to hit the streets as fast as they let him out of the prison gates.

I went on a visit the following week and talked to Libby about my plans on the streets once I got out. I told her what I intended to do, which was to give myself a chance to prove that I could make it on my own. I explained to her that I had never in my life paid one utility bill, let alone been responsible for anything that wasn't negative. I had to learn how to do those things without the help of anyone. She thought that was foolish of me. She wanted me to move in with her and the kids, but I didn't want to. I felt it would make me dependent on her. She agreed to support whatever it was I wanted to do. She said to me, "LaLa, I have a three bedroom house for rent. I will let you rent it out from me for $600 a month, and furnish it for you before you get out, since you want to be responsible." I asked her to allow Dirty Red to live there until I came home. She wanted to meet him, so I let him call her. They talked and agreed they would meet one another when he got out, but she told me she would allow him to stay in the house.

I hadn't even discussed my plans with Dirt yet when I got back from my visit with Libby. The next day on the yard I told Dirt I needed to talk with him. I told him I talked to my woman about him living at one of her houses that I planned on living in once I got out of prison. Dirt thought I was bullshitting. He said to me, "Cuzz, ain't no bitch going to give you no house. "

I said, "Cuzz, on everything I love, she's going to let you move in before I get out. I will let you call and talk to her."

He said, "If it's real, cuzz, I'll do it."

Libby furnished the house and put a lock on the room that I was going to sleep in. Dirt went home to our new home together. We talked often and he kept me informed about the comings and goings in that area which was the 83rd Street Gangster Crips area.

My brother Boxco had just arrived to Folsom around that time. Boxco didn't look strong like he had when I first saw him in Tracy. He looked weaker, but he was still my brother nevertheless. Something had happened to him in Tracy where he began taking medications of some sort that caused him to act crazy. He would just stand up in the dining hall where prisoners are told by the guards not to leave until instructed to. I surely didn't want to see or hear about the police shooting him, so they allowed me to go down to the building where he was being housed to talk with him.

When I saw him I was so happy. I thought about our entire lives together as brothers. In Tracy, I was in the hole when I first saw him, so I wasn't able to be in

AMERICA'S CONDUCT

his direct presence, but in Folsom I was finally given the opportunity to hug him and remember how much I loved him as my big brother. I remember feeling sorry for him, because something was definitely wrong with him.

I asked him how he was doing and what was he doing there in Folsom. He told me he was cool and they just sent him to Folsom, that he didn't know why. I asked him had he talked to our mother. He said he hadn't heard from anyone, but I know my mother had written to him while he was in Tracy because several of my homeboys had been calling her keeping her abreast of his condition. Lee Macc, from 118th Street Blocc East Coast Crips, was one of my homeboys in particular that called her often, informing her of Boxco's mental state. Boxco began telling me about our brother Terrence, as he had when I saw him in Tracy. I asked him what kinds of medicine do they have him taking. He told me he doesn't take any medication but I knew that wasn't true. Clearly there was something not right about my brother's conduct. He asked me to get him some cigarettes, so I brought him a can of tobacco. I also asked him if he had known the rules about not getting up from the tables in the dining hall until the police instructed him to. He said, "I be finished eating, so I leave. I'm not going to just be sitting there. Fuck the police." He then asked me had I heard from our mother. I told him I had, and that I would tell her that he was here with me, which I knew would make her feel much better.

I left and told him I would come down there as often as the guards would allow me. I thought my brother was sick in some capacity, but I also felt much better to know he could remember everyone in our family and that he was being defiant with the police. Still I didn't want to see them hurt him, which I knew they would do without hesitation. So I asked Legs Diamond, who was down there with him, to watch out for him. I asked the guards to consider that he's on medication, and asked if they would take that into consideration and allow him to leave as he pleased when he finished his meals.

I called my mother to tell her that Boxco was there with me. She was happy and didn't worry as much. She asked me how he was doing. I told her she knew how crazy Boxco was, but that I would look after him as long as he was there with me.

Right before it was time for me to go home, my homeboy Big Sike was killed. He was someone I was counting on being out there for me when I paroled. His death was a major setback for me, and it affected me hard.

Then Rodney King, a black motorist was pulled over by L.A.P.D. and beaten close to death. Scores of white Americans acted like they just couldn't believe the police department carried on this way, while many blacks couldn't believe these non-believers found L.A.P.D. conduct so surprising. This had been America's conduct towards African Americans from the beginnings of America's existence, so who were they attempting to deceive, manipulate or trick into believing this wasn't the norm against African Americans here in the United States? Sure, many blacks knew it to be, but there are African Americans that pretended it was surprising to them as well. That's part of the mental retardation I speak of that has affected so many people here in America.

I thought to myself, Rodney King was fortunate, like many of the slaves that had escaped death at the hands of white people way back when. Those that found his beating to be shocking ought to see firsthand how the correctional officers in prison beat the prisoners when there isn't anyone there to watch their criminal conduct, or should I say, their ways of correcting the behavior of those viewed by society as worthless human beings? Or how the Sheriff's Deputies in the Los Angeles County Jails beat the prisoners for minor violations. Who's holding any of them accountable for their actions? That shit usually gets swept under the rug because the system is set up for them to mistreat us, as it has always been. I thought Rodney King's ass-whomping wasn't shit compared to all the things I saw law enforcement officials get away with.

The time had come - July 10, 1992, my parole date. I woke up that morning feeling nervous and uncertain about my future. What would it be like for me not to have to fight for my life with the people claiming to be my loved ones? I had become accustomed to conflict and confusion; would I miss those things? The police allowed me to make a few rounds to my homeboys' cells in the building to give away some of my property. I went to Big Kill Kill's cell first to give him my television set and a few more things. Then I made a few more stops, said my goodbyes to some of the prisoners I knew I would miss. Then I took a shower. It was time to leave that life behind. I couldn't prolong the inevitable; it was time to push forward. The streets awaited my return. I had made all the preparations I thought were essential for my survival in society. Libby had sent my dressed outs, an all blue silk outfit with some fancy type leather tennis shoes and a blue pager, and some iron would be awaiting at my mother's house the minute I arrived.

As I was leaving, several guards came by to wish me well. A lot of inmates were literally sad to see me leave. I had stood up to those Imposters in there, and many of my homies were going to miss my presence.

When R&R (Receiving and Release) called for me to report for release it was all finally real for me. This nightmare had come to an end. I was finally going home to see my mother, sisters, brother, woman and all of my homies, in a matter of hours. My sister Debra and my homeboy Big Ricc Rocc were coming to pick me up, so my ride home would give me some time to think about all the things I wanted to do. But first, I had to make it out of the gates. I had seen many people fail to make that last transition, so I wasn't safe until I walked through those last doors and out of R&R.

AMERICA'S CONDUCT

On my way to R&R, I walked through the first gate, into the general population. Standing there awaiting me were Baby Bubble, Lil Sadd, Big Asmo and several more of my homeboys. My heart was broken when I saw Lil Sadd and Baby Bubble's faces. Their eyes were watery, and so was mine because I knew what they were feeling. I tried to stop both of them before a tear rolled down their faces. I felt their pain but it wasn't necessary for them to feel sad, because I wasn't going to forget them, like many of my homeboys had once they left them behind. They had become accustomed to being forgotten.

I was different from most of my homeboys in that regard. I truly loved my homeboys, and I knew what it felt like to be abandoned by those who claim to love you. I wasn't going to ever forget them. We had all been in prison together for 10 years and better; we had grown up from teenage boys to men in there. So of course we all were going to miss each other. We all hugged and I told them that I would write, and left my mother's number for them to call me. I went through the last gate to R&R. I got my dress out, and it felt good to get back into street clothes. The police in R&R asked me questions only I should know about my mother, then gave me $200 and allowed me to walk out the last gate, onto a bus. I was dropped off in the parking lot, where my sister and my homeboy Ricc Rocc awaited me in a sky blue 1992 Cadillac.

I hugged my sister and shook Ricc Rocc's hand. I told my sister to look at Folsom from the outside, and asked her how does it look to her from where she stands. She said, "Quiet." I told her shit there are some mentally retarded motherfuckers behind those walls. We drove off to their motel room, where they had spent the night before, to pick up their belongings.

I hadn't gotten high or drunk the entire time I was in prison. On the ride to the house I told my homeboy to stop by the store to get me some Old English 800 beer. He did, and then fired up some weed called Chronic. I never heard of it, but that didn't stop me from smoking it. I drank my beer and smoked some weed until I was as high as I could get. It felt good to be out of prison, but in my mind I was thinking how in the hell didn't these people know they had sent an innocent man to prison for a crime he hadn't committed, when they pride themselves on being so superior to everything on Earth?

I refused to believe that they didn't know what they were doing. Many people who are convicted for crimes they didn't commit are asked, "How were you able to do it?" Their responses are usually, "I prayed a lot and knew God would see me through this ordeal." Some straight bullshit. I knew I wasn't going to be asked how I felt because the government never acknowledged I was innocent, but in my mind and my actions I would be expressing how I felt loud and clear. I was upset that I had to miss all of those years of being around my family. I didn't want to hear anybody tell me anything about justice, freedom or righteousness when I knew firsthand society rarely followed the rules of law they expected everyone else to follow. I intended to make my own rule of laws as I saw fit, for at least 10 years and 4 months of my life, then call us even. Where was justice for people like me who were being crucified by the system every day of the year?

I knew what I had just left and what suffering looked and felt like for the misfortunate people in America.

On the ride back to my mother's house, Ricc Rocc was playing a song written by K-Solo, titled "You Can't Hold Me Back", and that's just how I felt. Ricc Rocc was telling me about one of my homeboys named Lil Fluxx. He told me about his oldest brother Roc that had been killed and how it had affected Lil Fluxx and fractured the foundation of the East Coast Crips. He also told me what I had been hearing for some time in prison, that Lil Fluxx was one of the baddest dudes in South Central Los Angeles. I loved that because it meant he was on our side. I hadn't met him yet but I looked forward to it. Lil Bubble had told me about him when I used to talk to him on the phone while I was in prison. He didn't think Lil Fluxx and I would get along, because he said we were just alike, but I disagreed with him because I never had any problem with any of my homeboys because they were aggressive. I was raised by Big Quake. He was as aggressive as they came, along with many others I was raised with, and I loved them all to death.

When I came home there was an entirely new crew of 6-Deuces out there that were like all the other crews before them. I kept hearing about Big Ray Dog who was vicious with his hands. I heard about Young Rob who was equally tenacious as Lil Fluxx and Ray Dog. Young Rob was smooth. He was all around in his game. He fit in anywhere with anybody. I liked his style more than all the ones I had met. There were Big and Lil Boxer, Lil and Tiny Monts, Baby Man, Baby Bam, Lil Moe, Baby Moe, Lil Gangster, Big T.C., and Big C-Bone who I had known prior to going in. He was the front liner and one of my most esteemed homies. Then there's The Young One, aka Young Sadd. You will learn more about him much later. I met him years later but I had to mention him because he is the cream of the crop. He alone taught me more about courage than anyone I have ever been around in my life.

Ricc Rocc told me that my neighborhood was at war with another East Coast Crip gang, the 69th Street. I knew about all of the details surrounding that situation, but what was new for me was fighting against East Coast Crips. I had just disciplined Lil Doc for talking about doing something to another East Coast Crip gang member and there I was being told about a war that was actually going on in the inner city where I was raised. I truly didn't know how I would act, but I did know I wasn't going to allow anyone to hurt me if I could prevent it. One thing I did have in me was Malcolm X's slogan "By any means necessary." Anyone wanting to try me would be foolish I was sure of that.

AMERICA'S CONDUCT

As we were driving to my mother's house, Ricc Rocc stopped by Bethune Park. Lil Bit, Ran, Big Casper, my cousin Sandra and Ray Rat from 59th Street East Coast Crips were standing around talking. They didn't see us, but my cousin Randy did and he ran over to the car, jumped in and rode to the house with us.

When we arrived, I spotted the love of my life standing on her front porch, not knowing when we were going to arrive. As the car pulled up she spotted me inside the car and she smiled a country mile as they say. I stepped out of the car as happy as I had ever been in my life to see her. She was so elated she quickly grabbed my face with both her hands and screamed. "My baby, my baby made it home. Thank you, Jesus." Then she just stood there staring at me. I reached in my pockets and gave her all the money I had in them. The $200 plus what I had left on my prison account when I paroled.

Libby was also there, standing on the porch with my mother. She was just as excited as anyone to see me. I had asked her when she came to visit me the week before I was paroled to get me a 45 semi-automatic pistol when I got out. She kissed me and told me she had something for me. We walked to the bathroom and she handed me a 45 semi-automatic pistol. I stuffed it in my waistband and walked back outside where I felt comfortable. There was a war going on and I didn't intend to be a victim. Prison hadn't confused my common senses. They were still functioning as well as any mentally disturbed human being that had lived under the stress, pressure and anxieties I had.

My mother told me that my younger sister, Shenette, had been involved in a car accident on the freeway earlier that day picking up things for the party they were giving me that night. Through all of that Libby wanted to make love to me right then and there. I told her we had all night to do that. I wanted to go see my sister. She was in the hospital because she was doing something for me. Tiger McCloud, my sister Shenette's husband, my mother and I rode to the hospital in my 1984 Cadillac Coupe that had awaited me in my mother's driveway. Before I was paroled, one of my homeboys Big Biscuit had asked me what kind of car I wanted. He gave me a choice between an Iroc, a 5.0 Mustang or a Cadillac. I chose a 1984 Coupe, because when I was last on the street I loved Cadillacs. Biscuit on the other hand had been on the streets since he got out of Fred C. Nelles in 1983, so he knew I was making the wrong choice. He asked me again, was I sure that was the car I wanted. I told him that I was. He then said, "Are you sure you don't want the Iroc or Mustang?" He was attempting to lead me in that direction, but because I was still 17 years old mentally, I wasn't able to forget the past. I lived in the past for many more years after my release from prison. Nobody understood why I wanted that big ass car, and after seeing all the new cars on the streets I started second-guessing myself also.

When we walked inside the hospital to see my sister she was laying in the bed looking like she was in so much pain. But when she raised her head up to see me walking through the curtain she smiled so widely. I recall seeing her, feeling like I hadn't protected her. I felt it was my duty to protect her; for whatever reason I had always felt that way. But there she was, vulnerable as ever. Shenette said, smiling, "They finally let you out, huh?"

I said, "Yeah, I should have never been in there."

She said, "I know Larry, I hope you stay out. You don't belong in that place."

In my mind I was thinking she doesn't have a clue how many people like me are stuck in prison for crimes they didn't commit, and some will never make it out and nobody gives a damn about them. It's a game and the families that are affected by these injustices are wounded for a lifetime.

I asked her how she felt, because she didn't look too good. She had a scar on her beautiful face. I knew she didn't like that. I didn't either. She said, "I feel okay." I told her it doesn't feel like I've been gone a day now that I'm out. We stayed a few more minutes then made our way back to mom's house where everyone was waiting for us to arrive.

Shenette had two children at the time I paroled. Quinnette was a little cutie, shy and thin as a tree branch. Her son Joshua reminded me of myself when I was younger. He was quite protective of his older sister, and like Boxco, when she got mad, look out, Josh. Shenette was also pregnant with her youngest daughter Ashley McCloud during the accident.

My eldest sister Debra also had two children when I was paroled. Myesha Johnson had gotten grown and started dating boys. I don't think I was out a week before she ran away with some young boy that lived next door to my mother. She thought she was doing something, but they didn't have any money, and they found her two hours later. Then there was Eric Johnson, aka Infant LaLa. Go figure, the line of retardation continues to be passed on. He was quiet and very attentive; I would learn just how attentive many years later. My little brother was standing there looking shy. He wasn't the little boy I had left behind. He was now a skinny little kid, elated to see his older brother, and curious to see what kind of brother he had just gained. They were all there to welcome me home and I was equally elated and grateful to be around them all.

Later that night East Coast Crips from every street were there. Lil Quake was running from the law on a murder they alleged he committed. I was happy to see him and hoped he never got caught. Big Vince, Lil Dev, Big C-Bone, Lil C-Bone, Baby Bam, Lil Bam, Mr. Low, Big Quake, Dirty Red and so many other Crips were there, I couldn't possibly name them all. I asked Dirty Red why Loco wasn't there and he told me Loco had to take care of some business but he would come by the next day.

The party finally got started and we partied until the next morning. I danced with my mother most of the night, but Libby wasn't having any part of that. She wanted in herself. She was so much fun to be around. We danced, kissed and enjoyed each other's company all that night. They started the Crip walking contest. My homeboys hadn't seen how much I had progressed in my storytelling abilities. I had something to say and anyone that stepped in front of me that night was in for something they had never seen or felt before in their lives. I was going to tell a story of what it felt like to be taken away from your family while everyone looked on helplessly as the judicial system pretended to be representing the best interests of society, with its citizens taking part in its trickery.

I wanted to compete against Mr. Low and Lil Bubble, who I couldn't outperform when we were younger. I started with Mr. Low. I walked him down; he just stopped altogether, recognizing he couldn't win. Apparently he hadn't been through too much since I had been gone. His golden feet were rusty. Then Lil Bubble; how could he tell a story equal to what I had gone through? He didn't even pretend to have anything to express with his feet. Everyone who stepped on the floor that night got walked down, without any defense to stop my expression of injustice! I was literally the life of the party.

Lil Fluxx was also there, and I saw in him the man everyone spoke of. I had the chance in my life to be amongst the roughest inner city thugs in Los Angeles County, and Lil Fluxx was one of them. He was what they called a hog, meaning a bad "MF." He was truly every bit of its meaning. I liked him and could tell he was a bully, but not the traditional type of bully we think of. He was a bully who sought out the baddest of the bad. I liked that about him. I remember thinking I wished he had been with me inside the prison walls when I had battled with those imposters.

As the party got started, Lil Fluxx took the mic from the DJ and started rapping free style. Let me tell you, he was not a rapper. He was the worst I ever heard in my life, but he was determined to get that party started right. I laughed so hard internally that I almost died from laughter, if you ever heard of such a thing. Lil Fluxx was what I always thought a Crip should be: rough, tough, tenacious. He was the King of the ghetto, a legend, all that plus more. If I was in a battle with anyone, I would want Lil Fluxx at my side, no doubt. But he was not a rapper.

With everyone shouting at Lil Fluxx to get off the mic, Baby Bam took over, and was as good as any professional rapper I had heard. Baby Bam's rapping was smooth and fierce, just like his Cripping, I knew I would like him. He reminded me a lot of Lil Sadd. Then I met Lil Snake and Baby Fox, who was up to no good. Everything reminded me of when I was a teenager. Everyone was still doing the exact same things as my generation of homeboys.

LARRY DAVIS

The next day I called Jackie and told her that I wanted to see her so we made plans to see each other that night. I drove to 37th and Normandie to meet her at her friend CoCo's house. I was happy to see her. Although we argued a lot, there was something about Jackie that I have always loved. She told me she had driven past my mother's house the night I had gotten out. I asked her why she didn't stop by, and she said, "I didn't want to cause any problems with you and your woman." After spending time with Jackie, I learned that statement wasn't true at all. If Jackie believed you belonged to her she would have caused problems with GOD. Jackie and I attempted to find my house that night but I didn't remember where I lived, so we agreed to meet each other the next day. I went home and told Dirt that I tried to find the house the night before but forgot where we lived. He laughed and told me how to always find the house. I never forgot again.

I called Jackie the following night and told her I wanted to see her again. She picked me up at my mother's house and we drove to my house and spent the night together, making love all night long. The next morning, Dirty Red took pictures of Jackie and me. I knew Libby would be coming by sometime that day, but I wasn't worried about her just popping up over there because we had talked about calling or paging me first.

Right after Jackie left that morning Libby paged me and told me she was coming by, so I attempted to hide all the pictures that Dirt had taken of Jackie and me. But it wasn't five minutes after she entered the house that Libby confronted us about the female in the pictures with me. Libby had bought me several pajama outfits and in the photos Jackie and I were wearing those pajamas. Libby asked Dirt who the woman in the pictures was, and he told her he didn't know. Then she asked me, over and over, who was this bitch? I told her I didn't know who she was, and for her not to be asking me any questions about those pictures. But I was caught blue-handed. I should have just told Libby from the very beginning, since she had told me several years back that she would give me my space. I needed the room to find out who I was and what I wanted in life, as opposed to trying to do what I saw everyone else doing. But no, I had to play the game. Libby said to me, "It's Jackie, MF." I never knew she had any idea who Jackie was or what she looked like. Libby was just too much for me. That was the end for me and Libby.

I knew then that my future was uncertain, because I understood with clarity that Libby wasn't enough for me. I wanted more. I craved the ghetto life, something no one had ever conquered but I wanted to try. I was after the crown. I wanted to be the King of the Ghetto and I vowed to myself I would wear that crown as Big Quake had when I was a youngster, walking along with my homies from 6-Duece Neighborhood East Coast Crips.

I knew even then that I was going to hurt the people that loved me and wished me well. There was a sickness in my mind that programmed me to fail. I wasn't going to deviate from failure; it was all I had ever known. What sense did it make for me to try to overcome all the odds stacked against me? Wasn't it easier for me to fail? How was it possible that all the inner cities in the United States were doing the exact same things at the same time? Where did that script come from, for us all to fail at the exact same time? Who wrote such a thing, and why were we so inclined to follow it?

Citizens of the United States, you who truly don't know what our lives are like in the inner cities, I have given you a true picture of our world. I have been your escort through the inner cities of America, and now you know. I was sent to prison for a crime I didn't commit. Ask yourself, if you were wrongfully convicted and truly innocent, at what point would you accept that you were guilty of that crime? I served 10 years and 4 months, with three additional years on parole. I had to report to a parole officer who couldn't care less whether or not I committed the crime. His job was to see to it that I was continuously supervised, so I had to pretend that I was being a good citizen and not committing crimes, acting as if I learnt my lesson for a crime I never committed in the first place. These are some of the mental games I had to go through just to be looked upon as being worthy of being amongst other citizens in society.

How in the hell is that not equivalent to slavery?

In those 28 years of my life, how had I ended up evolving into this kind of human being?

Was I a product, creation or reflection of America's Conduct?

Epilogue: Catastrophe

Over the next five years from 1992 until 1997, my life would spiral out of control into a complete unwinding. I continued to believe deep in my heart that the Crips, especially the East Coast Crips were worth dying for, because at that time I hadn't reversed my ways of thinking. I wasn't in search of reasons to live because I kept engaging in all the things that placed me in a greater position to encounter death. Most everything I touched, thought, or surrounded myself with aligned with payback, destruction or death. Subconsciously I think I wanted to die.

A few good things occurred around my life along the way. Both my sisters gave birth to daughters: Shenette had Ashley, and Debra had Erica. I somehow managed to get Jackie to marry me on April 20, 1993, my birthday. Marriage was something I thought was expected of me. We immediately started planning her pregnancy, but before we were successful in our attempts, three months after marriage, I was arrested for access to a firearm.

My brother-in-law Donnie and I had gotten into a fight over him disrespecting my wife. He ran off and called the police and told them I was on parole, so when they arrived to investigate the call, they searched the house. They found a gun that was registered to Jackie, and detained me until I was given a parole violation hearing to determine if indeed I had violated any of the terms I signed to. During the hearing it was found that I had violated my parole, so I was sent back to prison for at least one year.

For those that don't know what a violation is, I will explain. When you're sentenced to prison as I had been years earlier, all sentences aren't the same. Some people get 2, 3, 10 or 50 years. I was sentenced to prison for 18 years and 4 months in 1983. At the time, it was required by law that we serve three-fourths of the sentence before being eligible for release. However, I served 10 years and four months, due to a new law that passed during the time I was serving that sentence. The new law was called day for day, which meant I now could do fifty percent of the sentence instead of the 3/4 if I participated in the workers program. If I got a job doing something I could earn a day off my time for every day I worked. When I paroled I had three years remaining on my sentence. If at any time I violated any of the terms or conditions I signed to, it would place me in a position where they could send me back to prison for one of the three years, and add one year to the three years, making it four years of parole. Each violation would have been up to a year, but no longer than four years.

AMERICA'S CONDUCT

I was sent to Chino State Reception Center to be sent back to prison. I had no misgivings about where I was going. I assumed that I was going back to Folsom State Prison because I had paroled from there a year earlier. Plus I thought I still had 82 points, which kept me as a level four prisoner.

I was ducated to see the counselor to find out where I would be doing my violation and to my surprise it wasn't Folsom. The counselor informed I that while I was out on parole the point system in prison had changed, and I no longer had 82 points. I discovered I didn't have any points - zero. I was then told that I was Level One and would be going to a Level One institution. I thought for sure it was a mistake, that she had to have the wrong file, so I left well enough alone.

I was sent to C.M.C. WEST, a level one institution. I remember when I first arrived there I hated it. It was too open, too much freedom, no supervision. I was used to being caged up like an animal, always on the lookout for dangerous encounters. At C.M.C. WEST there wasn't any situation of danger. Most everyone there were programmers, following all the rules, looking to go home. However, there were some ghettos stars there, Blacc Dog from one eleven, East Side Blue from Four Trey Gangster Crips, Big Murk from Nine Seven East Coast Crips, Billy Bob, from Neighborhood Forties, Big Limes from 62nd Street East Coast Crips and a few more. I would complain to them every day that I wanted to leave and go back to Folsom. How mentally insane was I? Big Murk used to ask me to stay, but I wasn't used to all of this open space, so I went to see the counselor and told her that I didn't want to be there. I asked if she would put me up for transfer to Folsom prison. She sat there and stared at me. I know why she did now, but back then I didn't have a clue. She was staring at a mentally ill man that thought himself to be normal. She said to me, "Mr. Davis, just be patient and give this situation a chance. If you aren't comfortable, then come back to see me." In other words she wasn't going to transfer me - she couldn't.

I ran into Jeff, my football mentor, Lil Snoop, from Rolling 60 NHC, and my partner Ken Dog from Compton Crip. Snoop was wild, however Ken Dog was a fool. I recall one day when we were eating lunch in the prison dining hall, the correctional officer that was running the dining hall ordered us to get up and leave. But his tone was disrespectful towards us. One thing is clear - at that time, in 1993, inmates still stood for something, but today those standards have been stepped on and crushed by CDCR. The officer was an African American, tall, dark skin, and wore a Jerry curl. He didn't appear to be afraid at all to me. On our way out of the kitchen Ken Dog told him that he was a bitch. He said to Ken Dog, I'll be in your cell and I'll show you who the bitch is.

Ken Dog and I didn't give a second thought to the officer making a threat like that because at best he would write Ken Dog up for disrespecting staff, which is one of several million ways they attempt to control the inmates. I happened to be called out of my cell for something of no significance when the officer called me to come over to where he was. He said to me, "OG, watch the door for me." I had no clue what he was talking about until he went up to Ken Dog's door and asked him if he was ready. Before Ken Dog could respond, the officer was in on him and they rumbled briefly. The police had gotten the best of Ken Dog.

The police walked out calmly but Ken Dog wasn't satisfied. He was still shocked that the police had the heart to fight him without reporting it or writing him up for staff assault. I was impressed. I didn't think twice about it; he immediately earned my respect. However, Ken Dog wanted one more run. But the officer said to him, "Look man, you had your chance. I can't walk out of here with visible injuries without reporting them. All I'm asking you to do is to respect me."

There are officers in the system who are just as tough as the toughest convicts, and they will give you a squabble if they're allowed to get away with it. But now in prison they aren't allowed to take that kind of stand because the inmates today would tell on them as quick as they learned of any such thing.

Myself, East Side Blue, Blacc Dog, and Larry Watson lifted weights together five days a week. One day East Side Blue and I were in the day room, the area where all the inmates gather to watch television, play games etc. This particular day, March of 1994, I recall, there was a breaking news flash. Usually breaking news flashes were police officers in high speed chases of someone they suspected of breaking the law. However, this was different. It was a gathering of white men talking about a new law that had been passed that day, the Three Strikes and You're Out law.

They went on and on about crime and how the public was tired of a revolving door of prisoners, coming in and out etc. After they were done talking everybody started sharing with each other what they understood the men to be saying. They did their very best to interpret for others. I, on the other hand, had no idea what they were saying, because they were artful in communicating a double meaning in their rantings.

If you had one or more serious felony convictions then the law applied to you. If you were convicted of the same three crimes the law applied to you. If you been to prison three or more times the law applied to you. There were so many versions of how the law applied to you, you were left there not knowing if it applied to you or not and that's the way they wanted it. But I knew it didn't apply to me because I had only been arrested and convicted once as an adult, so I didn't care really what they were saying.

I paroled again June 10, 1994. Once I got out I hooked up with my childhood friend Mark Bond. He and I went to school together, played football together for Roger Mosley, the Magnum P.I. Star and Raymond Washington's mentor. Mark made it possible for me to relax and not worry about finances. I love him for that. Ole Mark Bond - who would've known he would be so daring.

One day I was watching TV and a breaking news flash came across the screen - "Wanted for Murder" - and they were showing the police following a white Ford Bronco truck with O. J. Simpson inside. I thought to myself that O. J. hadn't killed those people, so why would he be so stupid to do something like that when his life was good and white people had accepted him into their circle, in addition to being a football superstar? I also recall thinking damn, white folks don't give a damn who they go after.

In the inner city, many of us unlawful citizens know how dirty many of the police department officers are. They would plant guns, drugs, and a whole host of others things on someone innocent of that crime. As far as they were concerned, that person may be guilty of other crimes, so to them, who gives a fuck? Only people that have no dealings with the police think all of them are law abiding citizens. They're not.

It didn't take long for me to resume my stalking the streets with Loco, Lil Snake, Baby Fox, Big Moe, Ken Dog, Lil Mont, Tiny Mont, Baby Man, Maniac, Baby Moe, Tiny Bam, Baby Bam, Baby TC, Ray Dog, Lil Boxer, both C Bones, Lil Ed, Big Ricc Rocc, Big Sadd, and many others. Because of that very thing, it wouldn't take long before I was arrested again. This time the police claimed to have heard shots fired and suspected a truck carrying several occupants, including me.

Now this story is so unbelievable it makes my case about the judicial system and how fair or ridiculous it is depending on one's perspective. One night Loco, Big Moe and I were at Big Moe's body shop on Florence and San Pedro. I had a low-rider 65 Super Sport Impala that I had bought from Loco that needed some minor repairs so I took it there for Moe to fix. While waiting, I decided to walk to the store so I told them I'd be right back. I walked inside the store, purchased my order, walked out and was confronted by several men in a truck that were East Coast Crip hunting. They had gotten the jump on me. One of the dudes had gotten out of the truck already with a pistol in his hand, asking me where was I from? I told him that I didn't gang bang. They weren't the real Hunters of the night because they did too much talking. However I was wearing a tan color Dickies jumpsuit, Coast to Coast Trucking stitched in bold letters on the front of it, so there wasn't a doubt in the world that I was from East Coast in my hood, San Pedro and Gage. That was enough evidence for one of them. He told the dude that was confronting me to bring me along. I got inside the truck and they started talking about killing me, but in my mind I was thinking why hadn't they done it right there on the spot. So they decided they were going to take me to Denver Lane hood, a Blood area, kill me and make the police believe it had been the Bloods to have committed the murder.

Before I got into the truck one of my homegirls Donna had spoken to me, but I didn't acknowledge her. So she was suspicious of what was happening, plus she didn't recognize any of those dudes confronting me. As we drove down 108th and Figueroa, L.A.P.D. happened to suspect this truck of being where the shots were coming from. The dude driving the truck told the others that the police was following them. The second he said that, I jumped out of the truck while it was still moving. I assumed the dude in the back of the truck struck me in the head as I jumped out of the truck, and the gun fell out with me.

I passed out from the fall and when I woke up L.A.P.D. had their lights glaring into my face. This to me was the nightmare - wake up to see L.A.P.D. directing their pistol towards you. Instinctively I jumped up and ran, but to no avail. One of them yelled "Stop, motherfucker, or I'll shoot!" So I stopped.

Once they took me down to the station I saw a doctor and told the doctor what I thought happened to my head. When I was finished there the next day, the detectives came to interrogate me. They asked if I wanted to talk. I said yes, so they read me my rights, if there is such a thing. He began his questioning by asking who was driving the truck and who were you shooting at. I didn't acknowledge either question. I responded I was kidnapped.

He started laughing but I didn't see or hear anything funny. He said I saw the fucking gun in your hand. I had no idea what he was talking about. It's true that they found a gun however it didn't belong to me. It was a nine millimeter. I told him the same story I'm sharing with you all. He didn't believe me and he filed charges against me: ex-con in possession of a firearm, which carried 16 months, two years, or three years. Those are the sentences that I would receive if found guilty of the crime. But I wasn't guilty of that charge, so I had no intention of plea bargaining myself inside anyone's institution.

I was transferred to the Los Angeles County Jail. Worse than hell itself, if there is such a thing, the Los Angeles county jail is where it is located. From there I was arraigned on the charges. The lawyer called me out to explain what was about to happen. She began with you're facing 25 years to life under the Three Strikes and You're Out law. I couldn't believe what I was hearing. First and foremost, I didn't take her seriously; she had to be kidding. I had only been to adult prison once. I only had one arrest and conviction as an adult so she certainly had the wrong file.

The attorney explained to me that I had been convicted of five counts of attempted murder and each one of those attempted murders were strikes. That meant I had five strikes. I told her "Look lady I went to prison in 1982. I've only been arrested once as an adult. How the hell do I have five strikes? I thought you had to be in prison three times from the time the law was passed in 1994." She said a lot of people thought that but that's not how it works. Here in America, where black people were segregated their entire lives up until 1964, 30 years after allowing us to integrate into America's societies, 1994, they come up with a law that they trick mostly everyone into believing it to be one way but it turned out not to be. They punished blacks for every single crime they've committed since integrating into America's communities and they have yet to be held accountable for all the crimes they've committed against us. How in the hell did this make any sense and how did black activists allow them to get away with such a thing if they themselves aren't selling us out? I constantly read the **VIII AMENDMENT**:

> BAIL, FINES, PUNISHMENTS (Section 1.) Excessive bail shall not be required, nor excessive fines imposed, nor cruel and unusual punishments inflicted. Proposed September 25, 1789: ratified December 15, 1791.

Now for all you Constitution, Amendment loving Americans, what does the VIII amendment mean? How in the hell wasn't it cruel and unusual punishment to put somebody in prison for the rest of their lives for having a gun, when you can't recall anybody ever being sentenced to such a sentence? That's unusual. And it violates the constitution. How could the government come back to revisit those same crimes you have already served your time for, and then punish you again for them?

> **AMENDMENT V.**
>
> *SECTION 1*: No person shall be held to answer for a capital, or otherwise infamous crime, unless on a presentment or indictment of a grand jury, except in cases arising in the land or naval forces, or in the militia, when in actual service in time of war or public danger, NOR SHALL ANY PERSON BE SUBJECT FOR THE SAME OFFENSE TO BE TWICE PUT IN JEOPARDY OF LIFE OR LIMB, nor shall be compelled in any criminal case to be a witness against himself, nor be deprived of life, liberty, or property, without due process of law, nor shall private property be taken for public use without just compensation.

Just like the men explaining the three strikes that day in 1994, intentionally confusing those that couldn't comprehend their deceit, the V amendment explains what cannot happen to you, but then says it can happen if due process occurs. That's the position my grandfather, father, mother, and now myself were in - depending on written documents that were never meant to serve our best interest, and now my children would face the same exact challenges.

LARRY DAVIS

The lawyer said they're willing to offer you 16 months, double it up to 32 months, strike one strike and spare you a life sentence. Now I was supposed to feel like they were doing me a favor sending me to prison. Nobody could tell me the system wasn't corrupt. I was knee deep inside. I was victimized by it as so many others had been before me, and as I have victimized it. So I understood the game we were playing here and I was up for the challenge. I told the attorney there would be no deal - set me a trial date.

I wasn't going to allow them to run over me the way they had 12 years earlier. This time I understood better that it's not about innocence or guilt. It's about which side could convince 12 civilians that their story is more believable and that's the truth.

As I was preparing for trial, I often times would call my mother. She still would visit me and she would always tell me, "Larry, pray to your father. Ask him to help you." Most people pray to Jesus, Allah, Buddha and other Gods, but my mother always told me to pray to my Dad.

One day I was sitting in the cell I was assigned to and someone had left a small Bible there. I picked it up to thumb through it, and there was a number inside, Douglas McCann, attorney at law, out of the Santa Monica area. I didn't think anything of it, but I kept the number. While I was going back and forth to court preparing for trial, it became clear to me the attorney I had wasn't on my side. When I was out of prison I had visited the O.J trial to see how attorneys performed their duties, so I knew what was happening with me. I informed the judge that I would be hiring my own attorney and that I no longer wanted the attorney appointed to me. I had to have the attorney come to court and represent me, so I called the number I found inside the Bible. Douglas McCann answered. I told him that I found his number in a Bible and that I needed representation. He got all my information and said he would come to the jail to visit because he didn't trust the phones, since they were being monitored.

When he came to visit me, I walked down to the attorney room and there he was - a white man, five foot six, 135 pounds, blond hair, boyish looking. I thought he was quite young and maybe not the right person for this job. My wife and sister Debra were pregnant, and I was fighting to be a father and an uncle. My attorney had to be willing to rumble because there wasn't any doubt that I was. After talking to him I was convinced he too was a rebel, and we were a match made in heaven.

Now that I was inside the county jail, I was able to gauge the hatred people had for blacks. O. J. Simpson was on trial around the same time I was preparing for mine. The Mexicans and whites wanted him to be found guilty and most of the blacks wanted him to go free, whether he was guilty or not. During his trial, everybody was talking about race relations here in America, which didn't make any sense to me because everyone knows America is still racist. But I guess we have to all pretend it had vanished into thin air. To me, being unlawful as I was, and understanding how evidence is used in court, O. J. was guilty as hell. But it never was about innocence or guilt in the inner cities - it was about payback. Many blacks wanted O. J. to win to fuck the system for the injustices they and their forebears had endured and were still enduring. For the first time, people had the chance to see up close and personal how America's judicial system worked or didn't work. O. J. would benefit from the suffering of black people simply because he could pay for his defense and he had an attorney, Mr. Johnnie Cochran, who knew and understood that L.A.P.D. was corrupt, as we would learn more about after the O.J trial. The black communities had lived with their abuses, and Johnnie only had to show that they likely planted evidence, whether they had or not. If he could catch them lying about small things, it showed that it's possible they were lying about the big things too. Johnnie was magnificent.

While the O.J. jury was out deliberating they locked the jail down. I recall hearing the deputies making an announcement over the speaker system, "The jury has reached a verdict." The jail was silent. Then it came, "not guilty." The jail burst with joy; the black people inside that jail were so elated. It was their first time ever seeing white people feeling some of what we have been feeling all of our lives.

I was next; it was my turn. My trial date had been set. I had gotten my two witnesses together, Loco and Donna. The D.A. immediately started trying to intimidate my witnesses. They set up a meeting with Donna, asking her if she knew that I had tried to kill five people, why was she testifying for me? They said they knew she was lying and that she could go to jail for perjury. They told her that the police saw me with the gun. All sort of things they tried, to no avail. She still was willing to testify. They didn't even bother to question Loco; they knew that was a waste of their time and his. Jackie had our son, Lil Larry Hakeem Davis, our first child, and Debra had her third child Iesha Erica Johnson so the incentives were in place. I was ready to fight.

The D.A. called her first witness, the arresting officer who testified about receiving a call of shots fired. One witness after the other testified to the same exact thing, which was quite amazing seeing that they all had arrived at the scene at different times. If I recall correctly, one officer testified he first saw me riding a bike, and then I jumped off the bike and he caught me trying to run away. Of course he wouldn't be looking at perjury, right? Two sets of rules. The D.A. knew this man was lying and damaging her case, but she seemed not to care. I loved every second of it. Her next witness would contradict each other one. When it was my attorney's turn to question her witness, it would be the first time I would get a chance to see him in action. From the start he was pretty smooth. He would ask a question about something that had nothing to do with anything. Then one by one he started asking each of them questions that attacked the others' testimony. It was a mess. The

D.A.'s only chance of winning that case was if I just decided to jump up inside the court room and confess, which wasn't going to happen.

The D.A. redirected and rested. It was the defense's turn to call our witnesses. I think Loco was our first witness. Loco is a very proud man. He was a loving father to his girls. I can tell you in the streets people feared him because he didn't play games. He was an East Coast Crip Legend. I always was proud that he was on our side, but many others hated that he was, which he didn't know until years later when they would do the forbidden. I was happy to see him walk through the door; he had come to rescue his homeboy. He walked with an attitude, wearing the same type of jumpsuit I had on when I was arrested - a tan Dickies, with Coast to Coast running across his chest. The D.A. had to do something spectacular. Her case crumbled right before her eyes and mine. I couldn't believe what I was witnessing; only in my dreams could this happen. But there I was, feeling confident I would be going home just like years earlier. The D.A. gave up on Loco when he started toying with her. My attorney asked him one or two questions and then it was over for him.

Then came Donna; she was the star witness for me. She was the only eye witness that saw me being forced inside the truck. This is where the D.A. would have to do her very best, but didn't. Donna stayed consistent with her testimony during the pretrial motions. My attorney wanted to tell the jury that I had been kidnapped, but the judge wouldn't allow it because he ruled there wasn't any evidence to suggest that I had been kidnapped. So Donna and the D.A. got into a heated exchange. The D.A. was telling her that she was lying, all sorts of things. Then, unexpectedly, Donna said in front of the jury, "All I know is that night when I spoke to him and he didn't speak back it wasn't like him. I told my daughter something is wrong with Lala. Then I heard the next day that he had been kidnapped." The D.A. lost her mind in the court OBJECTION, OBJECTION, NOT IN EVIDENCE. The judge sustained, and informed the jury to disregard that last statement. But they couldn't. The D. A. knew she had lost her case. She let Donna go, and then it was my turn.

I honestly didn't need to testify, but I couldn't resist. She went at me hard, more out of defeat than anything else, but I walked right through her. Everyone rested and the judge gave the jury the case. I would sit in the holding tank all day wondering what's taking the jury so long. The police lied - it was so obvious. Finally, on the third day of waiting the bailiff came and said "Lala, they reached a verdict." I asked what did she think. She said it looked good for me, but you could never tell with a jury, I knew one thing, we were about to find out. The judge asked the jury had they reached a verdict. The Foreman responded they had. I scanned the jury for any hint of what the verdict was and there it was, this elderly black lady smiled at me wagging her finger like she was admonishing me. I acknowledged her because I knew what she was telling me. The clerk passed the verdict to the judge he looked

AMERICA'S CONDUCT

like he was shocked. He passed it back to the clerk, then to the Foreman and instructed him to read the verdict. "We the people in the above title action find Larry Davis not guilty." WOW!! I couldn't believe the judicial system was proud of itself for playing with people's lives every day. I thanked my lawyer and the jury and that same lady stayed back and whispered, "Stay out of trouble!" I winked my eye in appreciation.

It was time for me to be a father. I went back to the holding cell got on the phone to call Jackie. The first words out of her mouth were "What happened?" I said to her "Not guilty." She screamed and asked was I coming home tonight. I told her no, because I have a parole hold. It really didn't matter to me because I had been in the county jail eleven months and my violation was only twelve months, so wherever they sent me I'd have less than twenty days. I was sent back to C.M.C WEST where many of the same guys were still there wondering what was I doing back. I paroled again and Jackie came to pick me up with my son Lil Larry. He was a handsome child. As I reached to grab him he started crying. I said "Cry, Son, because I'm not going to put you down." I was so excited to be holding my son.

Jackie couldn't separate us. I fed him and changed his diapers. All the things men don't do, like women do all the time, I did with him.

I headed back into the streets with Young Rob, Lil Will, Loco, Lil Snake, Ray Dog, Young Sadd, Baby Fox, Baby Bam, Big Moe, Bam, Fox, both C Bones, Young Lala, Lil boxer, Baby Man, Limes, Lil and Tiny Monts, Baby TC, Lil Kev, Ricc Rocc, Ken Dog and others, but this time my life would change forever.

I was arrested again nine months later for a post office robbery. Once I was in custody, with Young Rob, Young Lala, and Lil Will, it was much serious than the post office robberies. They were alleging that Loco and I were the ringleaders of these armored truck murder robberies and that we were super predators. I couldn't help but think there they go again talking about themselves. In the post office robbery, there weren't any witnesses that could place me there until my childhood buddy Lil Will turned state witness against us. They filed three strikes against me again like the last time but I knew I would beat this rap also. I called Douglas McCann and he came down for my preliminary hearing and caught them lying as they do so well. The stage was set for trial when mysteriously my attorney went out for a recess and never came back. I spoke to his wife and asked her had she seen him? She said "Lala, Doug hasn't told you?"

"Tell me what?"

"They threatened him. They said he's the East Coast Crips lawyer and if he didn't walk away he would be in there with y'all."

So I had to represent myself because I refused to accept the trash they tried to appoint me. I remember sitting in court going over all the documents when the lead detective came over to me and said, "Damn, Lala, you wasted your life gang banging you could've been a damn good attorney."

The deck was stacked against me on this one. They wanted us off the streets. I was found guilty in the post office robbery and sentenced to 180 years to life. I couldn't help but laugh at the VIII amendment. Loco, and Ken Dog had been arrested. My homeboy Slim and several others testified against them and they were both sentenced to death in San Quentin State Prison. I was sent to Calipatria State Prison where I continued to get my Crip on. I ran back into many of my old childhood friends. I had two more Crip walk contests with Legs Diamond for Big Sparks which he won, then again for Cisco which I finally won. Legs didn't speak to me for a while because of it.

I learnt a lot from my experiences. I understand fully how I let my family down, my son in particular. I understand betrayal to the fullest extent. While I was in Calipatria State Prison I bent over backwards for the Crips, I taught them what strength and unity looked and felt like only to be betrayed by them. I met correctional officers at Calipatria that respected me and supported me because I represented truth. Many of them turned a blind eye because I tried to bring order where there hadn't been any except for our cause. You all know who you are. Always I will stay solid as y'all did for me good looking, especially you, Sparkles. I will never forget you, always know this. And to the realest Blood I have ever known, Maniac from Denver Lane, and my partna Silk, keep pushing. And to my road dog Young Rob, I love you with all my heart. You above all were able to witness firsthand how true I've been to East Coast. It has been my joy to ride alongside you. And to Young Sadd, you're the baddest mf I know. Stay focused.

And to the youth of America I wrote this book with the hopes of sharing with y'all the truth of what misery, betrayal, disloyalty, and deceit look like for many of us gang members. The path we took looked fun, exciting and worth any and all the sacrifices one could dream of. We all were willing to give our lives, and many of us did. But never once did we take the time out to think about what effects our actions had on others. What do I tell a two-year-old boy who was used to getting up every morning playing with his father, only to wake up never to be able to play with him again because we have chosen the streets over our loved ones? This life that looked so glamorous from the outside looking in doesn't look so alluring after you read my story. We owe it to ourselves to help our children, brothers, sisters, nieces, nephews, uncles, aunties, mothers, fathers, friends, and neighbors.

America has compelled us to expose our ugliest side, but at all times, we are the absolute owners of our destiny. We should choose the very best for ourselves and loved ones. We have great stars from our walk of life that are capable of making a difference in so many young people's lives, and we must be wise enough to do so. Young people, take control of your direction. Choose another path, different from ours because we have failed you all so miserably. Choose love, determination, success and joy for yourself and others.

I have always wanted to be treated with respect, dignity, and honor so here's my chance to do something meaningful in my life for somebody other than myself. I owe it to our ancestors, because of the sacrifices they made long before I was here on earth. My conduct has been shameful against other human beings, so I apologize to all that I have brought pain and suffering to.

To my son, I am so sorry that I abandoned you. I, like so many before me, really didn't understand. I lacked the courage as a young man to think for myself, so I followed behind others, emulating what I thought others wanted me to be, as opposed to being as I was.

And to my mother, the brightest star in the sky, you have always been so loving, kind, honest and the best example of truth. I apologize to you for causing you so much sorrow in your life, for you never bought this role I've been playing for so many years. Bless your heart. I hope this has made you proud of me. Finally, I've given back to society in the way that you always knew I would, to make you smile every single day. I love you so much.

To America, this is the result of your mistreatment of the human soul. Luckily for me, I awoke out of the ashes of death to recognize all the self-destruction I was inflicting on myself. You too can learn a lesson of humility. Learn to love the citizens you claim are yours.

And last, but certainly not least, my father, the love of my life. Pops, I've been on a ride, a journey of a life time. Hasn't one single day passed me by that I've forgotten you, nor has Momma allowed me to. I haven't always done my best, but I've always pretended that I had. But you rest assured Pops, this is an effort towards doing what I know you would be proud of. My journey continues until we meet again. Your Son, Poppa Cat.

Americas Conduct: The Inner City Escort.

Made in the USA
Middletown, DE
13 July 2017